CONTEMPORARY POETRY MEETS MODERN THEORY

Edited by

Antony Easthope and
John O. Thompson

University of Toronto Press
Toronto   Buffalo   London

First published in Canada and the United States
by University of Toronto Press 1991
Toronto   Buffalo   London

Printed and bound in Great Britain

Theory/Culture Series 10

Canadian Cataloguing in Publication Data

Main entry under title:

Contemporary poetry meets modern theory

ISBN 0–8020–2802–0 (bound) ISBN 0–8020–7677–7
(pbk)

1. Poetry, Modern – 20th century – History and
criticism.   I. Easthope, Antony.   II. Thompson.
John O.

PN1271.C66 1991   809.1'04   C91–095053–9

Contents

Acknowledgements

Grateful acknowledgement is given to the following copyright holders and publishers for kindly granting permission to reprint material in copyright:

'Sortes Vergilianae' by John Ashbery, Viking Press and Carcanet Press Ltd. Reproduced by permission.

'On Not Being Milton' by Tony Harrison, Rex Collings Ltd. Reproduced by permission of the author and the publisher.

Excerpts from 'The Grauballe Man' and 'Wedding Day' from *Poems: 1965–1975* by Seamus Heaney. Copyright © 1966, 1969, 1972, 1975, 1980 by Seamus Heaney, and from *North* and *Wintering Out* by Seamus Heaney. Reprinted by permission of Farrar, Straus and Giroux, Inc., and Faber and Faber Ltd.

Excerpt from 'Eye and Tooth' from *For the Union Dead* by Robert Lowell. Copyright © 1962, 1964 by Robert Lowell. Reprinted by permission of Farrar, Straus and Giroux, Inc., and Faber and Faber Ltd.

'Translational Response to a Stein Single' by Steve McCaffrey from *The L=A=N=G=U=A=G=E Book*, edited by Bruce Andrews and Charles Bernstein, Southern Illinois University Press, 1984. Reprinted by permission of the author and the publisher.

'My Lover is a Woman' by Pat Parker. Reproduced by permission of the estate of Pat Parker.

'Mirror Mirror on the Wheel' by Tom Raworth, originally from the volume *ACT* published by Trigrom Press, 1973. Copyright © Tom Raworth, and from *tottering state* by Tom Raworth, Grafton Books, a division of HarperCollins Publishers Ltd. Reproduced by permission of the author and the publisher.

'Aunt Jennifer's Tigers', 'For the Conjunction of the Planets', and 'Tear Gas' by Adrienne Rich, W.W. Norton. Reprinted by permission of the author and the publisher.

Introduction

This collection of essays brings together contemporary critical theory and a detailed analysis of individual texts by contemporary poets writing in English. In this brief introduction we want to outline why we think this is a fruitful conjunction likely to yield a greater understanding of both the poetry and the theory.

A conservative response to the great theory wars which have devastated conventional author-based literary criticism during the past two decades – structuralism, marxism, post-structuralism, feminism, deconstruction, postmodernism, new historicism (to name some of the great flags under which theory has sailed) – has been to claim that such theory has little or no relation to the practice of creative writing in the twentieth century. We would disagree entirely. For it is arguable that these powerful theoretical movements were themselves belated responses and theoretical reorientations made necessary by a previous artistic movement, namely the radical reworking of attitudes towards the representation of reality, the nature of the human individual (or 'subject') and the conception of historical and social forces exemplified in practice across all forms of art by modernism. To try to come to terms with the writing of Jacques Lacan one might well begin with his lifelong interest in the avant garde, and especially French surrealism.

The past two decades have witnessed what in the natural sciences would be termed (following Thomas Kuhn) a paradigm shift, even if this is as yet neither universally acknowledged nor universally instituted. If the previous dispensation in literary studies developed after 1930 in Britain by I.A. Richards and F.R. Leavis and in the United States by New Criticism, presumed the literary text as a *given* – 'the words on the page' or a verbal icon – in which the imaginative and sympathetic reader could participate on the basis of shared human values, the new paradigm denies that the text exists 'in itself' apart from the way it is read in a context of interpretation. The shift has been from the poem as point of origin to recognition of the poem as being in process in its reading, which is to say, without an absolute point of origin at all.

It would be hard to exaggerate the importance to that shift of the linguistic distinction introduced by Ferdinand de Saussure between the word as *signifier* or shaped sound and the word as *signified* or meaning. At this point 'reality' as the *referent* to which words may (or

vii

may not) refer becomes a secondary or derivative effect on human discourse, ceasing to be available as a foundation on which certain knowledge can be based. 'It is the world of words that creates the world of things' (Lacan); 'il n'y a pas de hors-texte' (Derrida). Philosophy can no longer conceive itself as a Mirror of Nature, to cite the title of Richard Rorty's enormously influential book of 1980.

And if reality, the world and 'physical nature' can no longer be known in itself except as it is construed within discourse, neither can there be a fixed and universal human nature realised in and by the self-conscious individual. Whether via the inflection of Marx (in which the individual is regarded as a personification of economic and social forces) or via the account of Freud (in which the I that I think I am is dependent on an unconscious I can never know), the idea of the individual as fixity and point of origin gives way to the conception of the subject as a partial and provisional *position*. Like Nietzsche's God in 1849, as the western world moves towards the year 2000, Man – essential, masculine, god-like Man – is no longer with us (something unlikely to be mourned by most women).

Whatever the causes of the Great Paradigm Shift, both poets and critics inhabit the same world and same historical space, however differently. Just as at a level of conceptual abstraction post-structuralist theory was anchored to the more immediate and intimate (for that reason perhaps chronologically earlier) development of modernism, so the forms of contemporary theory may gain a readier purchase on the postmodern texts of contemporary poetry. (Such poetry is postmodern in that it has surpassed the shock of the new characterising modernism if only because, coming two generations after modernism, it must accept that as already part of its own history.) Contemporary theory allows us to read poetry which arguably has already incorporated into itself such theory, though it has done so as it should, poetically rather than as conceptual discourse. Derridean deconstruction, for example, provides terms for understanding and enjoying the poetry of John Ashbery – this is the bet on which our collection of essays has been grounded. At the same time, as many of these essays will demonstrate, it is undeniable that literary theory has fed back into the thinking of poets working today and the ways they approach their project.

We believe that, as the theory wars with their concern to fight out the issues at a general level are drawing to an end, the time is right for interest to move back to a rereading of the text. It may even now seem brash to invite literary critics to name their chosen theoretical approach, 'apply' it to a particular poem and justify it effectively by means of 'practical criticism'. But the consolidation of the new paradigm encourages and legitimises the demand that critics frame their analysis with theory. Whatever the differences within the paradigm, it is structured around agreement that text and reader are terms in a reciprocal process so that any act of interpretation only becomes possible within an assumed theoretical context. Since it will in any case be present implicitly there can therefore be no harm and much good in making this context explicit.

Antony Easthope and John Thompson
Manchester and Liverpool, November 1990

For Jackie Jones

John Ashbery: 'Sortes Vergilianae'

You have been living now for a long time and there is nothing you do
not know.
Perhaps something you read in the newspaper influenced you and that
was very frequently.
They have left you to think along these lines and you have gone your
own way because you guessed that
Under their hiding was the secret, casual as breath, betrayed for the
asking.
Then the sky opened up, revealing much more than any of you were
intended to know.
It is a strange thing how fast the growth is, almost as fast as the light
from the polar regions
Reflected off the arctic ice-cap in summer. When you know where it is
heading
You have to follow it, though at a sadly reduced rate of speed,
Hence folly and idleness, raging at the confines of some miserable
sunlit alley or court.
It is the nature of these people to embrace each other, they know no
other kind but themselves.
Things pass quickly out of sight and the best is to be forgotten quickly
For it is wretchedness that endures, shedding its cancerous light on all
it approaches:
Words spoken in the heat of passion, that might have been retracted
in good time,
All good intentions, all that was arguable. These are stilled now, as the
embrace in the hollow of its flux
And can never be revived except as perverse notations on an indisput-
able state of things,
As conduct in the past, vanished from the reckoning long before it was
time.
Lately you've found the dull fevers still inflict their round, only they
are unassimilable
Now that newness or importance has worn away. It is with us like day
and night,
The surge upward through the grade-school positioning and bursting
into soft gray blooms
Like vacuum-cleaner sweepings, the opulent fuzz of our cage, or like
an excited insect
In nervous scrimmage for the head, etching its none-too-complex
ordinances into the matter of the day.
Presently all will go off satisfied, leaving the millpond bare, a site for
new picnics,

Author's Note: The title 'Sortes Vergilianae' refers to the ancient practice of fortune-
telling by choosing a passage from Vergil's poetry at random.

As they came, naked, to explore all the possible grounds on which
   exchanges could be set up.
It is 'No Fishing' in modest capital letters, and getting out from under
   the major weight of the thing
As it was being indoctrinated and dropped, heavy as a branch with
   apples,
And as it started to sigh, just before tumbling into your lap, chagrined
   and satisfied at the same time,
Knowing its day over and your patience only beginning, toward what
   marvels of speculation, auscultation, world-view,
Satisfied with the entourage. It is this blank carcass of whims and
   tentative afterthoughts
Which is being delivered into your hand like a letter some forty-odd
   years after the day it was posted.
Strange, isn't it, that the message makes some sense, if only a relative
   one in the larger context of message-receiving
That you will be called to account for just as the purpose of it is
   becoming plain,
Being one and the same with the day it set out, though you cannot
   imagine this.
There was a time when the words dug in, and you laughed and joked,
   accomplice
Of all the possibilities of their journey through the night and the stars,
   creature
Who looked to the abandonment of such archaic forms as these, and
   meanwhile
Supported them as the tools that made you. The rut became apparent
   only later
And by then it was too late to check such expansive aspects as what
   to do while waiting
For the others to show: unfortunately no pile of tattered magazines was
   in evidence,
Such dramas sleeping below the surface of the everyday machinery;
   besides
Quality is not given to everybody, and who are you to have been
   supposing you had it?
So the journey grew ever slower; the battlements of the city could now
   be discerned from afar
But meanwhile the water was giving out and malaria had decimated
   their ranks and undermined their morale,
You know the story, so that if turning back was unthinkable, so was
   victorious conquest of the great brazen gates.
Best perhaps to fold up right here, but even that was not to be granted.
Some days later in the pulsating of orchestras someone asked for a
   drink:
The music stopped and those who had been confidently counting the
   rhythms grew pale.
This is just a footnote, though a microcosmic one perhaps, to the
   greater curve
Of the elaboration; it asks no place in it, only insertion *hors-texte* as the
   invisible notion of how that day grew

From planisphere to heaven, and what part in it all the 'I' had, the
   insatiable researcher of learned trivia, bookworm,
And one who marched along with, 'made common cause,' yet had
   neither the gumption nor the desire to trick the thing into happening,
Only long patience, as the star climbs and sinks, leaving illumination
   to the setting sun.

Chapter 1

Points of Departure

Deconstruction and John Ashbery's 'Sortes Vergilianae'

Steve Connor

What, if anything, can deconstruction 'do', with, for, or to John Ashbery's poem 'Sortes Vergilianae'? To ask the question in this kind of way is to imply a certain relationship between a text and its reading, in which the text is seen as the pure and integral object of a reading which is absolutely exterior to it. What sort of relationship might there be, needs there in general to be, between a text and its reading for the reading to 'work'? Supposing we could describe this relationship in ways that satisfy us, would the same conditions need to apply for deconstruction in particular to 'work'? What does it mean anyway for a critical approach to 'work'? I have to confess to some uncertainties of my own right at the beginning of what I want to try to say about this (extraordinary, difficult, mesmerising, tangled, bizarrely unpoetic) poem. The problem is not that the poem resists a deconstructive reading so much as that it seems to me to respond in too reassuring, too obediently exemplary a way to what is known as deconstruction. Much of my essay will be concerned with spelling out what I mean by that suggestion, but here are a few of the topics I shall be attracted to: the difficulty of the poem (its sheer semantic intransigence), its complication of the experience of time as sequence, its questioning of the logic of punctuality or presence, its assault on traditional ideas of meaning as buried essence, its discursive multiplicity, its play with, and investigation of, figures of speech, especially metaphor and its self-reflexive interrogation of its own poetic powers and effects. All of these are characteristics that suggest a poem which one may claim is already on its own terms deconstructive.

So, everything looks propitious. Here is a poem that responds, as it were, in advance, and with only the faintest of promptings, to the requirements of deconstructive analysis, meeting its critical reader in spontaneous reciprocity. What more appropriate text could be imagined for a deconstructive analysis than one that could be claimed to be deconstructive in its own terms, in its undermining of meaning and certainty? But it is this very word 'appropriate' that kindles a risk. For isn't this exactness of fit suspicious as well as auspicious? Isn't there also a sense that some necessary resistance to theory is missing, that the text is too smooth a stooge in this exercise? I have no obvious answers to these worries at this point, but it will be necessary to return to them later on.

First, however, I ought to try to substantiate the claim I have been making about the complicity between poem and method. 'Sortes Vergilianae' seems to me to be a poem about a life-journey, a journey of some one person, addressed by the poem as 'you', in search of knowledge, of what is variously alluded to as 'the secret', 'the thing', or 'illumination'. The search is long, various, intermittently suspended and resumed; ultimately, it seems we are left not with access to the secret, but only with the achievement of 'patience', which may or may not be rewarded. Elusive though it is, this poem cannot be read, let alone read 'deconstructively', without assenting to some such narrative account as this. But at the same time, it will be necessary to point to the ways in which the poem actively or covertly prevents such a reading, or makes it hard to follow through properly; for deconstruction, all the popular usage of that term to the contrary, is not concerned with the undermining of structures of meaning, but with elucidating the ways in which those structures cohabit with and necessitate forms of uncertainty and indeterminacy.

One of the most obvious of the ways in which this appears in 'Sortes Vergilianae' is through the interruption and complication of the reader's sense of the time-scale and sequence of the journey. Even in the first few lines, the poem slides unpredictably from the finality of the perfect tense ('You have been living now for a long time and there is nothing you do not know'), and the actuality of singular, completed moments in time ('Perhaps something you read in the newspaper influenced you'), to the temporal indeterminacy of repeated actions ('and that was very frequently'). We are never sure where we are in the journey, at the beginning, in the middle, or at the end, for the poem keeps shifting its temporal vantage-point, continually suggesting, with words like 'lately' and 'presently', some stable point of reference or departure, in some present tense of speaking, but never adequately specifying that point.[1]

So the experience of time in the poem presents the reader with a lot of problems. Either we look for a smooth and continuous sequence of moments and events, which form themselves into orderly series, with direction and continuity – in which case we will be frustrated by the poem's false starts, embeddings and temporal disalignments;

or we assume that there is no sequence, only a series of separate moments, which have been arbitrarily put together in this order, but must really be apprehended as simultaneous – in which case we will be denying the very dynamism of the process by which sequence and direction are continually evoked by the temporal language of the poem. The poem actually requires the apparatus of time in order to effect its flip over into achronology. One characteristic deconstructive critical gesture here would be to insist on this form of doubleness in the poem, in which it is not a case of the logic of *either/or* – either this poem has a logical time-structure, or it doesn't – but a case of the mutual dependence of the *either* and the *or*.

It is not just the idea of sequence which is subjected to this kind of interior decomposition in the poem. Just as important (and closely related to the idea of sequence), is the poem's deconstruction of what we may call 'punctuality', which may be defined as the apprehension of time in separate instants, each with their absolute autonomy. In fact, the idea of sequence requires the idea of punctuality, since, without the capacity to separate out the differentiable elements of a sequence, we would be left only with pure duration, in which no moment could be isolated long enough to be recognisable as preceding or succeeding any other moment. The experience of punctuality is equated through Ashbery's poem with the idea of the privileged moment in time or understanding, a moment at which insight and significance seem disproportionately concentrated, as in Wordsworth's notion of the revelatory or epiphanic 'spot of time'. Such a point is lifted out of time and yet also radiates its significance through the rest of the sequence of events or instants of which the poem, or life, or life-poem, is made up. Ashbery's poem is organised around the hypothecation of such privileged points of revelation or summation, for example the following: 'Perhaps something you read in the newspaper influenced you'; 'Then the sky opened up'; 'It is this blank carcass of whims and tentative afterthoughts / Which is being delivered into your hand like a letter'; 'This is just a footnote, though a microcosmic one perhaps'. Organised, but also disorganised by them, for in fact what the poem offers is the gesture or syntax of organisation without its accomplished effect. These points stand out against the body of the poem like figure against ground, except that we have no way of measuring the exact difference between figure and ground. Such moments in the poem are turning-points, which do not allow us to see exactly what they turn, or turn upon. The uncertain relation of figure and ground, point and plane, is at work in these lines which occur toward the end of the poem:

> This is just a footnote, though a microcosmic one perhaps, to the
>   greater curve
> Of the elaboration; it asks no place in it, only insertion *hors-texte* as the
>   invisible notion of how that day grew
> From planisphere to heaven

The oxymoronic phrase 'insertion *hors-texte*' plays with the idea of
inclusion and exteriority. 'This' (though we do not know what this 'this'
refers to, if it is to the enigmatic event just recounted, in which the
pulsating orchestras are halted by the apparently scandalous or unnerv-
ing fact of someone asking for a drink, to the 'story' of the journey
which is alluded to a few lines earlier, to the entire poem, or to the
very words of the footnote themselves), turns out to be not the essential
fact after all, but only some kind of added extra. This seems to say
two contradictory things at once; first that it (the footnote, which may
be a footnote to the poem or a name for it) is unconnected to the main
business of the poem, lies outside of, or to the side of its central
concerns (but then what is this 'it' and where is its centre?); and
secondly, that if a central concern of the poem is to demonstrate the
lack of reliable and repeatable reference-points, then the 'tentative after-
thought' of the footnote becomes essential, becomes precisely its *point*.
In a poem of fragments, the unattached particle may come to stand as
a central principle. And, indeed, the footnote does make a claim to
provide the hidden secret of the unity of design and enactment, part
and whole, in that it contains 'the invisible notion of how that day
grew / From planisphere to heaven, and what part in it all the "I"
had'. Ashbery's poem therefore uses the hypothesis of the point to
elaborate a disassembling of the relationship of point and sequence.

As we have seen, this disassembling is achieved largely through
the uncertainty of reference of the word 'this'. There are in the poem
several other examples of demonstratives with such uncertainty or
variability of reference:

> Perhaps something you read in the newspaper influenced you and *that*
>   was very frequently.
> They have left you to think along *these* lines . . .
>
> All good intentions, all that was arguable. *These* are stilled now . . .
>
> Being one and the same with the day it set out, though you cannot
>   imagine *this* . . .
> creature
> Who looked to the abandonment of such archaic forms as *these* . . .

Demonstratives often act in a discourse as a powerful suturing
force, threading together sentences, keeping the reader's attention
fixed and conjuring a world of continuity-in-difference. But in Ashbery's
poem, the effect of these iterations is not at all to affirm continuity,

nor to allow the clear differentiation of separate points or ideas, of 'this' point from 'that', for in every case, it is not clear what the 'this' or 'that' refers to, nor what its relationship is with what has just been said.

Even more potent as a device is the use of the word 'it' in Ashbery's poem (and, actually, throughout his work generally). Like a demonstrative, the impersonal pronoun 'it' must always send the reader back or forward to some other noun or phrase. Throughout Ashbery's poem, the word 'it' imparts this momentum of allusion without ever supplying a clear referential destination. The poem is studded with instances of the word in which we have little idea what the 'it' means: 'When you know where *it* is heading / You have to follow *it*'; '*It* is with us like day and night'. In the following passage, the accumulation of impersonal pronouns creates an even more abundant poverty of attribution:

> It is 'No Fishing' in modest capital letters, and getting out from under
>   the major weight of the thing
> As it was being indoctrinated and dropped, heavy as a branch with
>   apples,
> And as it started to sigh, just before tumbling into your lap, chagrined
>   and satisfied at the same time,
> Knowing its day over[2]

The point is that these 'it's are not merely or simply vacant, for their vacancy is precisely relative to the 'major weight' that they carry in the poem; their fullness lies in their emptiness. We may say that the poem requires us to give a sort of privilege to the points in the poem that turn out not to be points at all, but to be traced through or cross-shadowed with the other (non)points that they evoke.

Poems usually employ one punctuating device of particular authority, in their titles. As many have noted, John Ashbery's titles are often puzzling, enigmatic, or plain daft. As he has indicated in interviews, his practice is to select a title before rather than after writing the poem, the idea being that the command exercised by the title over its text may thereby be made more oblique; naming the text, but naming it in advance, as a datum or starting-point, the title may be superseded or contradicted in various ways by the poem that follows, rather than serving as a genetic imprint containing in advance all its potential meanings. Lee Edelman suggests another way of describing this. Ashbery's titles, he says, stand to his poems in a metonymic relation-ship of chance and contiguity rather than a metaphoric relationship of likeness or substitution.[3] In fact, however, it is not so much a matter of the simple replacement of metaphorical authority by meton-ymic contingency, as a problematic mingling of the two, that makes it difficult absolutely to distinguish authority *from* contingency. For Ashbery, the title both regulates and does not regulate the poem which is governed by and exceeds it; its misnaming being a functional obverse of its naming function or will-to-naming. Ashbery's own comments on this process are interesting:

> The title almost amounts to the 'given' for me; it indicates a space in which I will work. In addition to introducing the poem, it introduces me to the poem.
>   Very often my poems diverge from the areas or concerns the title has announced, and I think it's possible in this way to add a further dimension to poetry. I mean, one can write a poem 'To A Waterfowl' that has nothing to do with waterfowls, and the reader is obliged to consider the poem as somehow related to the subject indicated only in the title and not in the text itself.[4]

In *The Double Dream of Spring*, the volume in which 'Sortes Vergilianae' first appeared, the poem is accompanied by a note which explains that the title, which means 'Vergilian Prophecies', or, perhaps, 'Vergilian Oracles', 'refers to the ancient practice of fortune-telling by choosing a passage from Vergil's poetry at random'.[5] The title therefore seems to be referring to a process which is something like the process of title-giving that Ashbery describes above. In this kind of fortune-telling, a passage chosen at random from a preexistent text (Vergil's) serves as the prompt or starting-point for a subsequent narrative, the narrative of the subject's 'fortune', just as Ashbery's titles are the arbitrary but authoritative starting-points for the fortunes of the poems that are extrapolated from them. In both cases there is an uncertain blending of choice and chance, since it is the surrender of conscious control which leads to the discovery of deeper, more fundamental laws of poetico-religious destiny. In this procedure, not to choose is always in the end to have made the right choice. Like Ashbery's arbitrary title, the very arbitrariness of the choice is what guarantees or legitimates the truth of the Vergilian '*sors*' or oracle, for, no matter what point in the text the hand lights upon, it will always prove to have a point, can never be beside the point. And yet this authoritative truth also remains vulnerable to the undermining force of the primal act of hazard, since its predictive authority is not self-derived, but dependent upon the conscious intention exercised at some point in the future to treat it as authoritative.[6]

One of the things that Ashbery's plural title ('*Sortes* Vergilianae') suggests is that his own poem is in fact a series of oracular fragments, rather than a coordinated narrative. What makes this difficult to cope with is that the principle of their fragmentariness seems to be missing; that is, we cannot be sure of the laws which would enable us to define the points at which one fragment begins and another ends. This is fragmentation deprived of the orderliness of fragmentation. One of the most obvious ways in which this experience of fragmentariness is enacted through this poem is in its use of metaphor. The poem is entirely typical of Ashbery's work in its use of mixed, splintered and partial metaphors, which lie with their edges uncomfortably askew to each other:

> It is with us like day and night,
> The surge upward through the grade-school positioning and bursting
>   into soft gray blooms
> Like vacuum-cleaner sweepings, the opulent fuzz of our cage, or like
>   an excited insect
> In nervous scrimmage for the head, etching its none-too-complex
>   ordinances into the matter of the day.

Here we are given a series of metaphorical attributes with no object to attach them to, or none beyond the proleptic 'it' at the beginning of the sentence. The metaphors seem to specify various sorts of struggle, for self-betterment and academic success – or the things for which these may be metaphors – and their dingy, if still oddly exotic rewards, the 'soft gray blooms' which are immediately modified to 'vacuum-cleaner sweepings'. The insect metaphor seems in its turn to modify this, substituting 'scrimmage' for ascent, instinct for purpose, and perhaps stressing the brutal scars left by the struggle for dominance rather than what might be achieved at the end of it. There is certainly a kind of logic in these metaphors, but it is a logic that forbids us to return to the 'it', satisfied that it has been defined. Like the title, or the Vergilian prophecy, the 'it' serves as a starting point, from which the metaphors are generated; the principles of association are local, and multiple, such that there is no underlying unity between the end and the beginning of the sequence, even as the desire for such unity is what provides the propulsive force of the association.

So the poem seems to work with and between two syntaxes of meaning: in the first, meaning is held to be organically latent in and determined by some preexistent source, in life or text (the text of Vergil, for example); in the second, meaning emerges as an undetermined prolongation of a starting-point which is not predictive but initiatory. If the tense of the first syntax is the future perfect, the tense of the second is the 'future imperfect'.[7] These two syntaxes interact in one of the most striking metaphors in the poem, a metaphor in which the poem seems to offer authoritatively to read itself:

> It is this blank carcass of whims and tentative afterthoughts

> Which is being delivered into your hand like a letter some forty-odd
> years after the day it was posted.
> Strange, isn't it, that the message makes some sense, if only a relative
> one in the larger context of message receiving
> That you will be called to account for just as the purpose of it is
> becoming plain,
> Being one and the same with the day it set out, though you cannot
> imagine this.

Let us hazard a translation of this.

> The meaning of your life is suddenly revealed to you, but revealed not
> as any single secret principle, latent from the beginning and applying
> indifferently throughout, but as the principle of your non-coincidence
> with yourself. Looking back on your past, you realise how little you
> share with it, even if you are its ultimate destination. Thus, out of
> discontinuity comes the recognition of a kind of continuity. The meaning
> of the letter is its own non-meaning; all along your life was destined to
> add up to this fragmentation.

As well as referring to the difficulties of understanding a single life,
this metaphor also seems to describe the very process, of open
accretion rather than closed synthesis, by which metaphor itself
works in the poem. This is to imply that this metaphor, and the poem
as a whole, is also concerned with the question of poetic meaning
and understanding. Ashbery's title may make particular reference to
Philip Sidney's comments on the 'Sortes Vergilianae' in his *Defence of
Poetry* (1595). These occur in the context of an argument in favour of
the historical dignity of poetry, which stresses the use of poetry in
the teaching of philosophy, in the composition of histories and
chronicles and, here, the use of poetry as prophecy in Ancient Rome:

> Among the Romans a Poet was called *Vates*, which is as much as a
> Diviner, Fore-seer, or Prophet, as by his conioyned wordes *Vaticinium*
> and *Vaticinari* is manifest: so heavenly a title did that excellent people
> bestow upon this hart-ravishing knowledge. And so farre were they
> carried into the admiration thereof, that they thought in the chaunceable
> hitting upon any such verses great fore-tokens of their following fortunes
> were placed. Whereupon grew the word of *Sortes Vergilianae*, when by
> suddaine opening *Virgils* booke, they lighted upon any verse of hys
> making: whereof the histories of the Emperors lives are full.[8]

The Vergilian oracles therefore seem to suggest the power of poetry
in particular, since, Sidney says, 'that same exquisite observing of
number and measure in words, and that high flying liberty of conceit
proper to the Poet, did seeme to have some dyvine force in it'.[9] Does
Ashbery's title suggest that his poem, or even contemporary poetry
in general, might have, or should have this sort of divine force? Or
does it suggest in a mock-heroic manner an ironic classical counterpart
for the various moments of pseudo-revelation around which the
poem is organised? This latter would seem to be suggested by the

conspicuously unpoetic nature of much of the poem's language, which (in contrast to the suggestion of the esoteric in the poem's Latin title) repeatedly sets the vapid against the vatic: 'something you read in the newspaper', 'they have left you to think along these lines', 'such dramas sleeping below the surface'. There may even be a degraded equivalent of the oracle in the poem, in the empty message '"No Fishing" in modest capital letters', while the phrase 'they have left you to think along these lines' may also encode a casual reference to the kind of prophecy and interpretation alluded to in the title. But the ironies here are not of a kind that can be easily stabilised, to yield either a message of regret for the loss of poetry as divine knowledge, or its glad abandonment along with the embrace of the fallen condition of everyday language. The question of the authority of poetry is rather a matter for tense negotiation throughout 'Sortes Vergilianae', and thus always lies somewhere between sacred authority and banal disposability.

There is one particular set of metaphors which bears the force of this negotiation by linking the various forms of revelation and understanding with the processes of astrological or celestial divination. Sudden understanding is suggested early in the poem by the fact that 'the sky opened up'; later on, the possibility that the forty-year old letter can be seen as a sort of horoscope suggests that the subject of the poem might once have been an 'accomplice / Of all the possibilities of their journey through the night and the stars'. Textuality and astrological fortune-telling are also compacted in the final lines, which suggest the presence of a 'microcosmic' footnote, which is 'the invisible notion of how that day grew / From planisphere to heaven'; and the various references to the alteration of day and night through the poem seem to resolve at the end into 'long patience, as the star climbs and sinks, leaving illumination to the setting sun'. There may also be more oblique evocation of processes of divination in a phrase like 'marvels of speculation, auscultation, world-view', and the later mention of 'expansive aspects'.

These references to the various forms of illumination offered by the text of the constellations and celestial bodies are mediated by the references to light and visibility through the poem:

> almost as fast as the light from polar regions

> Reflected off the arctic ice-cap in summer . . .
>   raging at the confines of some miserable sunlit alley or court
> Things pass quickly out of sight . . .

> For it is wretchedness that endures, shedding its cancerous light on all
>   it approaches . . .

> the battlements of the city could be discerned from afar . . .

the invisible notion of how that day grew . . .

The rut became apparent only later
And by then it was too late to check such expansive aspects as what
to do while waiting . . .

Only long patience, as the star climbs and sinks, leaving illumination
to the setting sun

As has often been observed, knowledge in our culture (and perhaps for our species) is profoundly identified with actual and metaphorical looking and seeing.[10] Perhaps because of all the senses it is the one which most allows, even requires, distance and separation rather than proximity or interpenetration between subject and object, looking is associated with a knowledge whose authority derives from the fact of its careful subtraction of itself from the objects it attempts to know. The metaphor of truth as light is an understandable extrapolation of knowing as seeing, although it complicates the clear differentiation of subject and object; for if light is the object of seeing, it is also what makes seeing possible, since in order to see light, it is necessary to have light to see by. This is to say that the metaphor of knowledge or truth as light simultaneously acts in the service of the abstraction of knowledge from what it surveys and serves to suggest the opposite of this – that knowledge is no more pure, placeless and insubstantial than light is.

'Sortes Vergilianae' participates in this double-reading of the knowledge–light association. The poem suggests both that knowledge is buried and may be brought *to* light ('Under their hiding was the secret, casual as breath, betrayed for the asking') and that knowledge *is* light ('Then the sky opened up, revealing much more than any of you were intended to know'). But the light in Ashbery's poem is a very imperfect and compromised medium, a miserable, declining, even 'cancerous' light. It is not clear what will be yielded to the 'long patience, as the star climbs and sinks, leaving illumination to the setting sun' in the last line of the poem, since the light that is apparently preferred to the inconstancy of starlight, is itself a light in decline. It may be that the literal and metaphorical meanings of 'illumination' are in conflict here; if the actual light of the sun is waning, then the metaphorical light of understanding and stoic resignation shed by this waning light ought to be positive and permanent. But the literal and the metaphorical may not be so easily separable. For the metaphor of 'illumination' derives its authority precisely from the permanence and reliability of the sun as source of all light, and source of the visibility of all metaphors. If this is so, then the diminution of the literal light, in the suggestion that the sun may slowly be fading out, must necessarily also complicate the force of the metaphor. With the discrediting of the metaphor of the sun, there would be no authority for the metaphor of the stoic illumination of awareness.[11]

The promise of a knowledge in the sense of an illumination which is beyond or beneath metaphor is the promise that 'Sortes Vergilianae' constantly holds out and betrays. The light of patient resignation at the end of the poem answers the image of light as revelation at the beginning, an image which already mingles light and movement:

> It is a strange thing how fast the growth is, almost as fast as the light
>   from polar regions
> Reflected off the arctic ice-cap in summer. When you know where it is
>   heading
> You have to follow it, though at a sadly reduced rate of speed

The implication of the light of knowledge and awareness with the dynamics of speed, movement and direction gives it an awkward materiality; there is something very peculiar about the idea of a light of truth or revelation which is not just the object of a spatio-temporal pursuit, but is itself 'heading' somewhere, moving through space and time. It is this idea of light in movement which connects the metaphors of illumination, astrology and punctuality in 'Sortes Vergilianae'. If light possesses materiality (velocity and duration), then the constellations, formed out of points of light in apparently invariant configurations, no longer offer themselves as any kind of prefiguration of human fortunes and meanings. They become an allegory of an illumination which is itself in motion, itself viewed from different points, cross-lit from different sources, none of them permanent; a projection, not of man's centrality in the universe, but of his Copernican decentring.

In one sense, of course, this examination of the function of light in 'Sortes Vergilianae' reveals nothing less than the resistance offered by the poem to the singling out of any metaphor as dominant; but it would be premature and homogenising to claim simply that the poem is – like the cosmos itself – nothing more than a decentred swirl of metaphors, none of which possess authority over the others. For such decentring is only perceptible, only has force and definition in the light of the particular forms of metaphorical dominant that the poem *seems* to offer, if only in order to undermine them.

It is in this sense that a deconstructive reading can claim to be following the authority of the poem, even in its questioning of final or transcendent authority. If the title of the poem tells us what the poem is unignorably about, the attempt to read the meanings of things, and the question of the authority of poetry in that reading, the poem also offers an internal critique of the process whereby meaning is abstracted and attributed. For what is this meditation upon time and meaning if not an unmistakeable demonstration of the impossibility of identifying any point in a poem, or a life, which is immune to the passage of time and the processes of metaphorical transference and narrative elaboration? The Vergilian oracle tells us that all attempts to assign fundamental, or hidden meanings are like arbitrary or random selections from a preexistent text; they pretend to bring a hidden destiny to light, but in fact only ever do so through a retroactive process whereby the text is made to refer to something in the future which it could not foreknow, drawing it out into a destiny which is always an interruption and a displacement, never a fulfilment.

This is the point at which we can return to the question posed at the beginning of this essay. The mode of analysis adopted here may seem more than ever to suggest its own redundancy as a generalisable procedure, since the claim has been that, in advance of any critical reading, Ashbery's poem itself performs the work of self-undoing. If the reading of the title and its relationship to the rest of the poem is correct, it seems to suggest a certain canny foreknowledge in this text of its deconstructive destiny; the poem seems to predict the future perfect of a reading which will bring to light its condemnation of prediction and bringing to light.

But we may also have seen how the very complacency of that gesture of self-cancellation is subjected to sceptical inspection by the poem, which insists above all that texts must be *read*. If a deconstructive reading such as the one offered here seems to be merely a restatement of what the poem already and in advance 'says', then that has only become apparent through a process of reading that is not reducible to the mere 'elaboration of a curve', the playing out of a central hypothesis. To translate the poem into the deconstructive lesson that it gives is actually to travesty that lesson, which insists precisely on process against proposition. In this it may seem again to redouble deconstructive thought itself, which cannot (or cannot without bad faith) be reduced to a set of protocols or critical routines; deconstruction is characterised not by processes and effects that may be reliably predicted in advance, but rather by what may ensue from a reading that does not in principle suspend itself at the point where coherence of meaning seems to have been achieved (and, as we have seen, incoherence at one level can function as a cohering force at another, as when a poem's uncertainties of meaning are construed as a coherent demonstration of the uncertainty of all meaning).

The questions of authority and responsibility that are enacted through these processes are what profoundly link the two bizarrely unprofitable activities of writing poetry and practising deconstructive criticism. In this respect, we may say that Ashbery's poem has an interesting and important address to its, that is to say, our, historical moment, for it is concerned markedly with the powers and functions of poetry itself, at a time when those powers seem to have been almost totally discredited. One point of 'Sortes Vergilianae' is the sardonic demonstration that poetry simply no longer has the divine authority which it once had; but the response made by the poem to this demonstration is neither romantically to hallucinate poetry back into its role as unacknowledged legislator of human fortunes, nor to reconstitute that authority negatively, in the equivalently romantic gesture of absolute self-denial. Rather, it is to compel a self-reflexive examination of the conditions of that authority, in a gesture that is neither uniformly positive nor uniformly negative. Charles Altieri, while noting the affinities between Ashbery's poetry and critical deconstruction, prefers the term 'decreation' for the former, on the grounds that, where deconstruction 'is primarily a critical act devoted to displaying the irreducible interchange of sense and nonsense in the overlapping codes on which any discourse is ultimately dependent', 'decreation' is a mode of disintegration which allows the exploration of new forms of integration.[12] But this is artificially to separate two moments – of disintegration and reintegration – that are in fact integral to both the 'deconstructive' and 'decreative' alternatives Altieri thereby produces. Ashbery's work does not allow us easily to counterpose the critical and the creative in this way, and certainly not to maintain this distinction between cultural affirmation and negation. The division between the two is a freezing of what is profoundly, if problematically, continuous in Ashbery's work. The shape of the reading which is portended by 'Sortes Vergilianae' runs together authority and surrender, affirmation and negation, insinuating that what poetry and critical deconstruction may have in common is the singular responsibility they assume for conducting the dissolution of forms of absolute authority.

NOTES

1. For a more detailed account of the temporal indeterminacies of 'Sortes Vergilianae', see Mary Kinzie, '"Irreference": The Poetic Diction of John Ashbery. Part II: Prose, Prosody, and Dissembled Time', *Modern Philology*, **82** (1987), pp. 389–92.
2. The indeterminacy of Ashbery's pronouns is a recurrent theme in criticism of his work. It is discussed, for example, in John Koethke, 'The Metaphysical Subject of

John Ashbery's Poetry', in David Lehman (ed.), *Beyond Amazement: New Essays on John Ashbery* (Cornell University Press, Ithaca and London, 1980), pp. 89–90, and Mary Kinzie, '"Irreference": The Poetic Diction of John Ashbery. Part I: Styles of Avoidance', *Modern Philology*, **82** (1987), pp. 274–5.

3. 'The Pose of Imposture: Ashbery's "Self-Portrait in a Convex Mirror"', *Twentieth Century Literature*, **32** (1986), pp. 96–7.

4. Interview with David Lehman, October 17, 1977, quoted in Lehman, 'The Shield of a Greeting', in Lehman (ed.), *Beyond Amazement*, p. 111.

5. *The Double Dream of Spring* (first published 1970; repr. Ecco Press, New York, 1976), p. 95.

6. In a prescient review of *The Double Dream of Spring*, Richard Howard notes this dialectic of choice and chance, but seems to see it as closed rather than open in direction and effect when he writes that 'what Ashbery calls "the secret of the search" is that its given, its continued existence in the world, makes all choosing certain to succeed, and therefore eliminates the necessity of choice', 'Sortes Vergilianae', *Poetry* (October, 1970), p. 53.

7. I borrow the notion of the 'future imperfect' from Geoffrey Bennington's 'Towards a criticism of the future' in David Wood (ed.), *Writing the Future* (Routledge, London, 1990), pp. 17–29. Many of the essays in this collection also bear on this question of the relationship between writing, prediction and retrospection.

8. Evelyn S. Shuckburgh (ed.), *An Apologie for Poetrie* (Cambridge University Press, Cambridge, 1938), pp. 5–6.

9. Ibid., p. 6.

10. Two critical accounts of this 'ocularcentrism' are David Michael Levin, *The Opening of Vision: Nihilism and the Postmodern Situation* (Routledge, London, 1988) and Martin Jay, 'In the Empire of the Gaze: Foucault and the denigration of Vision in Twentieth-Century French Thought', in David Couzens Hoy (ed.), *Foucault: A Critical Reader* (Blackwell, Oxford, 1986), pp. 175–204.

11. It will be plain how much this discussion of the relation between light and knowledge owes to Derrida's 'White Mythology: Metaphor in the Text of Philosophy', in Alan Bass (trans.), *Margins of Philosophy* (Harvester, Brighton, 1982), pp. 207–72.

12. 'Motives in Metaphor: John Ashbery and the Modernist Long Poem', *Genre*, **11** (1978), p. 661.

Chapter 2

'Sortes Vergilianae'

Richard Rand

I

What does it cost to read a poem by John Ashbery? What price does the poem 'exact'? What profit does it 'bestow'? What is the link, if any, between such profit and such price? (We read, in 'The System', that 'as it exacts, so it bestows.')

Ashbery has, on occasion, posed the problem of his poetry's 'price' in terms of attention: thus for example, a reader (the reader 'John Ashbery', for example), may wish to pursue the absent and cryptic meaning of a poem, or, accepting the fact of that absence and the unprofitability of that pursuit, may decide instead 'to stay in relation to these other things . . . whose installedness was the price of further revolutions':

> . . . gulls had swept the gray steel towers away
> So that it profited less to go searching, away over the humming earth,
> Than to stay in immediate relation to these other things – boxes, store
>   parts, whatever you wanted to call them –
> Whose installedness was the price of further revolutions . . .
>
> ('The Bungalows')

'These other things', initially and tentatively, may simply refer to anything recent or near at hand in one's everyday existence – to 'rectangular shapes', as the same poem also says, that 'became so extraneous and so near / To create a foreground of quiet knowledge . . . .' In 'The System', for instance, they comprise the contents of a 'scrap basket':

> . . . you turn away from the window almost with a sense of relief, to bury yourself again in the task of sorting out the jumbled scrap basket of your recent days, without any hope of completing it or even caring whether it gets done or not . . . .

These given things, however, soon start to assume a peculiar interest, taking on 'a life of their own':

> . . . a drowsiness overtakes you as of total fatigue and indifference; in this unnatural, dreamy state the objects you have been contemplating

19

take on a life of their own, in and for themselves. It seems to you that you are eavesdropping and can understand their private language. They are not talking about you at all, but are telling each other curious private stories about things you can only half comprehend, and other things that have a meaning only for themselves and are beyond any kind of understanding . . . .

('The System')

The 'scrap basket' of Ashbery's attention has become a library of story-telling pieces; the nearer things are like the things of language, of literary language with its 'curious private stories about things', signs whose meanings are 'only for themselves and are beyond any kind of understanding'.

It is a singular narrowness of Ashbery's work that everything does actually refer, in the end, not only to itself but also to 'the boxes, store parts, whatever you want to call them' of English – to the grammar, the syntax, and the rules of the English language. When, for example, in 'Soonest Mended', Ashbery tells the story of his poetic career in terms of the game of golf, he reports that the 'players' on the course are the 'rules' of the game itself – the poet and his readers being 'merely spectators':

> . . . though we knew the course *was* hazards and nothing else
> It was still a shock when, almost a quarter of a century later,
> The clarity of the rules dawned on you for the first time.
> *They* were the players, and we who had struggled at the game
> Were merely spectators, though subject to its vicissitudes . . . .

('Soonest Mended')

In his terms of 'price' and 'profit' this 'dawning' of the 'the clarity of the rules' is to be reckoned among the costs, the expense, of Ashbery's language when it plays the game of self-referral in earnest. The 'dawning' is felt as a 'shock', not just of learning, but of losing – of losses incurred, on the poet's part, of 'ownership' over language. For 'sentences' are detached from the poet: their separation is entailed by their legibility, their placement in a night-time sky whose 'message', stellified, is 'raised past us, taken from us . . .':

> Night after night this message returns, repeated
> In the flickering bulbs of the sky, raised past us, taken away from us,
> Yet ours over and over until the end that is past truth,
> The being of our sentences, in the climate that fostered them,
> Not ours to own, like a book, but to be with . . . .
> But the phantasy makes it ours . . .

('Soonest Mended')

The 'dawning' also imposes a cost on the reader's account: not only quitting the search for remote truths, the reader must also quit the search for some spontaneous insight into the poet – for some (confessional) revelation of his empirical person; such an inquiry, inevitably tempting, is deemed 'fantastic' ('the fantasy makes it ours . . .'). Detachment makes it so.

What then, do we gain when we watch the 'rules' at 'play' on the 'course of hazards'? Not, it seems a deep or cosmic insight of any decisive kind. In Ashbery's work, the truth is not to be told; reading becomes a test of patience, of renewed curiosity about the player-rules. The lines from 'Soonest Mended' provide a modest, though telling, example of that test: no doubt the pronoun 'they', in *They were the players . . .*', refers to the 'rules', which is the pronoun's nearest antecedent plural. But is the word 'rules', in fact, a plural antecedent of the pronoun, belonging, as it does, to a clause that is phrased in the singular ('the clarity of the rules')? The word 'hazards', on the previous line, supplies a more truly plural antecedent, however weak or implausible its meaning. Our reading is therefore unruly: it has watched, helplessly, as the rules of pronoun reference drive through the hazards of Ashbery's phraseology.

In a word, Ashbery costs us by challenging our readerly competence as well as our patience: he tests (and extends) our capacity for exactness, a capacity which he calls (in 'The System') our 'sensual intelligence'. Ashbery exacts of his reader a sense of exactness. Thus, in 'Litany', he asks:

> . . . Exactly whom are you aware of –
> Who can describe the exact feel
> And slant of a field . . .?

– a question which extends to the 'feel and the slant' of the written page:

> Just one minute of contemporary existence
> Has so much to offer, but who
> Can evaluate it, formulate
> The appropriate apothegm, show us
> In a few well-chosen words of wisdom
> Exactly what is taking place around us?
> Not literary critics, certainly, though that is precisely
> What they are supposed to be doing . . . .

It is the besetting misdeed, the impertinence, of critics to ignore the 'exact' or the 'precise' in favour of an 'approximate' view, a misdeed that leads to disasters of projection and tendentious reasoning:

> . . . Seeing things
> In *approximately* the same way as the writer or artist
> Doesn't help either, in fact, if anything, it makes things worse

> Because then the other person thinks he
> Or she has found whatever it is that makes
> Art interesting to them . . .
> And goes on a rampage, featuring his or her emotions
>   . . . but it's doomed
> To end in failure, unless that person happens to be
> Exactly the same person who is doing
> All this to them . . . .

As this passage indicates, moreover, exactness in reading a poem – unlike the exactness of reading a 'field' – takes on the particular charge of a rhetorical precision: someone 'is doing all this . . .' in language; someone is performing, acting or arguing to some effect, and precisely so (in 'Europe', Ashbery says that 'precise mechanisms / Love us'). The poet's precision is exactly argumentative, and it stands or falls according to the force, the pertinence and the acuity of its argumentation. The critic is a spectator in the sense that the critical questions shall have already been posed and explored by the poem, the insights of the reader deriving from the work that is read:

> Criticism should take into account that it is we
> Who made it, and therefore
> Not be too eager to criticize us: we
> Could do that for ourselves, and have done so . . .
>   . . . it knows
> Itself through us, and us
> Only through being part of ourselves, the bark
> Of the tree of our intellect . . . .

Does the reader risk, as it were, being coerced by the poet's arguments into some unreflective reiteration or paraphrase? The point to recall is the context of the given argument within the poem – the rules among the hazards, the conjunction or argument (or tendency) among the rules and the hazards at play. From this perspective, poet and critic alike are 'merely spectators'. Hence that the critic performs a pedagogical task – the task, indeed, of reporting to the poet precisely what happens in the rhetorical round of the poem:

>   . . . It behooves
> Our critics to make the poets more aware of
> What they're doing, so that poets in turn
> Can stand back from their work and be enchanted by it . . . .

Here, the term 'critic', like 'spectator', names a fissure in Ashbery's language – the non-concurrence of language as act and of language as cognizance – as well as a division of labour. Another designation for this fissure, in Ashbery's poetry, is the persistently reiterated pronoun 'you' – the enigmatic 'you' to whom almost every poem is addressed, apostrophically. 'You' is frequently a divided (anachronic-ally and anatopically) 'I'. Akin to John Bunyan's God, it often regards the work of 'I' (and of 'itself') with an ideal (or absolute) patience and lucidity:

> Each detail was startlingly clear, as though seen through a magnifying
> glass,
> Or would have been to an ideal observer, namely yourself –
> For only you could watch yourself so patiently from afar
> The way God watches a sinner on the path to redemption,
> Sometimes disappearing into valleys, but always *on the way*,
> For it all builds up into something, meaningful or meaningless
> As architecture . . . .

('The Bungalows')

What kind of poetry, at last, issues forth from the obsession with vigilance? As the allusion, above, to *Pilgrim's Progress* indicates, the fissures of Ashbery's work, and the fables arising from those fissures, are composed in an allegorical mode (Ashbery, at the close of 'The System', states that 'the allegory is ended, its coil absorbed into the past'). Throughout his poetry, Ashbery makes the kind of rhetorical move that Coleridge (in his 'Lectures on Literature' of 1818 published in the *Literary Remains* of 1836), remarking on Spenser's allegory, observes of *The Faerie Queene*:

> you will take especial note of the marvelous independence and true
> imaginative absence of all particular space or time in *The Faerie Queene*.
> It is in the domains neither of history or geography; . . . it is truly in the
> land of Faery, that is, of mental space. The poet has placed you in a
> dream, a charmed sleep . . . .

Ashbery's 'mental space' – a *constituted* space and time that keeps its difference and its distance from the *given* space of history or geography – is an 'allegorical' space akin to that of Spenser's verse, or of Euclid's geometry. His work is therefore not a work of initial appeal to those modes of analysis – psychoanalytic, sociological, or ideological – that posit an empirical 'desire' or purpose as the ground of the poet's rhetoric. Seeking only to reveal its language – not to have or to hold, not to win or to lose – his allegory is singularly lacking in occasional context: none of his almost four hundred poems, written over four decades, is written to intervene in any political process; none is addressed specifically to an actual person publicly linked to some place, or cause, or happening. In this respect, Ashbery's allegory goes far beyond the practice of Spenser or Bunyan, for whom the allegorical is a privileged elaboration of metaphysical or ethical questions in connection with current events, however obliquely mentioned. Ashbery, for his part, appears to limit his allegories to the issues of language in its most technical specificity: language, sheer language as such – that is his thing.

II

Like the rest, therefore, 'Sortes Vergilianae' is an allegory of language – of, in the first place, 'perhaps', the language to be found in 'the newspaper':

> You have been living now for a long time and there is nothing you do not know.
> Perhaps something you read in the newspaper influenced you and that was very frequently.
> They have left you to think along these lines and you have gone your own way . . . .

From the very first word, the one called 'you' is a figure somehow *subjected* – if not to 'the newspaper', then perhaps to a 'they' ('they have left you . . .'). A subject, perhaps of ideology? The subject *as* ideology? Does the poet belong to that subject? As elsewhere, the apostrophised 'you' is problematically coextensive with an 'I', nearly absent from this poem, never naming itself directly, never enunciating itself in its own person, rising, at most, to the oblique legibility of a 'we' (or, more precisely, of an 'us', as in the phrase 'it is with us like day or night', or the phrase 'the opulent fuzz of our cage') and, at the close of the poem, naming itself as that which is not itself, one among several topics in the poem ('what part in it all the "I" had'). Least of all does this virtual spacing of 'you' and 'I' – 'virtual' because reduced to a function of the person–system in English syntax – mark off a division of intellectual labour, as between author and reader; or between poem and commentary; or between poem and 'newspaper'; or between 'we' and 'they'. A division of this kind is baffled by the many dimensions of a demonstrative adjective and an ambiguous verb:

> They have left you to think along these lines and you have gone your own way . . . .

Variously: they have left you the lines and have assigned you the task of thinking along them; or, they have deserted you in order that they may think along these lines; or, they have deserted you in order that you may think along these lines – these lines being the ones that they have left you, or the ones that you have invented; these lines being either their legacy or your creation – such that, when 'you have gone your own way', it is either their way or yours or both. The poem does not tell us which: it does not let itself appear either to extend or to deviate from the given 'lines' (if indeed they are given) of the 'newspaper' (if indeed they are of the 'newspaper').

More generally, the ties of the poem's language to the givens of ideology are as uncertain as the ties between 'I' and 'you', felt – by any reader, at any given time, of any given passage – as at once an identity *and* a distinction, a confusion *and* a coincidence. At no point are we assured of the divisions between 'we' and 'they', 'I' and 'you', 'newspaper' and 'poem'. These improprieties of ideology are sustained, throughout the poem, by means of a curious stylistic discipline: the poem parades in an even masquerade of monotones – as in the length of its lines; in the length of its sentences; in the frequency of its endstopping; in the (loose) regularity of its stress-pattern; in a near-total use of sentences in the declarative mode (only one interrogative, and perhaps one exclamatory), and of sentences in the indicative mood; in the use of parataxis between the sentences, and, within the sentences, in an absence of periodic variety (no deferring of main clauses to the end).

Monotony of tone produces uncertainty of reading. Done, as here, at length, it gives rise to a block-like, impartial consistency which frustrates any continuous, curtailed or concentrated reading. In the process of thwarting a sustained reading, it produces random reading – readings, at least, of passages caught at random. Whence its title 'Sortes Vergilianae': the rhetoric of the poem compels us to read it in fragments, although the poem itself is self-evidently hyper-coherent. The monotone coherence of the rhetoric precludes, moreover, our *selecting* those moments according to any intrinsic feature of special notice or legibility. We read it in fragments, and the fragments are noticed at random. We engage the poem as the monks are said to have done with Vergil in the Middle Ages – as in, to cite the note by Ashbery, 'the ancient practice of fortune-telling by choosing a passage from Vergil's poetry at random'. But the poetry, in this instance, is the amorphous and anonymous idiom of the newspapers, duplicated, idiosyncratically, by the monochrome phrases of Ashbery's own language. Like Vergil, like ideology, 'Sortes Vergilianae' seems illegible in its consistency, its extension, its measured evenness of tone, and in the almost friable non-continuity of its ongoing narrative.

Is there, then, an ideology at work *within* this problematic effusion? Does its rhetoric espouse, or disespouse, a finite system of values of belief? And is there, in the problematic spacing of 'I' and 'you', of 'we' and 'they', a stable critical distance, or even a programme of distinctions that recalls some already existing critique or body of ideological analysis (Marxist, structuralist, Frankfurter)?

'Sortes Vergilianae' is, among other things, a poem of its own time and place: it thinks, in some parts, 'along the lines' of 1969, and of Paris and New York, which is to say, of ideology, of the critique of ideology, and of that critique *as* ideology. Thus, at the close of the poem, we happen upon some topics linked to the writing of Roland Barthes, Jacques Lacan, Louis Althusser, Michel Foucault, and Jacques Derrida – writers, like Ashbery himself, affiliated in various degrees to the Parisian periodical *Tel Quel*:

> This is just a footnote, though a microcosmic one perhaps, to the greater curve
> Of the elaboration; it asks no place in it, only insertion *hors-texte* as the invisible notion of how that day grew
> From planisphere to heaven, and what part in it all the 'I' had . . . .

Meditations, then, on the 'subject' and its position, and meditations on the nature of the text and of general textuality: these are topics of *Tel Quel* 'ideology', and of its critique; they can be absorbed in the anonymity of ideology as such, but they originate as modes of ideology's critique. 'Sortes Vergilianae' joins those topics: it does so, in the first place, by citing them; in the second place, by appearing to endorse them as principles of its own composition; and, in the third place, by contriving a context – 'Sortes Vergilianae' – in which the logic of that critique appears to be strung out to the point of incoherence (the 'part in it all the "I" had' is literally non-existent; the 'insertion' of the poem-footnote into the *'hors-texte'* subscribes, in its very syntax, to Derrida's celebrated remark that 'there is no *hors-texte'* – a footnote having no place, *qua* footnote, in the 'greater curve of the elaboration', nor being, *qua* footnote, *hors-texte*; nothing, for that matter, can be *in*serted, situated within, a thing or place that is *out*side, *dehors*. Subscribes, but also contradicts – by hypothesising the *'hors-texte'* as a place (that is not a place)).

In sum, 'Sortes Vergilianae' is *out of ideology* – at once the issue or product of ideology, the critique of ideology, and (that critique being grounded in structural linguistics and its deconstruction of ideological encoding) 'out of ideology' as one might be 'out of money' or 'out of fuel': as the allegory of a critique of (ideological) rhetoric, the poem is prevented, in advance, from venting its own values. That it may none the less come to do so, at the end, should not encourage us to ignore or to minimise its attenuated and circumspect atmosphere of the *uncertain* thing: to the verbal mass of its monotone is added the inaudible and invisible varnish of parody – between sentences, in the parodic pressure of parataxis, and within sentences, in a parodic overcharge of ambiguated syntax:

Things pass quickly out of sight and the best is to be forgotten quickly . . .

– meaning, to no obviously efficient rhetorical end, that it is best to be forgotten quickly; that it is inevitable that the best will be forgotten; or that the best way (for the best thing?) to pass quickly out of sight is to be forgotten quickly. 'Sortes Vergilianae' is a poem that haunts itself so as not to be itself; every sentence, if not every line, gleams with the parody of ripeness to excess, a stylistic feature, perhaps, since the exercise of unpacking ambiguities is not obviously destined in any way to advance an understanding of the poet's guiding allegory.

What allegory, therefore – what tale? What operation *out of ideology*?

Rather than dilate at too great length, a brief inventory of topics can serve to bring its ideological attention into view. Topics, in this poem, are ideologemes:

1. the poem tells a story, with a beginning, a middle and an end;
2. the story it tells is of a life (the life of 'you');
3. that life-story is told from its earliness ('the surge upward through the grade school') to its lateness ('by then it was too late') but not to its terminus, a future moment ('the larger context of message-receiving that you will be called to account for');
4. the story is one of loss (of initial power) and of knowledge gained ('there is nothing you do not know');
5. that life-story is also described as a journey ('as the journey grew ever slower');
6. that journey, in keeping with its own etymology, is described in terms of a 'day' ('it is with us like day and night');
7. the day, the journey, the life and the story commence with an apocalypse ('then the sky opened up') and end with a sunset ('leaving illumination to the setting sun');
8. the journey traverses a horizontal space; its complications of tempo, destination and interference are an affair of the ground; only its initial apocalypse is elevated ('then the sky opened up', or 'that day grew from planisphere to heaven');
9. the journey being implicated in its 'day', in the passage of the sun toward its setting, the movement on the ground, inferentially, passes from east to west; it is directional;
10. while the 'day' of *initial* apocalypse is punctual, or fugitive, the life of 'you' is represented also as a sequence of *subsequent* days that go nowhere, locked in the inertia of a diminished repetition, day following day of baffled passions and 'dull fevers', sustained by a mysterious 'patience' (by 'your patience only beginning');

11. the day, the journey, the life and the story are also a letter or 'message' ('the message makes some sense');
12. the 'you' who is the message is also its receiver ('delivered into your hand like a letter').

Long as this list may seem, it hardly exhausts the poem's ideological range. Indeed, we only mention these topics at this point to set them aside, for they form a system, a family of topics deriving from literature as such: they do not comprise an allegory of ideology, only the by-product of ideology in formation. Brutally, we may call them, as a group, a 'romantic ideology' of the kind so richly delineated in the critical writings of Harold Bloom. 'Sortes Vergilianae', as a tissue of Romantic topics, repeats or duplicates, parodically, the movements and themes of *Tintern Abbey* and the *Rime of the Ancient Mariner*.

Quite another topic in 'Sortes Vergilianae', also Romantic in its provenance, but not altogether so in its emphasis, is the topic of *prison* – of the police, of judgement; the narrative (if not the poem) commences in jail, in 'grade school', also described as 'the opulent fuzz of our cage', the place where 'perhaps something you read in the newspaper influenced you'. Such, it seems, is the prior terrain, the context, the ground of the (supposedly) inaugural 'apocalypse' ('*then* the sky opened up . . .'). And, the poem predicts, the life of 'you' shall terminate in a judicial moment ('the larger context of message-receiving that you will be called to account for'). In between the initial 'cage' and the terminal judgement (the life-time of Romantic questing) frustrations are those of spatial confinement – 'the confines of some miserable sunlit alley or court' – and of juridical stricture ('it is "No Fishing" in modest capital letters'). The journey is in jail. The journey is jail.

What, then, is *jail*, ideologically construed?

Jail is ideology. It is the system itself of Romanticism, and of literature. To borrow from 'Soonest Mended', it is 'the being of our sentences', and 'the avatars / of our conforming to the rules'. It is the time and the place of 'patience'.

Perhaps the most helpful gloss on 'Sortes Vergilianae' is the brief and quiet poem, immediately preceding it in *The Double Dream of Spring*, entitled 'The Chateau Hardware':

> It was always November there. The farms
> Were a kind of precinct; a certain control
> Had been exercised. The little birds
> Used to collect along the fence.
> It was the great 'as though,' the how the day went,
> The excursions of the police
> As I pursued my bodily functions, wanting
> Neither fire nor water,

> Vibrating to the distant pinch
> And turning out the way I am, turning out to greet you.

It is a remarkable memoir, in the confessional mode, of the poet's formation as a scene of the 'police' patrolling a 'precinct' with a 'fence' – a monotonous scene ('It was always November there'), marked by anonymous control ('a certain control / had been exercised') and the round of prison-like routine ('as I pursued my bodily functions'). It is a scene devoid of pathos, and the place where literary imaginings occur ('it was the great "as though"'): out of this setting, out of this police-state, the poet is 'turned out' to 'greet you' with his poems, 'Sortes Vergilianae' among them. And he never abandons this 'Chateau', a looming, Kafka-esque formation that shadows all his later movements. Grounds his movements.

What, at last, is this jail and its 'sentences', if not the syntax of English itself? To read 'Sortes Vergilianae' as a structuralist exercise, where the subject of the poem (be it 'I' or 'you') is 'caged' (caught or constituted) in the rules of syntax – sentenced, as the reckoning used to have it, to the 'being of our sentences' themselves – such a reading is not altogether implausible. As a poem of its moment, moreover, 'Sortes Vergilianae' ought to be read that way – at least provisionally so. The only shortcoming of such a reading is its lack of exactness: ideologically regarded, a 'sentence' – the prison-house of the constituted subject – consists of its principle parts of speech (subject, verb and object) in their grammatical relations. These are, as it were, the sentence; and they do indeed occur, with all due grammatical soundness, in all the various sentences of 'Sortes Vergilianae'. They do not, however, exhaust the grammatical force of these sentences; perhaps they do not, in the end, even furnish that grammatical force. A more exact accounting is called for.

To begin with, there is no such thing as *a* sentence in this poem, for the syntax of Ashbery's sentences serve to actuate not one, but two, rhetorics at one and the same time. Sentences like

> . . . When you know where it is heading
> You have to follow it . . . .

or

> Presently all will go off satisfied, leaving the millpond bare . . . .

or

> There was a time when the words dug in . . . .

are at once the syntagms of a narrative whose singular subject is 'you', and the detachable, free-standing apothegms of sententious rhetoric, whose subject is generalised to the point of being a plural 'you', and very nearly *im*personalised. As with the *Aeneid* of the Middle Ages, each sentence is at once the fragment of a unified, single, heroic life, and the free-standing, detachable phrase of the Chinese fortune-cookie (the '*sors*' of the 'Sortes Vergilianae'). Redoubtable problems of reading accrue to this double rhetoric: what, if any, is the link between the two rhetorics, the two subjects, the two sentences? Is there, between them, a relationship of dependence or dominance? An ideological bond? One, the subject of *narrative*, would seem to realise the topic of the Romantic subject, while the other, the subject of sententious *law-making*, would seem to realise the topic of the 'subject-position' as a formal effect of syntax. The poem could then be read as a meditation on the coimplication of the two topics, with one (the juridical topic) policing the other (the Romantic topic). Again, a reading of this kind is not only not false: it is unavoidable; and it is also incomplete. For the poem does more; it gives more, without saying more. How so?

For a clue to Ashbery's procedure, let us recur once again to 'The Chateau Hardware':

> It was always November there. The farms
> Were a kind of precinct; a certain control
> Had been exercised. The little birds
> Used to collect along the fence.
> It was the great 'as though,' the how the day went,
> The excursions of the police
> As I pursued my bodily functions, wanting
> Neither fire nor water,
> Vibrating to the distant pinch,
> And turning out the way I am, turning out to greet you.

Granted that the 'police' can be taken as a trope or figure for the juridical rhetoric of maxims, and that the 'I' of this 'confessional memoir' can be taken as a trope or figure for the Romantic rhetoric of a (sentenced) narrative self, what is the status, the place, the topology of 'the great "as though"'? Is it the *setting* of an empirical formation, the protective and policed environment of a 'Chateau', perhaps akin to the Deerfield Academy of Ashbery's boyhood? A hyper-space for the poet-in-training? Certainly so, provided we do not suppose that the poet has ever graduated (in 'Soonest Mended', we learn that 'none of us ever graduates from college'). The tense system of the closing sentence precludes any graduation ('it *was* the great "as though" . . . / As I *pursued* my bodily functions . . . / . . . turning out the way I *am* . . .') which is not a continuing process as well in the present time ('turning out to greet you'). Which is to say that the poet moves from a 'Chateau' called 'Hardware' toward an activity where 'hardware', acquired at the 'Chateau', is in use; the rhetoric of *this* poem is itself couched in the great 'as though': thus, the 'farms' / Were *a kind of* precinct', a *'certain* control had been exercised', 'it was . . . the *how* the day went', *'as* I pursued . . .', 'turning out *the way* I am'. The 'as though' cannot be reduced to a time, a place, or even a part of speech; it is the *milieu*, the space and the time, the spacing and timing, of Ashbery's infinite language, where 'as' and its innumerable synonyms or equivalences may be seen to operate *as* every part of speech – not only as conjunction, preposition or adverb, but as adjective, verb and noun. The point is widely and discreetly thematised throughout Ashbery's work; it admits of refinement and complexity; and it does not in any way submit to, or correspond to, a subject-centred ideology, or a syntax-centred critique of that subject as language. For 'as' is not human; it is not a subject, nor is it an object – least of all is it an instrument at some subject's disposal, be it the instrument of the police or of an inmate: it is a milieu, a process, a practice of 'hardwear' – of language in its impersonal persistence, its monotony.

In 'Sortes Vergilianae', all topics, tales, maxims, struggles, victories, enslavements, defeats, exercises, origins, duplications, revelations, concealments, delays – in sum, all life and death, all lives and all deaths – issue forth from the complex of 'as'. Were we to cite the incidents of 'as' *as such*, passing over its multiple cognates in all rhetorical registers, the compass of 'as' would only begin to let itself be scanned:

> . . . 'casual as breath . . .'
> . . . 'as fast as the light . . .'
> . . . 'as the embrace . . .'
> . . . 'as perverse notations . . .'
> . . . 'as conduct in the past . . .'
> . . . 'as they came . . .'
> . . . 'as it was being indoctrinated . . .'
> . . . 'heavy as a branch . . .'
> . . . 'as it started to sigh . . .'
> . . . 'as the purpose of it is becoming plain . . .'
> . . . 'such archaic forms as these . . .'
> . . . 'as the tool that made you . . .'
> . . . 'such expansive aspects as what to do . . .'
> . . . 'insertion *hors-texte* as the invisible notion . . .'
> . . . 'as the star climbs and sinks . . .'

Passing over such similar words as 'for', 'like', 'such', 'so', 'when', and 'where', and any of the other discernible words or phrases that carry out the like semantic or syntactic functions, we need only mention that they are operators, all, of analogy and of concomitance in space and time – operators, all (problematic, uncertain) of *relation*, the linguistic non-ground from which all relations and resemblances, *ideological* relations and resemblances included, may arise. All are the matters of 'as', from which all discourse arises, 'turns out' – 'turning out to greet you'.

The relationship of 'as' to 'subject' – does it admit of any phenomenal rendition, intelligible, formalisable, or comprehensible? Is there a trope of 'as', which might catch, in the mirror of language, the image of that mirror, the 'as' as it is or might be to the senses, to the cogitating grasp of a subject? 'Sortes Vergilianae' closes with a trope that seems to stage, in language, the operations of language as 'as':

> This is just a footnote, though a microcosmic one perhaps, to the
> greater curve
> Of the elaboration; it asks no place in it, only insertion *hors-texte* as the
> invisible notion of how that day grew
> From planisphere to heaven, and what part in it all the 'I' had, the
> insatiable researcher of learned trivia, bookworm,
> And one who marched along with, 'made common cause,' yet had
> neither the gumption nor the desire to trick the thing into happening,
> Only long patience, as the star climbs and sinks, leaving illumination
> to the setting sun.

In this terminal passage – Ashbery leaves us to think along these lines – the principal topics, terms and concerns of the poem appear to converge, or to settle down, like 'the little birds' that 'used to collect along the fence' of 'The Chateau Hardware', in the paired formulae of an oppositional logic, dispersed throughout the cloven openings of the poem's multiple contexts. As the coda, or tail-piece, of the poem, the passage forms a part of the whole from which it stands apart; the subject it poses (an ' "I" ') is at once of the poem and yet out of it, playing a part apart; ensconcing the poem within the tale that the poem tells, the passage absconds from tale and poem alike (as 'insertion *hors-texte* as the invisible notion'). So doing, the passage appears to be the (represented) inside of its own outside, and the (represented) outside of its own inside, the 'notion' as apprehensible schema – a burrowing 'bookworm' that none the less 'marched along with, "made common cause" . . .'. Passage, subject, tale and poem all seem to be *somewhere*, namely everywhere – a topical deployment which may be hard to account for, but whose accounting, at least in principle, is not beyond all conjecture. According to this flexible project of representation, they are, in principle, *representable* 'notions', and as such, they are eventually recognisable, comprehensible, susceptible of ideological framing. They would cohere, finally, in a figure or trope at some critic's vigilant command. Ashbery, in the fullness of time, would then be reduced to the ashes of conceptual finitude: critics, aiming for that sort of thing, could count on that outcome for the validity of their own ingenious probings.

What, however, actually takes place? How does 'Sortes Vergilianae' leave the determined reader?

It ends itself – in a move of absolute exposure, of vulnerability to critical recuperation – with a trope or figure, an image (it seems) of itself:

> And one who marched along with, 'made common cause,' yet had
>   neither the gumption nor the desire to trick the thing into happening,
> Only long patience, as the star climbs and sinks, leaving illumination
>   to the setting sun.

This 'patience' (of the '"I"', of the poem, and of the poem's tale), which is like the patience of a star – perhaps a nameless, invisible daytime star, whose movements are hidden by the light of the sun, or perhaps a night-time star, whose movements are legible only in the absence of sunlight – is, as it were, a principle of comprehension that lets itself be comprehended in its turn; that comprehension (that representation) is relayed through the reading of 'as' in its analogical function: anything that is *like* something is representable, susceptible of formulation. What, however, occurs when we read the 'as' in its conjunctive function – 'as' in its meaning of 'while', concomitantly? 'Patience' is then absconded from likeness, it leaves all likeness, all representation, to the miming movements of 'star' and 'sun'. 'Patience' itself is elsewhere, gone, nowhere – detached. And that detachment, for its detachment, depends upon its removal from something – namely, from the representative movements of sun and star. 'Patience', which lets analogy happen, becomes the other of analogical, and notional, representation – by departing from 'patience' as *analogy* (from 'patience, as a star . . .'). Divided from the 'as' of analogy, and from the pairings of analogy that enable representation to be, 'patience' becomes the 'as' itself of concomitance.

Of this, be it noted in passing, the poem says nothing at all, elliptically, silently doing so; for the poem itself is 'as', it is the 'patience' of 'as' as 'as' (while 'as') is (an analogy), in a movement of spacing (of identification and articulation) that spins out, ineluctably, all that happens (to be) there, represented or representable or otherwise – not excluding, at last, the invisible, ungraspable, silent thing that signs itself as 'Ashbery'.

Chapter 3

Charles Bernstein's 'The Simply'

Jerome McGann

> being less interested in representing than enacting.
>
> (Charles Bernstein, 'State of the Art/1990')

Charles Bernstein's poetry is (in)famous for its difficulty. Yet the work is difficult, it seems to me, only if read within an informational or communicative or representational framework – only if you assume that the poetry is there to be explicated for some allegorically or symbolically coded meaning. The poetry of course deploys representational forms – no language can dispense altogether with its communicative function – but those forms are subordinated in Bernstein's work to other kinds of intention.

For Bernstein, poetic 'meaning' is never a product, and hence cannot be coded or decoded. It is a process of writing through which 'the before unapprehended relations of things' have to be *attended to* (in both senses of that phrase).[1] Among the most important of those unapprehended relations are the ideological formations – the constellated sets of different social opinions and understandings – which define (sometimes even dominate) 'the way we live now'. The poet's office, for Bernstein, is to put those constellations at the reader's disposal.

Like Shelley, Bernstein pursues this revelation not for its own sake, but to break the spell of ideology by dislocating its forms of representation. To read Bernstein is to take part in a (comic) play wherein 'meaning' is dismembered. The 'difficulty' arises from a process by which we are alienated from the meanings of things that we thought we knew, that in fact we *did* know. As Brecht might have said, 'the fourth wall' between poet and reader is taken away.

To do this means dramatising the linguistic and semiological forms by which social relations are constructed and managed. Bernstein's poetry often reads like a catalogue of current clichés (drawn from various social groups and institutional contexts), advertising slogans, nonce expressions, and the like:

> *Something like* after
> a while I'm reading my book, go to store to get

more stuff. 'You're about as patient as the flame
on a match.' After the ceremony lunch was served
by Mrs. Anne MacIssac, Mrs. Betty MacDonald, and Mrs.
   Catherine
MacLeod, and consisted of tea, bannock, homemade cheese
oatcakes and molasses cookies. We thank the ladies. Waste
not, want not; but there's such a thing as being shabby.
Which seems finally to move the matter, but in despair
seeing 'lived experience' as only possible under
the hegemony of an ideology, an 'imaginary'. Started
to do this, I corrected, he (they) demurred, I
moved aside. Don't look up but she goes off. 'Pleasant Bay
   news
really hasn't dropped out, it was just on holiday'.

('The Simply')[2]

This passage is a collage (or mobile) of social texts whose arbitrary
juxtaposition forces a clearer awareness of the specialised character
of each one, and of the local world from which each one draws its
peculiar life. The collaged structure may be taken as a minimally
representational image of a modern or postmodern field of experience.
Unlike a modernist mobile, however, this ordering of randomness –
the 'meaning' of collage – is not the object of our attention. The text
preserves its nervousness and incompletion, as one would see even
more clearly if the quotation were allowed to continue.

This text does not have, that is to say, an order of finality. In terms of
'meaning', collage itself is a recognisable *convention* of meaning in a
postmodern scene of writing (whereas in a modernist scene it appears
as an innovation, an 'original' meaning). In the present case the convention serves, on one hand, as another problem of meaning (e.g. 'fret
which is whirled / out of some sort of information'); and, on the other,
as a *selva oscura* where one may find one's way, but only with difficulty
(e.g. 'guided by irritation'). I quote here from the opening section of
the poem (see below); and I signal both quotations by 'e.g.' because
neither *means* precisely what my commentary might be taken to have
said. Rather, the parts of this poem work by suggestion and are always
dissolving away from the meanings we are tempted to bring to them.

The heart of this poetry lies in those temptations toward meaning.
The test is not so much a secret communication as 'a vocabulary and
a set of rules by which it is processed'.[3] What comes of such a text
depends upon how the reader reconstructs the linguistic relationships:
because choices will and indeed must be made if even the simplest
act of reading is to proceed.

But even that simplest act of reading emerges as a difficult operation
to perform, in this sense – that readers can only go on if and as they
are paying attention to their (chosen) act of reading. To read this text

is to be forced, as Thoreau would have said (had his subject been texts rather than nature), to *read* deliberately. The ultimate subject of a text like this is the reader. It is a linguistic/ideological field, with textual units mirroring (or quoting from) a wildly various group of subject positions: from New Left discourse (perhaps an allusion to Verso Books) to society column news.

To read the text one must construct relations and relationships. As soon as one does so, however, the text responds by (as it were) reading the reader. For 'the poem itself' does not 'have a meaning' which the reader is expected to discover and articulate. The poem's 'difficulty' arises exactly from its having refused to proceed according to those conventions of language-use. The text assembles units of (various) conventional meaning-forms, but as a poem – as a field in which those units are ordered and encountered – their relations are left to the reader's devices. As soon as the reader acts within the textual field – as soon as he chooses certain options of reading – he is immediately drawn into the poetic space and reflected back to himself.

In these last comments I deliberately used the pronouns 'he' and 'himself' in order to emphasise the highly particular forms which every reading decision always involves. (Had I used the pronouns 'her' and 'herself' this fact would have been patent.) Those pronouns are a sign that the reader's subject-position is always gendered – masculine, feminine, neuter – whatever the sex of the reader. It makes a difference, according to the poetic logic of this kind of poem, how (and of course by whom) the reading is gendered. This is part of the *subject* of the poetry, just as 'the reader' is always a specific individual.

The passage above is preceded by the following, which is the opening of the poem:

> The Simply
> Nothing can contain the empty stare that ricochets
> haphazardly against any purpose. My hands
> are cold but I see nonetheless with an infrared
> charm. Beyond these calms is a coast, handy but
> worse for abuse. Frankly, hiding an adumbration of
>   collectible
> cathexis, catherized weekly, burred and bumptious;
> actually, continually new groups being brought forward for
> drowning. We get back, I forget to call, we're
> very tired eating. They think they'll get salvation, but
> this is fraudulent. Proud as punches – something like
> Innsbruck, saddles, sashed case; fret which is whirled
> out of some sort of information; since you ask. We're
> very, simply to say, smoked by fear, guided by
> irritation. Rows of desks. *Something like* after . . . .

The title itself 'enacts', as Bernstein might say, a problem of reading, and thereby puts the reader in an acute state of attention. As one moves through this text one searches out relations and (inevitably) discovers various kinds: the odd sequence of adverbs, for example; the repetitions with variations ('something like' and *'Something like'*; 'we're / very tired eating' and 'we're / very, simply to say . . .'; 'The Simply' and 'simply to say'; etc.); and possible thematic rhymes among different parts of the sequence. For the latter, one cues to several phrases and images which suggest boredom, irritation, and a general condition of quandariness. The text as a whole seems to take no particular attitude toward its various units, but in that very appearance of indifference, certain possibilities of meaning emerge. One wonders, for example, if the first sentence is not indeed the poem's 'topic sentence', a statement about the rich (uncontainable) value of the poem's flat and 'empty stare' back at us. In this reading the 'purpose' would be an equivalent of the reader's search for meaning, and the 'empty stare' would be the poem's device of indifference, which might only increase the reader's imperative toward meaning.

Other readings are of course possible. Indeed, the way the units of this poem 'ricochet' off each other may be taken as a sign that it is enacting its own stimulus toward reading and meaning.

Bernstein's poetry turns out, as a result, a kind of comedy of errors, with the reader (we are many) playing the principal role(s). American traditions of screwball comedy – the Marx Brothers, Laurel and Hardy – have had a deep influence on his work. There is a wonderfully comic moment about half-way through 'The Simply' when the text turns to satirise 'the reader of poetry'. The passage appears as a random quotation from (evidently) some missionary's journal or letter to a friend or superior.

> 'For all that
> we have not up to the present noticed any more
> Religion among these poor savages than among *brutes*;
> this is what wrings our hearts with compassion, if
> they could know themselves what they themselves are
> worth, and what they cost him *who has loved us all*
> *so much*. Now what consoles us in the midst
> of this ignorance and barbarism, and what makes us hope
> to see the Faith widely implanted, is partly the *docility*
> they have shown in wishing to be instructed, and partly
> the honesty and decency we observe in them; for
> they listen to us so diligently concerning the mysteries
> of our Faith, and repeat after us, *whether they understand*
> *it or not*, all that we declare to them.'

Part of the joke here is plainly the double-take which such a passage encourages. This text's 'we' will be read to mean something like 'the sentences of the present poem' or (more generally) 'poets'; and 'these poor savages', with their 'honesty and decency', are . . . ourselves? Yes, of course. The joke is especially wonderful and outrageous because the passage is so elaborate, and yet every one of its details may be translated to an immediate application for 'the reader'. Once again, not a representation but an enactment of meaning, with the reader as a key player in the events. And the passage allows its further implications to wind out – for example that reading is a social act just as practical behaviour in the world is a way of reading; or, that acts of appropriation break open the world in ways that power cannot contain and control; or even, that anything can (and does, or does not) mean anything.

As the poem proceeds, its subject – the enactment rather than the representation of meaning – becomes, I think, more strongly thematised *at the level of the enactments*. The missionary passage is blatantly thematic, and so is the following, toward the poem's conclusion.

> Don't you find it chilly
> sitting with your Silly? Yet things
> beguile us with their beauty
> their sudden irascibility: the hay of the
> imagination is the solace of a dry soul; which
> is to say, keep yourselves handy since
> you may be called on at any hour.
> One wants almost to shudder (yawn, laugh . . .) in disbelief
> at the hierarchization of consciousness in such a dictum
> as 'first thought, best thought', as if recovery
> were to be prohibited from the kingdom;
> for anyway 'first thought' is no thinking
> at all. There is no 'actual space of'. So
> quiet you can hear the clouds gather. Weep
> not, want not; but there's such a thing as being
> numb.

'First thought, best thought' is a reference to Allen Ginsberg, who likes to take this 'dictum' as an essential truth about poetry. Bernstein's text moves against such a 'thought' – rethinks it – by situating us in a text that foregrounds the process of reflection. At all points Bernstein's text seduces us with imaginative options ('shudder (yawn, laugh . . .)'). Its religious faith is the 'disbelief' which Brecht said would move mountains, and its 'kingdom' is the world of imaginative reflection and recreation.

One particularly traces the movement of this poetry at its many odd transitional points, where the reader is forced to swerve out into unexpected directions. These may be simple moments of syntactic conjugation – the 'Yet' of the second quoted line; the colon and the semicolon of the fourth and fifth – or semantic dislocations ('beauty'/ 'irascibility') – or unexpected connections to other moments in the poem (e.g. the arbitrary rhyme that the last sentence of this quotation makes with the seventh and eighth lines of the first passage I quoted).

The closing lines of the poem are, in all these respects, typical of the work:

> 'You have such a horrible sense of equity which
> is inequitable because there's no such
> things as equity.' *The text, the beloved?*
> Can I stop living when the pain gets too
> great? Nothing interrupts this moment.
> False.

The joke of that final word is that it also, simultaneously, means its opposite. But not only its opposite. The movement away from fixed meanings is not always, or even principally, a binary recoil. It takes place rather at tangents and Dickinsonian 'slants', at what Tennyson called the 'strange diagonal' of poetry. In the last two sentences, for instance, the reader may observe that the 'Nothing' which does or doesn't 'interrupt this moment' recalls the 'Nothing' from which the poem originally set forth:

> Nothing can contain the empty stare that ricochets
> haphazardly against any purpose.

Not for nothing is 'The Simply' placed as the opening poem of a book Bernstein has titled *The Sophist*.

NOTES

1. The quotation is from Shelley's 'Defence of Poetry', in David Lee Clark (ed.), *Shelley's Prose; or, The Trumpet of a Prophecy* (University of New Mexico Press, Albuquerque, 1954), p. 278. And compare: 'poetry . . . awakens and enlarges the mind itself by rendering it the receptacle of a thousand unapprehended combinations of thought' (p. 282); or 'Poetry . . . arrests the vanishing apparitions which haunt the interlunations of life and, veiling them, or in language or in form, sends them forth among mankind, bearing sweet news of kindred joy to those with whom their sisters abide' (pp. 294–5).
2. 'The Simply' is printed as the initial poem in Bernstein's collection titled *The Sophist* (Sun & Moon Press, Los Angeles, 1987). I quote here from that text.
3. I take this phrase from Ron Silliman's 'The Chinese Notebook' in *The Age of Huts* (Roof Books, New York, 1986), pp. 54, 63.

Chapter 4

Toward Gay Reading

Robert Glück's 'Reader'

Joseph Chadwick

The word *reader*, according to one of the *OED*'s definitions, may be 'used as a title for books containing passages for instruction or exercise in reading'. Taking that word as its title, Robert Glück's latest collection proclaims itself such a book, and it sustains that generic self-identification by explicitly defining many of the texts that compose it as exercises in reading – as readings *of* other texts ('Burroughs', 'Keats', 'F O'H'), as texts *for* others to read ('A Genre Novel for Dennis Cooper to Read'). The crucial implication of the title *Reader* and the texts grouped under it is thus that whoever reads this book needs instruction in reading. In its broadest sense, that's a very safe claim to make. But that claim turns out to be a riskier one if, recognising that reading can never be simply a matter of purely neutral technique applied to a fixed and stable object but always involves some kind of ideologically charged transaction with a text, we post the question: in what specific strategy or practice of reading does *Reader* instruct and exercise us? For the best answer to that question, as I will argue, involves a form of reading the very existence of which, as Eve Kosofsky Sedgwick suggests, has been masked by the regimen of evasions and frustrations which in part constitute it and through which one must usually learn it (if one ever learns it at all):

> I don't know whether there can be said to be for our culture a distinctive practice of 'homosexual reading', but if so, it must surely bear the fossil-marks of the whole array of evasive techniques by which the *Britannica*, the *Reader's Guide*, the wooden subject, author, and title guides frustrate and educate the young idea. (132)

One crucial feature of the practice of (what I will call) gay reading in *Reader* does indeed consist of negotiating the evasions of powerfully institutionalised discourses. Many of the volume's texts disrupt the coherences that lend officially sanctioned psychiatric, political, journalistic, and literary discourses their ideological force, their sense of naturalness or inevitability. Subjecting the syntactic, narrative, discursive, and generic coherences that underpin such discourses to a process of allegorical fragmentation and decomposition, *Reader* awakens what Sedgwick calls a 'skepticism about the representative adequacy of language, . . . a pressing sense that there [is] something somewhere else for it to be adequate to' (132). And such scepticism has much to do with a need to resist the institutionalised discourses, codified categories, and redemptive or essentialising interpretations that continue to play an inescapably constitutive but also deeply oppressive role in the shaping of gay identities and desires in a virulently homophobic social order. This disruption of coherences is complemented, however, by a second crucial feature of gay reading in *Reader*: a textual erotics, perhaps best called 'cruising', that engages its reader (as well as the texts it reads) in a play of masks in which one is read as one reads, in which one's gaze solicits a reciprocal gaze from an unexpected, unknown other. This self-transformative play of masks, as I will show, constitutes the affirmative, Dionysian aspect of the volume's allegorical undermining of coherences.

Reader offers something like a definition of the allegorical–fragmentary element in gay reading in the second section of 'Burroughs':

> I cut up his cut-ups, allegory of an allegory of an allegory of an allegory of a waterfall of mental curlicues whose new meaning is no meaning in extremity. Is a Burroughs to eat? I am timid, abstract, complete, light, fever, timid. Barefoot, yells Hey Pop, got any more Dick Tracys? (46)

'[A]llegory', in this passage, names not an extended analogy that encodes, for those capable of deciphering it, a divine truth in a set of tropes which (in contrast to a symbol) claim no essential relation to that truth, but rather the shattered or ruinous fragments that remain of such a system of figuration once the principle of divine truth is abandoned. In this version of allegory, as Walter Benjamin argues, one encounters a language 'constantly convulsed by rebellion on the part of the elements which make it up', a language 'broken up so as to acquire a changed and intensified meaning in its fragments' (207–8).[1] Defining the radically fragmentary cut-up as a paradigmatic allegorical figure, this passage puts fragmentation to work in attacking coherences of referentiality, syntax, and grammar. The repetition of 'an allegory of' implies a perpetual deferral of any arrival at a stable point of reference (though not a complete elimination of the possibilities of reference). And the trope that culminates that repetition – 'a waterfall of mental curlicues' – extends that implication by using vivid physical–visual figures (waterfall, curlicues) to name a quite abstract mental process and thus suggesting that such figures play a constitutive, rather than a purely representative, role in the referent's discursive existence. The passage's remaining sentences show how rebellions in the domains of syntax, diction, and grammar foreground the reader's role in making meaning from sentences 'whose new meaning is no meaning in extremity'. The indefinite article in 'Is a Burroughs to eat', for example, enables us to construe the question as asking either whether someone (or something) named Burroughs is going to eat, or whether someone (or something) named Burroughs is to be eaten. The following sentence begins with the kind of declaration of identity ('I am . . .') that, as Marjorie Perloff puts it, 'posit[s] the self as the primary organizing feature of writing' (100), but immediately switches to a series of adjectives and even one noun (or two? what part of speech is 'light'?) so 'timid, abstract', and *in*complete as to undermine the very assertion of identity that the subject and verb set up. Finally, the sentence beginning 'Barefoot', can be construed either 1. as a speech by someone named Hey Pop addressed to someone named Barefoot; or 2. as a speech by an unnamed but barefoot speaker that begins with the interpellative exclamation 'Hey' and is addressed to someone called Pop. These sentences' shifting, unstable subject-positions undermine not only syntactic but also narrative coherence. Rather than telling a story about 'Burroughs', then, these sentences propose a way of reading 'Burroughs' that consists of cutting up cut-ups, that engages the reader in a process of making explicitly arbitrary but none the less changed and intensified meanings by fragmenting language.

What makes such allegorical fragmentation effective as a specifically gay reading practice, especially given that Benjamin finds it at work in Baroque tragedy, that Peter Bürger finds it in Modernist *montage*, that Paul de Man makes it into something like a paradigmatic trope of deconstructive reading, and that Ron Silliman defines something very much like it as a principle of sentence-construction in those works of 'L=A=N=G=U=A=G=E poetry' that deploy what he calls the 'new sentence'?[2] At a general level, one might answer this question by citing Lee Edelman's claim (which draws on Derrida's 'Plato's Pharmacy') that '[d]econstruction, as a disseminative project . . . can be subsumed beneath the rubric of the homosexual' in that, by questioning the logic by which Western philosophy has claimed to distinguish the true from the false, the natural from the unnatural, it 'enacts the law of transgression . . . operative in "both the writing and the pederasty of a young man named Plato"', a '"transgression . . . not thinkable within the terms of classical logic but only within the graphics of the supplement or of the *pharmakon*"' (309).[3] Western

notions of the true and the natural, that is, have been in part
constituted through the exclusion or devaluing of disseminative,
'wasteful' practices like writing or homosexual activity. Just as deconstructive appropriations of Benjamin's notion of allegory tend to elide
the social–historical specificity that informs Benjamin's uses of that
notion, however, so Edelman's claim tends to elide the question of
the strategic advantages of allegorical reading in resisting specific
forms of discourse – a question that *Reader* takes up in a text like
'WWII', which poses a medical essay on 'The Gag Reflex and Fellatio'
(dedicated to arriving at a reliable method of detecting which individuals may be assigned to the category 'sexual psychopathology,
fellatio') against passages from Foucault's *History of Sexuality* and
from personal letters by gay servicemen:

> In conclusion, it is felt the test is a definite aid in screening candidates
> not only for the military services but for positions where the sexual
> deviant must be eliminated.

> *and conversely, how were these discourses used to support power relations?*

> 'This morning I saw the psychiatrist. I went in his office and after a few
> routine questions he asked me to stand up in front of him – he had me
> pull my shirt up and my pants down. He starts running his hands
> around my back and chest and slowly working his way down to the
> inevitable – he asked me to say whatever came into my mind – but after
> he went through this routine we settled down to the $64 question.' (33)

In this passage, fragmentation occurs primarily at the level of discourse, the passages from the medical essay, from Foucault, and from
the personal letter each interrupting the other and partially disrupting
the continuity of argument or narrative. A certain coherence does
emerge from the juxtaposed passages, in that the discourse of the
medical article clearly supports the power relations at work in the
situation narrated in the personal letter, and that coherence is
strengthened by the privileged position given to the Foucault passage
by italicised print and by its status as a question (to which the other
passages thus provide answers). At the same time, however, the
fragmenting and interrupting of these discourses catalyses certain
shifts and intensifications of meaning, even at the level of individual
words. The term 'positions' in the medical article, for example, takes
on sexual as well as occupational connotations, just as the term
'eliminated' connotes extermination as well as discrimination (those
connotations combine to disclose this discourse's dream of a sexuality
utterly free of 'deviance'). In the personal letter, the slang-term '$64
question' could refer either to the question of whether the letter's *I*
is a 'homosexual', or to the psychiatrist's following up his supposedly

diagnostic caresses with some more intensely gratifying act. The result is much the same either way, however, since both the power-relation set up by the psychiatrist's discourse and that discourse's categorising of the *I* are confirmed in either case. The very term '$64 question' confirms this by highlighting the power-relations at work in the series of questions that it culminates: 'after a few routine questions'; 'he asked me to stand up'; 'he asked me to say'. The question itself as a rhetorical device, that term suggests, may institute a power relation by delimiting a discursive field, by defining what can and what cannot be spoken within a given situation. That implication extends even to Foucault's question, calling attention to the limitations imposed by its terms even as it calls attention to the limitations imposed by those of the medical article. Although the term 'power relation' provides a strategically apt name for whatever occurs between the psychiatrist and the serviceman, that term can never hope to encompass the ironic discrepancy of value also summed up in the term '$64 question', the discrepancy between the psychiatrist's insistence on making a certain form of sexual response, the ultimate criterion of individual identity and the serviceman's awareness of the hollow conventionality of that insistence (an awareness also evinced in his repeated use of the word 'routine').

The strategic usefulness of allegorical fragmentation as a practice of gay reading, then, as 'WWII' suggests, derives not from its enabling an escape from canonical discourses of sexuality to some utopian space of liberation, but rather in its enabling one to infiltrate those discourses, to deny them the coherence that their argumentative or narrative continuities seek to establish, to turn them against themselves, to confront them with counter discourses. Such fragmentation does not deny the constitutive role played in the formation of gay subjects by discourses like those of the psychiatrist or the medical article, but it does pose Sedgwick's question of the adequacy of those discourses, the question of the 'something somewhere else'. And that question, as 'Genre Novel for Dennis Cooper to Read' suggests, needs to be posed not only against discourses that have made obvious contributions to Western forms of homophobia, but also against the discourses, including certain literary ones, that have played a constitutive role in the shaping of gay desire:

> He let out his breath slowly,
> Relaxing his swollen muscles,
> And shut off the spray.
> He stood shivering, water   emotion, There was a cry

                    Dripping upon the tiles
                    From the shiny wetness
                    Of his nude flesh. He
                    Grabbed for the towel,   of tortured agony.

            Ruffled it through his tawny hair,
            Over the rounded firmness of his
            Shoulders and tobogganed the rough

    Terrycloth down the rugged columns   The knife rose quick

            Of his legs. (24–5)

This poem's left-hand column presents a formulaic description of the male body as macho ideal: an image of the male emerges which such verbs as 'shut off', 'grabbed', 'ruffled', and 'tobogganed' define as brusquely active; which such adjectives as 'tawny' and 'rough' define as slightly animalistic; which such objects of prepositions as 'swollen muscles', 'nude flesh', 'rounded firmness', and 'rugged columns' define as something close to a walking erection. A quality of willed control is added to that image by the passage's succession of declarative sentences that begin with 'He' as their subject (a sentence-pattern that extends through much of the rest of this left-column text as well). Finally, the passage's steadily cumulative listing of physical attributes marks it as the sort of text that incites that 'pleasure of corporeal striptease or of narrative suspense' which Roland Barthes defines as 'an Oedipal pleasure (to denude, to know, to learn the origin and end)' (10). Slicing up the physical description to fit into what seems a quite arbitrarily chosen four-line stanza form and parodically emphasising the single-line units by capitalising each one's initial letter, however, the poem undermines that pleasure by disrupting the steady flow of coherent prose toward some revelatory climax upon which it depends. The stanza- and line-breaks, that is, call attention to the devices of vocabulary and syntax which shape and incite such pleasure; or rather, they call forth the sort of analytic-fragmenting reading that I have just offered by examining the passage's parts of speech and sentence patterns. Those breaks thus expose the body described in this passage as one of what Leo Bersani calls 'those (in large part culturally invented and elaborated) male bodies that we carry within us as permanently renewable sources of excitement' – bodies which, even though gay men may idealise and strive to replicate them, constitute 'representations of masculinity on the basis of which [gay men] are in fact judged and condemned';

bodies which demonstrate that the internalisation of such oppressive representations 'is in part constitutive of male homosexual desire' (208–9).

The deeply insidious ideological thrust of such representations meets a certain resistance in the fragment juxtaposition of the left-column's formulaic description against the right-column's explicitly disconnected shifts from an *I* in crisis ('Yes I believed nothing – / now the eclipse is a face / like L.A. where air is / emotion'), to a third-person narrative of violence ('There was a cry / of tortured agony. / The knife rose quick / as a serpent's tongue / slicing across Ian's / features'), to a general claim ('The mind dreams / prevent boredom'). Even as the left-column text both confirms and exposes the role that an oppressive representation of masculinity (given ideological coherence by a formulaic, climax- or knowledge-oriented narrative) plays in the construction of gay male desire, the right-column text seems to invoke a 'something somewhere else' – perhaps the threatening anonymity and violence of the left-column text's stereotype, perhaps simply an aimless sequence of meditations and recollections that counter the left-column text's insistently goal-oriented coherence. In either case, the discursive fragmentation effected by right-column text suggests that what left-column text offers is not enough, that other and *different* constructions of gay desire must also be explored.

In addition to its usefulness in exposing the insidious roles of institutionalised discourses on sexuality and conventional representations of masculinity in the formation of gay identities and desires, allegorical fragmentation takes on a special aptness as a strategy of gay reading now, in the midst of an epidemic that has so far killed tens of thousands of gay men in the United States alone, because of allegory's refusal to subject death to a redemptive transformation. The implications of that refusal can best be outlined through an extended quotation that juxtaposes Glück's 'Learning to Write / Basho' against a passage on allegory from Benjamin's *Origin of German Tragic Drama*:

		family	as-for	
all	staff-with	leaning		white-hair
	go	grave-visiting		

	3	2	
1	2	2	2
	1	4	

A visit to the family graves in my native village in remembrance of the recent death of my common-law wife. There are present (in addition to myself) my wife's mother, my two older brothers and their wives, and also my wife's brother. My two daughters are still in Edo. The 'family' is small and certainly made up of elderly people. My oldest brother has no children, and my second brother's oldest son, whom I had adopted, died within the year. I'm already looking forward to my own death and, on this occasion, it seems to me, looking forward to the probable extinction of my whole family as well. (Glück 26)

Whereas in the symbol destruction is idealized and the transfigured face of nature is fleetingly revealed in the light of redemption, in allegory the observer is confronted with the *facies hippocratica* of history as a petrified, primordial landscape. Everything about history that, from the very beginning, has been untimely, sorrowful, unsuccessful, is expressed in such a face – or rather in a death's head . . . this is the form in which man's subjection to nature is most obvious and it significantly gives rise not only to the enigmatic question of the nature of human existence as such, but also of the biographical historicity of the individual . . . . Significance and death both come to fruition in historical development . . . . (Benjamin 166)

'Learning to Write / Basho' (the haiku-section of which could describe just as aptly a group of gay men with AIDS – 'all   staff-with   lean-ing   white-hair' – as a seventeenth-century Japanese family) is a version of what Benjamin calls 'a death's head': a representation of something in history that, 'from the very beginning, has been untimely, sorrowful, unsuccessful'. It represents, that is, a gay experience of AIDS. And it represents that experience allegorically at a wide range of levels. First, there is the extended analogy I have already indicated between the threatened family and a group of gay men with AIDS. Second, the text draws on Basho's own concerns with fragments, ruins, and unredeemed death, as exemplified by the first haiku of *Records of a Weather-Exposed Skeleton*:

Determined to fall
A weather-exposed skeleton
I cannot help the sore wind
Blowing through my heart. (51)

Third, the fragmenting juxtaposition of the haiku against both the formal skeleton of its syllable count and the fleshed-out explanation of its context suggests that none of the three provides a language fully adequate to the situation at hand, that none embodies any transfiguring or redemptive essential truth of that situation because no such truth is to be found beyond the mere fact of death. This allegorical representation, refusing to move beyond the domain of 'historical development' or of the 'biographical historicity of the individual', the realm of man's subjection to nature and to death, thus also refuses the sort of redemptive interpretation of AIDS that appears in suggestions that the epidemic has made gay men (or those gay men who have so far survived it) more psychologically mature and socially responsible (the implicit message of Randy Shilts's claim that in fighting the epidemic, San Francisco gay people 'had forged a gay community that was truly a community, not just a neighborhood' [571]). Instead, it insists that the significance of AIDS must be a matter of writing, or of 'learning to write' (or, that is, of learning to read allegorically) – a matter of learning to make meaning or knowledge with history's fragments and ruins rather than looking beyond history to a transfigurative, essential truth; a matter of visiting graves rather than (as another text in *Reader* puts it) 'looking down from the Great Divide' (13).

From the allegorical perspective, indeed, the very absoluteness of meaning that would legitimise any redemptive (or, for that matter, any scientific–objective) 'truth' of AIDS can only be identified, as Edelman argues, with death itself (312). For it is death, as 'Keats' suggests, that puts an end to the meaning–destabilising tropological substitutions at play in the language that speaks in and through us as long as we remain alive:

> We are sentimental
> in my kitchen; on TV
>   Baryshnikov does
> everything the body can.
>   Don't think about dying –
> how is a grand jete
>   cut flowers in a glass.
> Sharon glided to death
>   on the freeway.
> She was younger
>   than I am now. (Glück 38)

The way not to think about dying is to think 'how is a grand jete / cut flowers in a glass'. Except that because the transformation of grand jete into cut flowers reveals no absolute meaning about either, the play of substitutions must continue until, sooner or later (in this case, sooner) it brings one back to the only end it will ever have: 'Sharon glided to death / on the freeway.' The narrative *I* of 'Wordsworth' sums up the dynamic at work here when he writes: 'I suppose I will have to use language to manufacture distance as my resemblance to the dead increases . . .'.[2] Language, infected by the allegorical principle by which '[a]ny person, any object, any relationship can mean absolutely anything else' (Benjamin 175), provides a way to resist, if not escape, death. Just as important, however, it provides a way to resist attempts to confer upon death or its causes the deathly fixity of some 'great meaning' (Glück 1), attempts that in the case of AIDS almost invariably involve a moral repudiation of both the sexual practices and the styles of behaviour that played such a fundamental role in forming the '"family"' of 'Learning to Write / Basho'.

As a strategy of resistance, the practice of allegorical reading that I have outlined in the texts of *Reader* is perhaps inevitably shadowed by feelings of melancholy and mourning: the melancholy of analytically examining and calling into question the constitutive elements of one's very identity and desires; the mourning of contemplating the decimation of one's '"family"' and one's own impending death. These feelings, however, are complemented by a counteraffect, perhaps best called Dionysian, that shows up in the erotic–tropological transformation of the reader him/herself in 'F O'H':

> And for the welling and serious mounting
> of what everything could be
> and for the person who reads one page too many
> just lie back and watch the light glow
> like the moon in daytime. (17)

Although the repeated locution 'and for' in this sentence sets up an apparent parallel between 'the welling and serious mounting / of what everything could be' and 'the person who reads one page too many', the admonition that ends the sentence disrupts that parallel by suggesting that to 'just lie back' is 1. a way to enter into that 'welling and serious mounting' (in which case 'for' means 'in order to'); and 2. a remedy or therapy for reading 'one page too many' (in which case 'for' suggests that the admonition is directed toward a certain kind of person). This false parallelism impels the reader to engage (at the syntactic–semantic level where 'for' is assigned its meanings) in the play of transformations that continues for 'the person who reads one page too many' even if he (I use the pronoun advisedly) obeys the admonition to 'just lie back', the play of transformations by which 'the light' turns into 'the moon in daytime'. Reading, this sentence suggests, doesn't stop when one puts down the book; rather, it continues as long as one remains alive to the possibilities of 'what everything could be' rather than becoming immured in fixed definitions of what and how things are. The energy of 'welling and serious mounting' that impels this unceasing reading has much in common with the force that Nietzsche, in *The Twilight of the Idols*, calls Dionysian:

> In the Dionysian [frenzy], . . . the whole affective system is excited and enhanced: so that it discharges all its means of expression at once and drives forth simultaneously the power of representation, imitation, transfiguration, transformation, and every kind of mimicking and acting . . . . It is impossible for the Dionysian type not to understand any

> suggestion; he does not overlook any sign of an affect; he possesses the
> instinct of understanding and guessing in the highest degree. He enters
> into my skin, into any affect; he constantly transforms himself. (519–20)

The overflowing transformative impulse that Nietzsche defines here
shows up not only in 'the person who reads one page too many' in
'F O'H' (a person who remains a 'Dionysian type' even – or especially?
– when he 'just lie[s] back'), but also in the various ways that *Reader*
as a whole positions its readers and readings. Through such means
as 'representation, imitation, transfiguration', or even quotation, for
example, the writer of this volume (whom its spine, cover, and title
page identify as '*Reader* [space] Robert Glück') to some degree
becomes whomever or whatever he reads: 'Burroughs', 'WWII',
'Basho', 'Keats', 'Wordsworth', 'F O'H'. By the same token, anyone
else who takes the place that 'Robert Glück' has so kindly vacated
and (as I have done here) rewrites the text via his own reading must
enter into that same play of transformations by assuming the various
masks the text offers. That demand is made especially explicit in the
texts addressed to specific readers, texts which invite any other
reader to try to read as the addressee would and which thus impel
that other reader to assume the mask of that addressee's identity (a
mask that must be constructed from whatever traces the text in
question offers in addition to whatever knowledge the reader may
already have).

Through these multiple dynamics of Dionysian transformation,
Reader defines allegorical reading not only as a strategy of resistance,
but also as a version of the textual erotics that Barthes defines when
he writes:

> I [the writer] must seek out this reader (must 'cruise' him) *without
> knowing where he is*. A site of bliss is then created. It is not the reader's
> 'person' that is necessary to me, it is this site: the possibility of a dialectics
> of desire, of an *unpredictability* of bliss: the bets are not placed, there can
> still be a game. (4)

Reader is created as a 'site of bliss' insofar as it responds to the texts
it reads with an unexpected, unpredictable, desiring gaze (a gaze that
reads 'WWII' with an eye to its role in the formation of categories of
sexual pathology, that reads 'Keats' by watching TV). And *Reader*'s
reader is so created insofar as he is neither the reader whom the
volume identifies as its writer ('Robert Glück') nor the reader whom
any specific text addresses (and in this sense, even Dennis Cooper
could never quite be the 'Dennis Cooper' to whom 'A Genre Novel
for Dennis Cooper' is addressed). These transformative encounters
between readings and readers thus depend upon the element of
unpredictability that gives 'cruising' whatever subversive edge it may

have as a practice of gay desire. Such encounters may not enable an escape from the threats of 'great meaning' posed by regulatory discourses and categories (even categories like poetry and prose, quotation and invention, reader and writer, 'person' and text are never simply discarded here), but they do constitute a practice of reading that at once offers some resistance to such discourses and categories and affirms some elements of gay desire (transformation, unpredictability) that have recently come under renewed attack. Just now, we can use all the 'instruction and exercise' in such reading we can get.

NOTES

1. For Benjamin's most detailed discussion of this notion of allegory, see the chapter 'Allegory and Trauerspiel' in *The Origin of German Tragic Drama* (pp. 159–235). For a helpful contrast between more traditional, religious versions of allegory and the version that Benjamin ascribes to German Baroque drama, see Miller.
2. For Bürger's argument for the centrality of Benjaminian allegory in Modernist avant garde art, see his *Theory of the Avant-Garde* (pp. 69–82). For de Man's discussion of the deconstructive implications of allegory, see the chapter 'Allegory (*Julie*)' in *Allegories of Reading* (pp. 188–220); de Man acknowledges the link between his notion of allegory and Benjamin's in his essay 'Lyric and Modernity' (pp. 173–5). Silliman, despite his interest in Benjamin's work, never to my knowledge draws on Benjamin's notion of allegory in his writing on poetics, but his account of the 'new sentence' as 'blocking . . . the integration of sentences one to another through *primary* syllogistic movement' (through consistency of diction, tense, etc.), even while maintaining the sentence's syntactic structures constitutes in part, I would argue, an exploration at the level of the sentence of ideas about fragmentation, relative arbitrariness of reference, and quotation that Benjamin develops through that notion (p. 92).
3. To be fair to Edelman, his discussion of various discursive constructions of AIDS shows a keen awareness of such strategic advantages, even if his Derridean approach seems to lead him to argue for the inherently – rather than strategically – subversive force of deconstructive or allegorical reading.

WORKS CITED

Barthes, Roland. *The Pleasure of the Text*. Trans. Richard Miller (New York, Hill and Wang, 1975).
Basho, Matsuo. *The Narrow Road to the Deep North and Other Travel Sketches*. Trans. Noboyuki Yuasa (London, Penguin, 1966).
Benjamin, Walter. *The Origin of German Tragic Drama*. Trans. John Osborne (London, Verso, 1985).
Bersani, Leo. 'Is the Rectum a Grave?' *October*, 43 (1987), pp. 197–222.
Bürger, Peter. *Theory of the Avant-Garde*. Trans. Michael Shaw (Minneapolis, University of Minnesota Press, 1984).

de Man, Paul. *Allegories of Reading: Figural Language in Rousseau, Nietzsche, Rilke and Proust* (New Haven, Yale UP, 1979).

de Man, Paul. 'Lyric and Modernity'. *Blindness and Insight: Essays in the Rhetoric of Contemporary Criticism* (New York, Oxford University Press, 1971), pp. 166–86.

Edelman, Lee. 'The Plague of Discourse: Politics, Literary Theory, and AIDS'. *South Atlantic Quarterly*, **88.1** (1989), pp. 310–17.

Glück, Robert. *Reader*. (Venice, CA, Lapis, 1989).

Miller, J. Hillis. 'The Two Allegories'. *Allegory, Myth, and Symbol*. Morton W. Bloomfield (ed.) (Cambridge, MA, Harvard University Press, 1981), pp. 355–7.

Nietzsche, Friedrich. *The Twilight of the Idols. The Portable Nietzsche*. Walter Kaufmann (ed. and trans.) (Harmondsworth, Penguin, 1976).

Perloff, Marjorie. 'New Nouns for Old: "Language" Poetry, Language Game, and the Pleasure of the Text'. *Exploring Postmodernism*. Matei Calinescu and Douwe Foukkema (eds.) (Amsterdam, John Benjamins, 1987), pp. 95–108.

Sedgwick, Eve Kosofsky. 'A Poem Is Being Written'. *Representations*, **17** (1987), 110–43.

Shilts, Randy. *And the Band Played On: Politics, People, and the AIDS Epidemic* (New York: St Martin's, 1987).

Silliman, Ron. 'The New Sentence'. *The New Sentence* (New York, Roof, 1987), pp. 63–93.

Chapter 5

Tony Harrison's Languages

Rick Rylance

The question of the social determination of language has been a key issue in much recent literary theory. Indeed, the loss of the relative innocence of language is often both the justification and subject of much recent work. Critics have, against Leavisite and New Critical theories of 'organic' form, stressed the tensions and contradictions in both the formal and substantive elements in poetry. A poem, for New Criticism, was an integrated whole, harmonious and reconciling. Its formal equanimity provided a glimpse of a mythic world lived more fully in preindustrial ages, and thus provided consolation for the spoliations of twentieth-century experience. By contrast, recent criticism has tended to stress textual disarray. Language itself is often described as in crisis, partly because of its deep connection with social power.

The investigation of the social basis of language has taken a number of forms. Writers such as Foucault and Said have investigated 'discourse' – the structure of concepts and assumptions which hold together the understanding of social groups and which are derived from relationships of social power – and literary critics have had a greater sensitivity to ideological determination and constructedness. However, some recent theory's appetite for totalising accounts of complex processes, for epochal history, and a language which, heavy with neologism, has become a transatlantic argot fondly satirised by David Lodge, has threatened to turn these insights into blandly arcane repetition. Literature's communicative powers, its capacity to intervene and create, and to render human situations and histories meaningful, have been neglected in the emphasis on textual 'signifi-cation', the epistemological difficulties of sceptical rationalism, and psychoanalytic speculation. None the less, I wish to preserve and extend some of the responsible guiding insights of this work. It seems clear to me that 'discourse' exists; that it bears very heavily upon human beings and works of literature; that language does carry the 'traces' (to appropriate a Derridean term) of a history within it; and that human identity is often a matter of crisis and dislocation. This essay therefore considers these ideas in relation to Tony Harrison's poem 'On Not Being Milton'. I have, though, tried to avoid much of the terminology usually used to discuss them.

> In 1799 special legislation was introduced 'utterly suppressing and prohibiting' by name the London Corresponding Society and the United Englishmen. Even the indefatigable conspirator, John Binns, felt that further national organization was hopeless . . . When arrested he was found in possession of a ticket which was perhaps one of the last 'covers' for the old LCS: *Admit for the Season to the School of Eloquence.*
>
> (E.P. Thompson, *The Making of the English Working Class*)

ON NOT BEING MILTON

for Sergio Vieira & Armando Guebuza (Frelimo)

Read and committed to the flames, I call
these sixteen lines that go back to my roots
my *Cahier d'un retour au pays natal,*
my growing black enough to fit my boots.

The stutter of the scold out of the branks
of condescension, class and counter-class
thickens with glottals to a lumpen mass
of Ludding morphemes closing up their ranks.
Each swung cast-iron Enoch of Leeds stress
clangs a forged music on the frames of Art,
the looms of owned language smashed apart!

Three cheers for mute ingloriousness!

Articulation is the tongue-tied's fighting.
In the silence round all poetry we quote
Tidd the Cato Street conspirator who wrote:

Sir, I Ham a very Bad Hand at Righting.

Note. An 'Enoch' is an iron sledge-hammer used by the Luddites to smash the frames which were also made by the same Enoch Taylor of Marsden. The cry was: 'Enoch made them, Enoch shall break them!'

In some senses the verbal and intellectual organisation of Tony Harrison's work might lend itself to post-structuralist method. He has a strong sense of the social ground of language, especially its silences and occlusions, and of the suppression of variations across an apparently homogeneous language community by the dominant discourse. His techniques, too, have some resemblance to those of post-structuralist criticism. He has a highly self-conscious relationship to earlier literature, and his work is packed with quotation, allusion and intertextual citation. He also, like many post-structuralist writers, makes agile use of punning and wordplay to release meaning. Yet the tone, idiom and mood of his work are quite different.

Harrison's biography is well-known for his own experience is emphasised in the poetry. Born in a working-class family in Leeds, educated as a 'scholarship boy' at Leeds Grammar and subsequently a graduate in classics, Harrison uses his own cultural shifts as representative of broader social dislocations which have been a major feature of postwar life for many working-class families in Britain. (This aspect of his work has been very usefully described in Ken Worpole.)[1] His poetry therefore is an extended meditation on class and generational differences, and an examination of the guilt and pain involved in some experiences of cultural transition. Recently these issues have found focus in mourning for his parents. The mood of the poems is sombre and self-absorbed, therefore, and, as in most elegies, they dramatise a personal crisis as representative of larger problems.

Language, and therefore education, are frequently among his central concerns. Many of the poems turn upon his distance from his parents' language, 'the English that I speak at home' ('Classics Society').[2] He sees language differences as contributing to, and representative of, wider class differences. 'Marked With D.', for instance, a moving poem for his father, a baker, uses the nursery rhyme alluded to in the title to explore the separations of class, language and education. It grimly superimposes his father's daily work (making bread) onto his cremation ceremony. D. stands for Dad, death and of course dunce. His father is seen as an educational victim, a source of anger and guilt for the educated and socially mobile poet:

> The baker's man that no one will see rise
> and England made to feel like some dull oaf
> is smoke, enough to sting one person's eyes
> and ash (not unlike flour) for one small loaf. (153)

Restraint reveals and suppresses strong feeling. The punning on 'rise' brings together political anger at his father's social disadvantage (he could not rise socially) with ideas of rising dough and religious resurrection (the poem is also about Harrison's rejection of his parents' Christianity). The conclusion, too, makes its point through clenched teeth. The appalling resemblance between the cremation ashes and flour switches the poem from tense adult grief to the intimacy of childhood recollection: the echo of the nursery rhyme at the start ('Pattercake, pattercake, baker's man . . .'), the embarrassed hiding of his own tears, the ghastly reference at the close to the northern child's penny-loaf.

A poem like this poses interesting questions for our modern sense of how we read as literary critics. It is technically accomplished and verbally dextrous, but its primary impact is emotional. Like much of Harrison's work, it bids for sentiment through its virtuosity, though the heart strings it plucks are familiar ones, and some find these poems clichéd. This is partly because the poem invites a response which professionally we are not accustomed to give. It is populist in cast, draws upon the sentimentality of popular entertainment, and wants to make us cry. This embarrasses the tough, conceptualised manner of much recent criticism, which has not wished to attend to such effects. Indeed, it has been suspicious of frank appeals to emotion, preferring the complexities of disruption and difficulty. Even when 'the pleasure of the text' has been stres ed, this emotion has been sophisticated and cerebral; and rather chillingly, and often bafflingly, couched in a language which it takes a very sophisticated stylist indeed – like Roland Barthes, for instance – to make at all vivid.

I wish now to turn to 'On Not Being Milton', but before doing so I want to remark that I am not implying that this populism means that the poem by-passes a critical analysis which might focus on the poem's discourse as defined in my opening remarks. I will return to this, but for the time being I simply want to emphasise that any assessment must begin to pay attention to the recognisable and openly expressed human situation described in the poem, in a particular social and literary context, and that I have a reservation about the adequacy of the language of post-structuralist criticism to express this.

'On Not Being Milton' is a studiedly literary poem, packed with reference and allusion. The opening self-consciously places it in a literary framework. It also has the rather odd effect of beginning belatedly, as though the poem had already been written and the poet was now giving his retrospective introduction. This, too, encourages the feeling of self-consciousness established by the title and formal dedication, and develops a mood of persisting meditation, as though a problem has obsessed the poet for some time, to which he keeps returning.

The second part begins an argument with an analogy between art and early nineteenth-century industrial militancy. Just as the Luddites smashed the knitting-frames that were depriving them of their livelihoods, so the Leeds accent smashes the 'frames of Art'. Art is capitalised because it is identified with 'owned language' – the established voice and accent of the culture. Hence the title of the poem: Milton's Latinate language and his learned classicism stands for that essentially southern English definition of the mainstream which has rejected Harrison's native culture. Line twelve uses a famous phrase from Gray's 'Elegy' of 1750, which sadly mourns the 'mute inglorious Milton' who died in poetic silence, his potential unrealised.

The final section returns to the early nineteenth century. It announces a general political and cultural proposition – 'articulation is the tongue-tied's fighting'. If language is owned, then expression is a political as well as a cultural activity. Poetry emerges from, or is appropriated by, a society which suppresses and undervalues the non-literary. The poem therefore concludes with an aptly appropriated quotation from the shoemaker Richard Tidd who was executed, with his coconspirators, in 1820 for his part in the attempt to assassinate the Cabinet, planned in Cato Street. Harrison uses the pun produced by Tidd's spelling 'error' (at a time when English spelling was only just coming to be standardised) to clinch his connection between articulacy and political activism: writing and setting to rights.

The argument of the poem raises two questions immediately. Is Harrison's championship of the inarticulate compromised by the highly literary manner? Is the analogy between political and linguistic violence valid? Harrison acknowledges the first problem. The allusion to Gray sets the poem in the persisting tradition of mournful alienation in English writing about the dispossessed. This tradition sees victims sympathetically, but does not speak in their voice. Distance is its governing rule. Gray's language (the language of this tradition), therefore, is jostled by others: that of Richard Tidd, for example, or of the popular cry 'three cheers', or of the deliberately difficult allusiveness and vocabulary of the poem's restless general 'voice', which does not fall into a settled manner or tone. Therefore, the poem sets aside the tradition in which it participates. But the puns on 'framed' and 'forged' make clear that this does not mean that it somehow leaves the literary in naïve solidarity with its unliterary 'other'. 'Art' is 'framed'. It is constructed, it is false and exclusive, and it is related to the dominant economic interests, the owners of the means of production, the knitting-frames. But, by the same token, the opposing language is 'forged' which implies imitation, and deceit. Most efforts to get a working-class voice into literature are compromised because 'literature' is produced outside the working class, even when that class is its subject. The poem can only recognise the inevitable problem and make it part of its theme.

A similar difficulty is detectable in the poem's attitude to Milton. Milton represents what is to be rejected, but his poetry is admired. An interviewer recalls Harrison's remark that 'Milton could go in a moment from the public and political to the "privately tender". That was one of the things that he, Harrison, tried to do in his work.'[3] In Harrison's *Continuous*, 'On Not Being Milton', the first poem, is preceded by a sixteen-line epigraph – which therefore looks like a Harrison poem – from Milton's Latin elegy 'Ad Patrem'. Harrison's poem, therefore, could be saying, humbly, my elegies are not as good as this. The ambivalence about Milton is part of a wider ambivalence in Harrison's work which celebrates the literary as it criticises it.

I'll now turn to the second problem. Is the analogy between political and linguistic violence valid? There are two elements here: a judgemental one (the analogy is perhaps factitious) and a historical one (why return to the nineteenth century?). The latter bears upon the former. In his recent study *The Politics of Discourse*, Tony Crowley examines arguments over the 'standard language' question in Britain in the nineteenth and early twentieth centuries. He demonstrates that the creation of a 'standard language' was stimulated by the militant politics of the early nineteenth century. As Crowley observes, 'Whenever political or cultural crisis threatened, the English language was offered as evidence of the underlying or unconscious unity that held together despite all superficial differences.'[4] For many linguists (a word which dates from this period in fact) the construction of standard forms was a way of stressing social-bonding and a shared cultural heritage. In reality it meant the non-recognition of 'deviant' or non-standard forms.

Later, linguists like A.J. Ellis and Daniel Jones took as their models for 'received pronunciation' and 'standard English' the – as Ellis put it – 'educated pronunciation of the metropolis, of the court, of the pulpit, and the bar'.[5] Allegedly this was not prescriptive, but the arguments in Jones's *English Pronouncing Dictionary* (1917), for instance, in effect were so. Non-standard forms, it was claimed, were intellectually and socially disadvantageous, whereas standard forms offered common intelligibility and literary, cultural and educational access. They were also intrinsically superior aesthetically.[6] At the same time, in response to international rivalries, patriotic linguists and critics were keen to stress the 'Mediterranean' (southern) rather than the Germanic (northern) origins of English, and Milton's work became representative of the rule, as Arthur Quiller Couch put it, that 'always our literature has obeyed, however unconsciously, the precept *Antiquam exquisite matrem*, "seek back the ancient mother"; always it has revealed itself, kept pure and strong, by harking back to bathe in those native – yes, native – Mediterranean springs'.[7]

Harrison, of course, is aware of this history. 'Them & [uz]' is a poem about the recovery of a native voice suppressed by schooling in the tradition of 'dozing Daniel Jones', and, in short, there is some historical justification for the kind of analogy Harrison makes in 'On Not Being Milton' between political activism and the suppression of regional language. But there is another reason for the poem to look to the nineteenth century for its details and sources. It was originally published in 1978 in a collection entitled *From The School of Eloquence and Other Poems*. It was then reprinted in *Continous: 50 Sonnets from the School of Eloquence* (1981). In both collections it is the lead poem, as it is in the 'School of Eloquence' section of *Selected Poems* (1984). 'The School of Eloquence' was one name for the London Corresponding Society, an eventually banned radical organisation of the 1790s whose history was written by E.P. Thompson in *The Making of the English Working Class*, from which *Continuous* has an epigraph. In other words Harrison is looking back to the nineteenth century not just in this poem but more widely, and especially to the continuities in working-class experience at a time when a return to 'Victorian values' is urged. Harrison's 'poetry from below' is continuous with the 'history from below' of socialist historians like Thompson.

Continuous has a more perceptibly deliberate structural organisation than *From the School of Eloquence*. It was published a year after the death of Harrison's father, and has three sections, of which the second is a sequence of elegies for his parents, the dedicatees of the collection. This is another meaning of continuous: the continuation of mourning (his mother had died four years earlier), and the continuation of his parents' lives – and way of life – in personal memory and his poetry. The retrospective mood in which 'On Not Being Milton' begins is part of a continuing meditation and structure of feeling which is all the more deliberate because it is the first poem one reads. Furthermore, the pages of the collection are unnumbered which encourages the reader, looking for one poem, to continuously read the others, and there are two further sections to *Continuous* which flank the elegies.

The first (which includes 'On Not Being Milton') deals mainly with communally based issues, such as those focused on language or nineteenth-century subjects. Again the continuity between personal and general experience is stressed in a way easily recognisable, as a theoretical position, in Raymond Williams. The third section of *Continuous* also deals with the relationship of art to socio-political events. The meditation on dislocation, on family and class history, and the place of art in a class-bound culture, remains, but to these are added meditations on ecological catastrophe ('Art and Extinction') and, again resuming an issue raised in section one, imperial history, particularly that of southern Africa. Other kinds of continuity are therefore established: between our present and our posterity (Harrison's is a profoundly historicised imagination), and between the various elements of a global situation. Some poems – including 'On Not Being Milton' – connect British experience with the independence movements in the African colonies.

Harrison taught for four years in Nigeria and much of his early work – for instance *The Loiners* (1970) – uses African settings and themes. 'On Not Being Milton' is dedicated to two leading members of FRELIMO, the marxist governing party of Mozambique. Sergio Vieira reorganised the national bank after independence in 1975, and is presently Minister of Agriculture. Armando Guebuza, a member of the central committee of FRELIMO, was political commissar of the armed forces after independence, and served as a provincial minister and Vice-Minister of Defence in the 1980s. Both are poets, and have a particular concern for education. This is the subject of Vieira's best-known poem '4 Parts for a Poem of Education Left Incomplete, because education is for all of us to build'. Guebuza, too, began his work for national independence as an educational activist and teacher, and FRELIMO has throughout put particular emphasis on cultural and educational issues. Several other leading members of FRELIMO are also poets, including Marcelino Dos Santos (pen-name Kalungano), the Vice President after independence and another dedicatee of a Harrison poem – 'Dichtung und Wahrheit' – in *Continuous*.[8]

The emphasis on the relationship between poetry, education and politics, so strong in FRELIMO, relates to Harrison's work directly. This is partly a generational matter. Guebuza, for instance, was born in 1942, Harrison in 1937, and Harrison, in this poem and elsewhere, invites analogies between the postwar educational enfranchisement of his generation of the working class, and the history of colonial and postcolonial independence movements. The experience of writing in a condition of cultural exile is another feature of this analogy. Though Harrison's exile is neither politically nor experientially of the same kind as that of the Mozambican poets, there are interesting points of contact and difference which the poetry explores. For example, Harrison's attitude to his cultural origins is understandably ambiguous. He feels both loss and separation, and a recognition of the limits of the culture left behind. (He is alert to the baleful racism in some working-class life and writes about this not only in the well-known *v*, but also, more startlingly, in relation to his father in the 'Next Door' poems in *Continuous*.)

I will comment more freely on this in the conclusion, but for the time being I want to note that a similar ambiguity pervades postcolonial experience. In Mozambique, typically, this involves both a celebration of native culture, and a recognition of the need to develop beyond it in new circumstances. Sergio Vieira, for instance, comments on the problem of reconstituting popular authority after independence:

> How is it that any person becomes a chief? There was a customary feudal law, a customary political law, as venerable perhaps as the British constitution. It was necessary to abolish this system of entitlement to power, to modify the conception of customary law as the foundation of power, to affirm the principle that sovereignty belonged to the masses as opposed to the ancestors, or the spirits, or a lineage.[9]

There are similar problems in art. For example, Makonde sculpture – adopted by FRELIMO and one of Mozambique's more visible international cultural exports – draws upon 'traditional' motifs. But, like much colonial culture, it is not in any meaningful sense 'traditional' art. Though it uses certain craft skills, and expresses certain experiences of subjugated peoples, its motifs and even materials are dictated by the market or politics. Makonde softwood carving was abandoned for black hardwood work because it was durable as a product, and felt to be more 'ethnic' by white visitors and customers.[10]

'On Not Being Milton', then, is concerned with the politics of art and language in relation to not only the history of the English working class, but also of empire. Harrison calls 'On Not Being Milton' his *Cahier d'un retour au pays natal*, notebook of a return to a native land. The reference is to the celebrated poem by the Martinican writer, Aimé Césaire. Like the Mozambican dedicatees of 'On Not Being Milton', Césaire combines poetry with cultural activism and a political career. He founded the socialist Martinican Progressive Party in 1958 and has served as a member of the French parliament thereafter. (Martinique has not opted for independence.) Césaire's work has also powerfully affected postcolonial aesthetics, particularly through the *négritude* theories which influenced much African writing (including that of Mozambique), and radical European intellectuals such as Sartre whose 'Black Orpheus', a rather breathless appropriation of *négritude* ideas, was translated into English in *Stand* magazine in 1962 in an issue in which Harrison published an early story.[11]

Négritude writing (the term was coined by Césaire) discovers a distinctively black aesthetics and cultural identity after the psychological and cultural traumas of the colonial diaspora. *Négritude* poems are frequently stimulated by the techniques of European modernism and use a formal and verbal range appropriate to the cruel and fragmented history on which they comment. *Cahier d'un retour au pays natal* is a long, freewheeling poem organised by tone and image. It exuberantly celebrates anti-colonial resistance, black belonging and relatedness, and the release of sexuality from its savage regulation under slavery. It also documents appalling black living conditions, colonial privilege, French cultural hegemony, and the madness which lurks as the psychological legacy of colonial domination. There is also the poignant loneliness of the returnee. The poem is set – in so far as it has a stable setting – 'Au bout du petit matin', a twilight area between desire and anger, hope and remorse, transformation and guilt, communion and solitude. Alongside new possibilities, there is the peccancy of complicity with the educational and cultural structures which degrade one's people.[12]

There is plenty, then, to appeal to Harrison in Césaire. *Cahier* was written, in 1938, on the eve of Césaire's return to Martinique after seven years of education abroad. Like much of Harrison's work, it is preoccupied with the social context of language, and dual feelings of sympathy with, and separation from, a native culture. 'On Not Being Milton', therefore, describes 'growing black enough' to return to his roots – a phrase with a distinctively black resonance after Alex Haley's *Roots* of 1976. But Harrison, again, uses his verbal dexterity to gain a distance on the idea even as it is advanced. For behind the identification with (even appropriation of) this black experience, lurks a northern phrase invited by the rhyme between lines two and four: growing too big for your boots – becoming conceited, having grand ideas. The poet sees himself through the eyes of his family (he now has cultural pretensions), but he also implies he is too assuming in aligning himself with Césaire's black predicament. The uniting idea is found in the blackness of coal. Harrison's family worked in the mining industry which forms so much of Yorkshire working-class culture. (This issue is raised in various *Continuous* poems and in *v.*) One meaning for the initially puzzling opening of 'On Not Being Milton' is therefore: I have read (been educated) and committed this older culture, like coal, to the flames, but am now returning.

The lines also have a religious ring, and another meaning is offered by Harrison's quarrel with his parents' Christianity. They can be glossed: I, having become cultured, have turned atheist and thus am 'committed' (meaning both sentenced and determined by choice) to the flames of hell. The religious register of Harrison's work is widely evident. His atheism is partly political, and concerns the relationship between the clergy and the legitimation of the status quo – Armando Guebuza makes a similar point about the Christian apologists for slavery in his poem 'Obscurantism'. But Harrison also – particularly in his later work – associates Christianity with guilt and psychological repression. None the less it provides a useful mythological motif in the story of the pentecost – the gift of tongues of fire. Harrison uses the story's ambiguity. Fire brings pain, but also eloquence; articulation, but also the suggestion of fanaticism. 'Dichtung und Wahrheit' (poetry and truth), a poem about Marcelino dos Santos, then – 1971 – FRELIMO's spokesman in Dar-es-Salaam, is a worried meditation on the relationship between propaganda, poetry and the inevitable violence of the war of independence. The image that unites these ideas is that of the tongue of fire: the gifts of poetry and eloquence for the dispossessed, but also the flame at the end of a gun barrel. In 'Fire Eater', an elegy from the second section of *Continuous*, the image is applied to his own work. He makes poetry from his family's inarticulacy: 'Their's are the tongues of fire I'm forced to swallow / . . . and though my vocal cords get scorched and black / there'll be a constant singing from the flames.' In 'On Not Being Milton', the pentecostal image at the beginning of the poem implies a scouring return to his native land.

Beginning with personal circumstance and developing outward to wider contexts is Harrison's usual practice. This analogical mode risks overdramatising the central personality, and blurring the differences between cases and situations. But the virtue of the method is that in making connections he also expresses difference. The comparison of his poem to Césaire's *Cahier* is a case in point, and in earlier work Harrison is more explicit about the difficulties of analogical borrowing. 'The White Queen' sequence (1970) uses dramatic monologue to explore the sexual psychology of colonial exploitation. In Part 5, 'The Zeg-Zeg Postcards', sexual exotica is the speaker's only idea of *négritude,* and an essay on Cuba from the same year voices suspicion of *négritude* theory – is it only an 'Africa in the head'?[13] What interests him, however, are the interlockings and frictions of the bits and pieces of the colonial diaspora, the cross-fertilisations, connections and jostling cultural horizons. Clearly, this reflects a central aspect of his own work, but it also reflects a wider situation. His personal predicament risks factitiousness to represent a modern condition which is personal, regional and international. It is the drama of expression with a language pressured by problems of power; in Raymond Williams's memorable terms, it is written within the interaction of dominant, residual and emergent.

In their introduction to *The Penguin Book of Modern African Poetry,* Gerald Moore and Ulli Beier comment on the difference between writing in the Francophone and Anglophone traditions. Francophone poets have, in *négritude* forms, an alternative, expressive and oppositional language within reach. In Anglophone areas, however, English 'has acquired a life and flavour of its own . . . but is still perceived by many as a colonial imposition which must sooner or later be rejected'.[14] Many therefore compose in an African language and translate into English, a practice which is widespread among colonised linguistic groups. (Sorley Maclean, Scotland's leading Gaelic poet, does this, for example.) The language problem is symptomatic of the wider political and cultural situation in a way which is true for users of variant forms within 'English' also. Thus Anglophone Caribbean writers are creating a 'nation language' which uses English elements, but draws on a wider repertory of popular forms (from music, oral performance and demotic, for instance) to express a Caribbean identity distinct from that offered by the English education system. Nation language, as Edward Braithwaite puts it, tries to record the hurricane, and not the weather of the Shropshire hills.[15]

Braithwaite works in the Caribbean, but the situation is similar for writers outside the mainstream in England itself. In a recent essay, also entitled 'On Not Being Milton' (but subtitled 'Nigger Talk in England Today'), the black poet and critic David Dabydeen contrasts Milton's language with Caribbean creole. 'Milton's ornate, highly-structured, Latinate expressions . . . are still the exemplars of English civilisation against which the barbaric utterances of black people are judged', he argues.[16] Creole, on the other hand, expresses black experience authentically without the imperialist distortions of 'standard English'. It is energetic, lyrically and sexually lively and draws vitally on ordinary speech. Interestingly, Dabydeen analogises the black experience of language to 'the ancient divide between north and south in Britain'. The 'sheer naked energy and brutality' of non-Chaucerian alliterative verse 'reminded me immediately of the creole of my childhood'. So the connections go the other way too. Just as Harrison connects the experiences of a northern Englishman to that of a black writer in the Caribbean in his 'On Not Being Milton', so Dabydeen, in his 'On Not Being Milton', looks from creole to the language of the *Gawain* poet.

Meanwhile Harrison translates not just the medieval *Mysteries*, but Palladas of Alexandria (*Palladas: Poems*), Martial (*U.S. Martial*), Aeschylean tragedy (*The Oresteia*) and Sophoclean satyr writing (*The Trackers of Oxyrhynchus*) into a modern northern idiom. Recalling the 'standard English' arguments, and Quiller-Couch's reorientation of British culture towards a certain construction of Mediterranean classicism, it is easy to see that Harrison is very deliberately reannexing this literature in his translations. In 'On Not Being Milton', in the fifth line, Harrison changes the focus from *négritude* writers to the Old Norse poet, the 'scold' (or 'skald') stuttering 'out of the branks / of condescension'. This is typical Harrison wordplay. A scold is also a trouble-maker; branks are both gagging devices (used on a medieval scold-cart) and swaggerings typical of the condescending ruling establishment. Recently, *The Sunday Telegraph*, in patrician annoyance at Harrison's continual return to working-class subjects, advised him 'to throw off his muddled sense of obligation to his past, accept himself calmly as the person he has now become, and put an end to the bluster and self-assertion that mar his work'.[17] Thus are whole areas of experience written out with cold disdain in the mandarin accents Harrison deplores.

It is best, then, to see Harrison's 'On Not Being Milton' as engaged in a cultural exchange and borrowing typical of the postwar period. Its discourse, that is to say, is formed by a *bricolage* of international elements, using techniques of intertextual allusion, punning, self-conscious analogy and juxtaposition characteristic of a certain contemporary manner (as in the ubiquitous postmodernism). But it articulates that condition with particular regional and generational emphases, engaging with a familiar postwar argument concerning the history of the British working class, and these features are not happily absorbed into post-structuralist theory. Like Harrison's poetry, much of this argument has centred on education, and the cultural dislocation of the most academically able of working-class children. It has been a characteristically male discourse (in so far as it has tended to centre on male experience), and has stressed both achievement (of fuller cultural participation), but also loss (of background, values and community). At its strongest – as, for example, in Raymond Williams – this tradition can accept the problem, and the inevitable ambiguity of feeling, and move on to fuller analysis. At its weakest it is nostalgic, and understands not just working-class, but *most* postwar experience, as tragedy. This strand effectively begins with Leavis and shades into, on the one hand, Richard Hoggart, and, on the other, 'Black Papers' Toryism.

At the centre of the discussion stands the forlorn figure of Tony Harrison's father, and the class and generation he represents. In-articulate, deprived and tragic, he is portrayed only as loss, a victim whom 'England made to feel like some dull oaf'. The working class is – in Harrison's characteristic motif – all but dumb. This is the negative, and sentimental, limit of the argument. But it goes in another direction, too, in which 'articulation is the tongue-tied's fighting'. In this argument (which connects interestingly with writers such as E.P. Thompson and Raymond Williams) 'the long revolution' in education, material conditions, cultural access, and so forth, is, though always difficult and bordered by defeat, a developing and participatory process. This argument has, subsequently, become international as a common predicament is perceived in the relations between the dominant and the suppressed – which is one central strand of Williams's revision of his earlier thinking in *Towards 2000* (1983).

Through the 1970s the work of, for example, Williams and Thompson was known, rather negatively and undiscriminatingly, as 'culturalism' by marxists influenced by French structuralism.[18] These younger theorists were suspicious of its emphasis on human agency and individual experience. Theory itself, therefore, was stressed over history, structure and ideology over agency, the unconscious over willed creativity. Literary forms which were dislocating rather than representational were valued, as was an abstracted, erudite and generalising language, rather than one that was plain, detailed or emphasised feeling. These shifts involved gains, but also losses. Among the losses were attention to specific history, and to individual or non-metropolitan experience. In this context, Harrison's work is important in its effort to find a language which is self-conscious about its own history and difficulties, but which is also adequate to speak of human loss and aspiration in divergent, but continuous and particular, human and social contexts.

NOTES

1. Ken Worpole, 'Scholarship Boy: The Poetry of Tony Harrison', *New Left Review*, **153** (1985), pp. 63–74.
2. Tony Harrison, *Selected Poems* (Penguin, Harmondsworth, 1984), p. 120. All subsequent quotations are taken from this volume.
3. Michael Davie, 'How to Get Poetry Out of its Corner', *The Observer*, 8 November 1987, p. 12.
4. Tony Crowley, '*The Politics of Discourse: The Standard Language Question in British Cultural Debates* (Macmillan, London, 1989), p. 70. See also Olivia Smith, *The Politics of Language 1791–1819* (Clarendon Press, Oxford, 1984).
5. A.J. Ellis, *On Early English Pronunciation* (1869–89). Quoted by Crowley, p. 146.
6. Crowley, pp. 198–200.
7. Arthur Quiller-Couch, *Studies in Literature* (1918). Quoted by Crowley, p. 40.
8. Information on these careers, and subsequent information on Mozambique, is drawn largely from Luis Bernado Honwana, 'The Role of Poetry in the Mozambican Revolution', *Lotus: Afro-Asian Writings*, **8** (1971); Allen Isaacman and Barbara Isaacman, *Mozambique: From Colonialism to Revolution* (Gower, Aldershot, 1983); and Barry Munslow, *Mozambique: The Revolution and Its Origins* (Longman, London, 1983). There are translations of relevant poems in Honwana's article and in Chris Searle (ed.), *The Sunflower of Hope: Poems for the Mozambican Revolution* (Alison and Busby, London, 1982). The latter contains work by Vieira and Guebuza, including those poems referred to in various parts of this essay. Searle's *We're Building a New School! Diary of a Teacher in Mozambique* (Zed Press, London, 1981) is an interesting and informative account of the educational policies and experiments of FRELIMO. See also Richard Gray, '"Khalai-Khalai": People's History in Mozambique', *History Workshop Journal*, **14** (1982), pp. 143–52.

9. Quoted in Munslow (note 8), p. 106.
10. Chrissie Iles *et al.*, *Makonde Sculpture from East Africa from the Malde Collection* (Museum of Modern Art, Oxford, 1989). Noémia de Sousa's poem 'If You Want to Know Me' develops Makonde motifs in relation to Mozambican nationalist politics. It is translated by Honwana and Searle (note 8) – both difficult to find – and in Gerald Moore and Ulli Beier (eds.), *The Penguin Book of Modern African Poetry*, 3rd edn. (Penguin, Harmondsworth, 1984), pp. 162–3.
11. T.W. Harrison, 'The Toothache', *Stand* 5, **2** (1962), pp. 41–5.
12. Locha Mateso, 'Négritude: traditions et developpement', *Présences Africaine*, **109** (1979), pp. 126–30; A. James Arnold, *Modernism and Negritude: Poetry and Poetics of Aimé Césaire* (Harvard University Press, London 1981). There is a useful bilingual edition of the *Collected Poems of Aimé Césaire*, translated and with an introduction by Clayton Eshelman and Annette Smith (London, University of California Press, 1983). Ellen Conroy Kennedy (ed.), *The Negritude Poets: An Anthology of Translations from the French* (Thunder's Mouth Press, New York, 1989) includes an abridgement of the *Cahier* and a selection of African work.
13. Tony Harrison, 'Shango the Shaky Fairy', *London Magazine*, **10** (1970), pp. 5–27.
14. Gerald Moore and Ulli Beier, 'Introduction', *The Penguin Book of Modern African Poetry* (note 10), p. 21.
15. Edward Kamau Braithwaite, *History of the Voice: The Development of Nation Language in Anglophone Caribbean Poetry* (New Beacon Books, London, 1984).
16. David Dabydeen, 'On Not Being Milton: Nigger Talk in England Today', in Christopher Ricks and Leonard Michaels (eds.), *The State of the Language: 1990 Edition* (Faber, London, 1990), p. 4.
17. 'A Yorkshire Poet Who Speaks for England', *Sunday Telegraph*, 6 August 1989, p. 17.
18. For a level-headed, but revealing, discussion see the Centre for Contemporary Cultural Studies volume on *Working-Class Culture*, John Clarke, Chas Chritcher and Richard Johnson (eds.) (Huchinson and CCCS, London, 1979).

Chapter 6

Ana-; or Postmodernism, Landscape, Seamus Heaney

Thomas Docherty

'Back – up – again'; or, in Greek, 'ana-, ana-, ana-'. 'The Grauballe Man', ostensibly about a man who is 'back up again', is an exercise in what I shall call 'anagrammatology': it is a writing elaborated in various modes of this 'ana-': anamnesis, anagogy, anamorphosis and analysis. In the present essay, I will show the poem as a writing which occurs as an *event* in these four modes. This status of the writing, as an event and not a work, nor even a 'text' in the conventional sense, is important. 'Eventuality' opens writing to a postmodernism, as an anachronic or untimely meditation, countering the 'punctuality' of the Modern, which is concerned to map two points in time as if they were two stable points in space. Eventuality releases the interior historicity of those 'spots of time'. To think this writing as event enables an analysis which will be, literally, a setting free of its elements into a movement of emancipation. A philosophy of postmodernism will raise the stakes of the poem, disabling the conventional reading of it as a neo-Modernist exercise in myth-making and replacing the usual banal reading of its politics with something literally more compelling. Three elements construct the argument: the issue of historicity; an exploration of the poem's cinematism; and a consideration of the poem as an engagement with the issue of justice, judgement and criticism: a 'cutting' which attempts to *trancher la question*.

'THE BEARINGS OF HISTORY'

> Once imagined, he cannot be seen
> > (Seamus Deane, 'A Killing')

On the face of it, Heaney's 'The Grauballe Man' seems an unlikely contender for the title of 'postmodernist poem'. In terms of obvious theme and style, it seems that most critics would think of it in terms of a 'late Modernist' text, Heaney as a late Modernist poet, the ephebe influenced by Yeats and by a Romantic tradition which was crucially concerned with landscape and a particular kind of eco-relation to the land.[1]

This 'economy', or law of space, however, is no longer available in the same way to Heaney as it was to the Romantics or even to the Modernists who were all so famously concerned with the issue of 'exile'. Contemporary space is what Virilio thinks as an 'espace critique', a space in which geometry is giving way to chronometry: our socio-political being is organised not primarily by spatial or geo-political mappings, but rather by temporal, chrono-political determinations.[2] Heaney lives in this different eco-consciousness of the aesthetic of space proposed by (for example) Beuys and Long, sculptors whose work is uncannily 'temporal' in that it is marked by its internal historicity and temporal mutability. A typical piece by Richard Long, say his 'A Line Made by Walking, England' is, in a certain sense, no longer 'there', except in the photographic record or image. Heaney's 'sense of place' is also – inevitably – now a sense of time. He writes:

> We are dwellers, we are namers, we are lovers, we make homes and search for our histories. And when we look for the history of our sensibilities I am convinced . . . that it is to . . . the stable element, the land itself, that we must look for continuity.[3]

This land is also a repository of history and continuity across time. It is the case that for Heaney, space has become critical in precisely another way close to this. Ireland itself is, of course, a 'critical space', a space built upon a 'critical difference' called 'the border' between North and South; it is built on that *stasis* or civil war which problem-atises any sense of its identity, specifically any sense of its historical identity. It is for this reason, of course, that the Field Day company, with whom Heaney works extremely closely, is crucially concerned to forge a history, to *remember*, as a therapeutic – and political – act which aims to 'suture' the wound to Ireland which is the border.

'The Grauballe Man' is, in a sense, a poem on poetry itself; its writing is precisely this kind of therapeutic anamnesis:

> I have always listened for poems, they come sometimes like bodies come out of a bog, almost complete, seeming to have been laid down a long time ago, surfacing with a touch of mystery.[4]

But it is a poetry which lies uncertainly between image (the photograph which prompted the poem) and memory (where 'now he lies / perfec-ted'), between history and its representation. If anything, then, this is a poem which is about poetry as mediation or about a specific act of reading. Heaney is confronting the bog as 'the memory of a landscape', the palimpsest record of history which is now conceived as 'a manuscript which we have lost the skill to read'.[5] Most importantly, 'The Grauballe Man' is what we should think as a kind of 'interstitial' event, a writing half-way between image and text, figure and discourse.

For the neo-Romantic and Modernist traditions with which Heaney is conventionally aligned, 'imagination' forges a link between the Subject of consciousness and History as its Object. This enables the formulation of a transcendental Subject in Romanticism or – less gloriously – a Self capable of persistence in Modernism. This trans-historical or mythic Subject is, however, no longer easily available to Heaney, for the postmodern has problematised the relation between the Subject and History, or between the 'real' and its 'representation'. If, in the 'society of the spectacle' or the 'hyperreal simulacrum', everything is now of the status of the image, then the 'real' has simply disappeared. The reality which is supposed to ground our representations, be it the presence of History as exterior fact or the presence-to-self of the supposed transcendental Subject, has itself become an image.[6]

This, in fact, is Heaney's problem, both a political and an aesthetic problem. The 'ground' for his poetry, history itself in the Irish context, has disappeared, gone underground. As a result, a series of reversals takes place in 'The Grauballe Man': what seemed a tomb is a womb; what seemed a man gives a kind of birth while also being the baby itself; to dig is to discover not the past at all (history) but rather 'the presence of the past' (anamnesis). When Heaney wrote the poem, he was deeply aware of the presence of the past, not just in terms of his search for 'images and symbols adequate to our predicament',[7] but, rather, in terms of the very historicity of the present, his present as a moment in flux, his spatial present as a moment bifurcated, divided, a moment when space has gone critical, differential, historical rather than antiquarian. As Deane suggests, the mythologisation of history is more of a wound than a salve.[8]

The poem's crucial turn lies in a stanza which is itself an interstitial stanza:

> Who will say 'corpse'
> to his vivid cast?
> Who will say 'body'
> to his opaque repose?

This stanza asks: is history dead, a thing of the past; or is it alive, vivid, a presence of the past? It is the very posing of the question which opens the text to a postmodernism, to what I shall call its postmodern cinematism.

THE CINEMATISM OF THE POSTMODERN

'Postmodern' is frequently misunderstood: many follow a particular inflection of Fredric Jameson who, while theoretically aware of the complexity of the postmodern, takes it in his practice to mean a rag-bag of the art produced since 1945. But postmodernism, if it is to be taken seriously, is not to be understood as a simple periodising term like this. Rather, the postmodern calls into question this very manner of thinking history. Lyotard, for instance asks:

> What, then, is the postmodern? What place does it or does it not occupy in the vertiginous work of the questions hurled at the rules of image and narration? It is undoubtedly a part of the modern. All that has been received, if only yesterday . . . must be suspected. What space does Cézanne challenge? The Impressionists'. What objects do Picasso and Braque attack? Cézanne's. What presupposition does Duchamp break with in 1912? That which says one must make a painting, be it cubist. And Buren questions that other presupposition which he believes had survived untouched by the work of Duchamp: the place of presentation in the work. In an amazing acceleration, the generations precipitate themselves. A work can become modern only if it is first postmodern. Postmodernism thus understood is not modernism at its end but in the nascent state, and this state is constant.[9]

Postmodernism is, as it were, the moment in the modern work when a critical difference becomes apparent; it is, for instance, the critical distance between Cézanne and Picasso when the latter paints in such a way as to call even the experimentalism of Cézanne into question; Picasso – postmodernist to Cézanne – becomes modern when a critical space is introduced by the works of Duchamp, and so on.

'Postmodern' does not describe a work, but, rather, an event; it is not a point in history, but event in its historicity. The effect of this is to question a prevalent understanding of history itself. One view of history suggests that the past can be 'sliced into', and that certain nodal 'points' can be identified and epistemologically understood: thus, say, the 'history' of '1848'. Call this the 'Modernist' view, one shared by Jameson whose periodisations necessitate the location of some crucial 'points' in history. Another view suggests that this 'point' is merely an epistemological hypothesis: '1848' is not a point in time, but is itself internally historical, in the sense that within 1848 there is only a series of differing 'becomings' or events whose flux and mutability cannot be arrested. There is, as it were, an overlap between, say, January and February 1848, and it is this *overlap* or interstice which is history, not the points 'January' and 'February' between which the overlap eventuates. Call this the postmodern view: in this, epistemology becomes difficult; but the historicity of history is maintained. The Modernist view is, properly, the very contradiction of history.

This can be more easily explained in terms of a kind of cinematism which is extremely appropriate to Heaney's poem, which itself hovers undecidably between discourse and figure, between the photographic still and the properly cinematic moving image. Heaney's task in the text is not to discover an archaeological remnant of the past in its antiquarianism, but rather to write in the interstices of history itself, to be historical and to be aware of the flow and movement of history, history as 'becoming' even as he writes – or because he writes – the poem. It is an attempt to make movies out of the still image, which is, of course one of the reasons why most of the descriptions of the body describe it in fluid movement or flux.

Cinematism is precisely aligned with the postmodern. Bergson characterised 'old philosophy' as the belief that the flow of Being could be reduced to a series of *'coupes immobiles'* or 'stills'. Deleuze follows Bergson in the rejection of the still and its replacement with the *'coupe mobile'*, a 'cut' which releases the temporality or cinematic hetero-geneity (*'l'espace critique'*) held within the apparently still or homo-geneous photographic image itself. For Bergson, according to Deleuze,

> le mouvement ne se confond pas avec l'espace parcouru, l'espace parcouru est passé, le mouvement est présent, c'est l'acte de parcourir . . . les espaces parcourus appartiennent tous à un seul et même espace homogène, tandis que les mouvements sont hétérogènes, irreductibles entre eux.[10]

> (movement is not mixed with space traversed, space traversed is past, movement is present, it is the act of traversing . . . spaces traversed all pertain to a single, same and homogeneous space, whereas movements are heterogeneous, not reducible to each other.)

The reading of Heaney as a Modernist has to view this text as one in which there is an established homogeneity – a late symbolist 'corres-pondance' à la Baudelaire – between Jutland and Ireland which, as Deane has pointed out, can only be maintained by some 'forceful straining'.[11] Such a reading, further, has to ignore the literal movement of the text, which delineates not the past but the presence of the past as a living present and the mutability of that present, its fluidity or flux.

'The Grauballe Man' is an example of a kind of montage, which Eisenstein had described as a kind of dialectical process. Montage 'arises from the collision of independent shots',[12] as, for example, the collisions between Jutland and Ireland, the Iron Age and the IRA, the description of the man prior to the 'corpse/body' stanza and the child hinting at a Christian iconography, raising the issue of justice which dominates the latter half of the poem, and so on. Montage such as this gives what Deleuze calls l'image indirecte du temps, de la durée. Non pas un temps homogène ou une durée spatialisée, comme celle que Bergson dénonce, mais une durée et un temps effectifs qui découlent de l'articulation des images-mouvement.[13]

(the indirect image of time, of duration. Not a homogeneous time or spatialised duration, like that which Bergson denounces, but a real duration and time proceeding from the articulation of the image-movement.)

It is a common misconception, deriving from much literary criticism, to suggest that Bergson had argued for the prioritisation of some kind of subjective time, a time which was to be measured within the Subject. Deleuze points out the fallaciousness of this. Far from time being within the Subject, the Subject is, that is, 'becomes', only through the agency of Time itself.[14] Virilio raises this to a sociological status:

Au temps *qui passe* de la chronologie et de l'histoire, succède ainsi un temps *qui s'expose* instantanément. Sur l'écran du terminal, la durée devient 'support-surface' d'inscription, littéralement ou plutôt automatiquement: *le temps fait surface*.[15]

(A time *which manifests itself* instantaneously thus takes the place of the time *which passes* of chronology and history. On the screen of the terminal, duration becomes 'support-surface' of inscription, literally or, rather, automatically: *time becomes surface*.)

Time surfaces, a little like the body in the bog which is also, for Heaney, the poem itself in which time – or in my preferred term here, historicity – exposes itself.

This 'temps qui s'expose' is prefigured, as Virilio points out, in the techniques of photography and cinema.[16] Those techniques, of course, were precisely the techniques which Benjamin feared, on the grounds that they would make history less accessible, would derealise it in some way. However, this derealisation is nothing more nor less than the denial of the availability of the *coupe immobile*, the denial of the still; and it bears repeating that the still itself is the very opposite of historicity as such; the still, or the *coupe immobile* which enables a stable knowledge of the past, the pastness of the past, is a kind of epistemological myth, however necessary. Heaney's text, however, is not about the pastness of the past but its presence. This is in accord with the living in a critical space of Ireland which Virilio would see as a paradigmatic postmodern condition. As a result of the movement away from perspectivism and its pieties towards cinematism, the inhabiting of time has supplanted the inhabiting of space itself. It is this issue which Heaney's poem is addressing: the anamnesis of history.

In anamnesis, according to Plato in *Meno*, we have something which Modernism articulated much later as a Proustian *souvenir involontaire*. In this, there is not so much a moment of knowledge of the past, but rather an actual recreation of the past, now present fully:

it is, as it were, the actualisation of the virtual.[17] It is this process of 'actualisation' which is central to Heaney's poem. The body in the photograph starts off as a fluid being:

> As if he had been poured
> in tar, he lies
> on a pillow of turf
> and seems to weep
>
> the black river of himself

As the poem continues the description, we have what is in fact a process very like Robbe-Grillet's well-known description of a painting, 'La défaite de Reichenfels' in *Dans le labyrinthe* which, as it elaborates itself, becomes less static painting and more mobile scenario. A soldier, described fully as an image, begins to talk with a little boy, himself fully delineated within the frame of the painting; but as the description progresses the frame is transgressed and the boy and soldier leave 'La défaite de Reichenfels' (the title of the canvas: figure) and engage with each other in a fully narrative situation, *'dans le labyrinthe'* (the title of the novel: discourse).[18] This tendency towards the mobility and the mutability of narrative, the actualisation of the virtual, of that which seemed to be merely a representation – in short, the presentation of the unpresentable – occurs also in Heaney. The poet describes the corpse/body to the point where it is unclear whether it is alive or dead, on which side the grave it is; then recalls the photograph; and moves towards the perfection of the man in the memory of the poet, at which point the presence of the past becomes all the more telling in the issue of justice which the poem is addressing. It is 'the actual weight / of each hooded victim' which the poet feels. 'Actual' means 'current; present'; and the issue of justice is itself realised as now and present for the writing/reading of the poem. Through anamnesis, the virtual or hypothetical issue of justice which is proposed by the atrocity of the Northern Irish situation is made actual, current, an event. Its currency or fluency is also, of course, realised in the fluidity of the bog man, who is seen not as a still but as a moving image: as a *coupe mobile*.

CURT CUTS

> the curt cuts of an edge
> Through living roots awaken in my head
>   (Heaney, 'Digging')

In this cinematic poem, then, there is an arrangement around a crucial 'cut' or rupture. Within the text itself, that cut is the slashed throat of the bog man; and a slashed throat is also a throat which cannot speak. Heaney writes a poem about the difficulty of writing poetry within the problematic of injustice which determines the situation of the poet and his poem; both live in a terrain marked by a savage cut or critical space which lodges them in history rather than in place. If people have no clearly demarcated terrain within which to identify themselves, they must turn to time and live in it. But the time is 'out of joint', in the sense that the history of Ireland is itself 'cut' or slashed, interrupted by a long colonial sojourn. These are Heaney's 'living roots' which quicken or come to life in his head. As Virilio indicates, 'le temps n'est un temps vécu . . . que parce qu'il est interrompu' (time is a lived time only as and when it is interrupted).[19] The poem enacts this living time through its cut and montage organisation.

But this slashed throat raises another issue: that of justice and revenge. The text is clearly related to Heaney's 'Trial Pieces', poems exploring Viking culture in relation to his own:

> I am Hamlet the Dane,
> skull-handler, parabalist,
> smeller of rot
>
> in the state, infused
> with its poisons,
> pinioned by ghosts
> and affections,
>
> murders and pieties,
> coming to consciousness
> by jumping in graves,
> dithering, blathering.[20]

The Jacobean revenge motif in Heaney is closely related to the idea of 'finding a voice', with 'Feeling into Words', those 'words, words, words' which Hamlet reads/says when confronted with the not so wily spy, Polonius, who finds a 'pregnancy' in Hamlet's talk.[21]

Heaney's first prose collection, *Preoccupations*, opens with the word 'Omphalos' repeated three times ('words, words, words'), with which he 'would begin'. This is important to the Oedipal impetus in Heaney. In his poetry, the land frequently occupies the position of the maternal womb, a womanly space to be 'quickened by penetration' as Deane puts it.[22] Heaney 'speaks daggers' to this Gertrude earth, this 'Bog Queen'. Oedipalisation is, of course, a setting of time 'out of joint', for it enables the mythic attempt of the son to be at once both son and father of himself. In Heaney, this temporal *décalage* is made more evidently a 'presence of the past' in the ghostly apparition of Hamlet in 'The Grauballe Man' and his other 'Danish' poems.

This bog man is strangely androgynous. Firstly, we find that a 'ball' is like an 'egg'; there is a dark linguistic hint here that the testicle is like an ovary; and this linguistic slippage or ambivalence, this metaphor itself, merging ball and egg, produces that theme of pregnancy which dominates the latter half of the poem. Further, even his body takes on a female cast:

> His hips are the ridge
> and purse of a mussel . . .

There is a kind of *anamorphosis* going on here, as the male character mutates into something female. A mussel typically is a container of sorts; and here it is as if the man's hips contain a 'currency', a pearly fluency. This fluency or fluidity in the cast of the body makes it an example of what Irigaray thinks as a *mécanique des fluides*,[23] a 'mechanics' which enables the poem to become mobile, a mutable *coupe mobile*. It is also a mechanics which enables the poem to articulate a 'becoming womanly'; and again, the drive towards becoming rather than being is a drive towards the historicity of eventuality rather than to the fixity of a punctuality. This engagement with gender places the text in the mode of anamorphosis.

The man is 'pregnant' in these lines: but what he is pregnant with is, of course, the presence of a future. The poem, then, is written in this peculiar future anterior tense which, according to Lyotard, describes the typically postmodern event. Further it again recalls Deleuze who cites Augustine's notion:

> il y a un présent du futur, un présent du présent, un présent du passé, tous impliqués dans l'événement, enroulés dans l'événement, donc simultanés, inexplicables. De l'affect au temps: on découvre un temps intérieur à l'événement . . . .[24]

> (there is a present of the future, a present of the present, a present of the past, all implicated in the event, rolled together in the event, and thus simultaneous with each other and inexplicable. From affect to time: one discovers a time which is interior to the event . . .)

This slipperiness of the 'actual', the constant and fluid actualisation of a virtual which organises the poem, is manifest in all the slipperiness which threatens to be arrested but which the text constantly strives to release or to loosen. If the man is in a sense giving birth to himself from the female bog in which there lies a 'Bog Queen', then it follows that the poetry is in a sense also giving birth to itself, originating itself or authorising itself in this peculiar act. The poet is Hamlet giving birth to himself, the poet as ephebe delineating a birth to himself through a violent act of self-wounding. For the poem is itself paradigmatic of poetry for Heaney; it is a poem about his own writing, which comes from the bog or from anamnesis, but it is also thus a poem which delineates how the poetry must derive from an act of self-wounding anamorphosis.

In my epigraph to this section, Heaney has described himself as the man suffering from the cut or bruise to the living root which is not in the Grauballe Man's head but in his own. The poem is his epithalamium, in a sense, the wedding text which tries to wedge together the wounding, a suturing which is involved in the act of love. It is the 'Wedding Day' on which:

> I am afraid.
> Sound has stopped in the day
> And the images reel over
> And over . . . .[25]

It also brings to mind his dream of freedom:

> I had to read from Martin Luther King's famous 'I have a dream' speech. 'I have a dream that one day this nation will rise up and live out the full meaning of its creed' – and on that day all men would be able to realize fully the implications of the old spiritual, 'Free at last, free at last, Great God Almighty, we are free at last.' But, as against the natural hopeful rhythms of that vision, I remembered a dream that I'd had last year in California. I was shaving at the mirror of the bathroom when I glimpsed in the mirror a wounded man falling towards me with his bloodied hands lifted to tear at me or to implore.[26]

The Grauballe Man is, as it were, the image in Heaney's mirror: it is his Imaginary, his dream of freedom. As an Imaginary, it fits in with the idea of anamnesis in the poem. For what we have is a situation in which the world, that alien space, turns out, according to the logic of the poem, not to be an unknown alien realm at all, but rather simply what the poet always knew but had simply forgotten: it is as if the world is, as it were, a latent unconscious for the poet, his Imaginary; and the writing of the poem is the therapeutic act of recovering what had been repressed and facing it. In these terms, the atrocities of violence in Ireland are a return of the repressed pagan rites of sacrifice. Paganism, of course, is itself aligned by Lyotard with a certain postmodernism.[27]

But there is another image which fits this in the text as well. That image is an image of Robert Lowell, who ghosts this poem. Lowell ghosts the poem in the stanza which describes the head of the Grauballe Man:

> The head lifts,
> the chin is a visor
> raised above the vent
> of his slashed throat . . .

What we have here is a situation again reminiscent of Hamlet, especially that Hamlet who tests the veracity of Horatio when the latter is testifying to seeing Hamlet's dead father, returned from the grave rather like a proto-Grauballe Man. In that scene, Hamlet asks whether the ghost was armed:

> Hamlet: Armed, say you?
> All: Armed, my lord.
> Hamlet: From top to toe?
> All: My lord, from head to foot.
> Hamlet: Then saw you not his face.
> Horatio: O, yes, my lord. He wore his beaver up.[28]

This can be easily translated back into Heaney's text. Here, the idea of the chin as a visor which is raised above the throat suggests a literal 'disfiguration' in the sense that the face disappears in a particular way. It implies a closeness of the eye and the mouth, or, as Lowell would have thought this, a closeness of 'Eye and Tooth'. In Lowell's poem of that name, we have an examination of a particular kind of justice, the justice of a biblical mode (eye for eye, tooth for tooth, etc.) which is placed at the service of a political ideology, that which is identified in Lowell's poem by the imperialist American eagle:

> No ease from the eye
> of the sharp-shinned hawk in the birdbook there,
> with reddish brown buffalo hair
> on its shanks, one ascetic talon
>
> clasping the abstract imperial sky.
> It says:
> *an eye for an eye,*
> *a tooth for a tooth.*[29]

In a certain sense, then, Heaney's 'bog poems' become his version of a text 'For the Union Dead': a volume which is, of course, a validation of America's 'North'. Heaney's 'Act of Union' sees the relation of imperialism in precisely the same Oedipal terms which 'The Grauballe Man' explores.

In the interstices of the poem, then, there comes a pressure which breaks it from within. It is, in a sense, an allegory of Ireland's situation. But whereas the Modernist reading would see this in terms of a spatial allegory: in which the text would be regarded as falling into two halves, marked by the interstitial line of Lowell and/or Oedipus, and would thus think of this breakage or interruption in spatial terms, what my own reading shows is that this Irish situation, this 'curt cut', is itself a temporal cut, hence allegory as *anagogy*, one which involves history and which sees the poem as itself a historical event. Heaney here is not map-making, but history-making: one of the 'history boys'.[30] When Lowell appears as the ghostly father figure in the way I have described, we have 'the presence of the past', not its pastness.

Lyotard suggests that the 'post' of postmodern be understood in terms of 'ana-': it is a 'procès en ana-':

> Tu comprends qu'ainsi compris, le 'post-' de 'postmoderne' ne signifie pas un mouvement de *come back*, de *flash back*, de *feed back*, c'est-à-dire de répétition, mais un procès en *'ana-'*, un procès d'analyse, d'anamnèse, d'anagogie, et d'anamorphose, qui élabore un 'oubli initial'.[31]

> (You understand that understood in this way, the 'post-' of 'postmodern' does not signify movements of the type *come back, flash back, feed back*, that's to say of repetition, but rather a process in 'ana-', a process of analysis, of anamnesis, of anagogy, of anamorphosis, a process which elaborates an 'initial forgetting'.)

Heaney's poem is precisely such a process. It is analysis: literally a setting free and into mobility of elements which had seemed to be irreversibly conjoined. It is anamnesis, in its articulation of and actualisation of the presence of the past, even of disparate pasts. It is anagogical in its allegorical enactment of the historical split which is the *espace critique* of Ireland. It is anamorphic, a distorted drawing or representation with its abnormal transformations of Heaney into Oedipus, Oedipus into Lowell, Ireland into America, *North* into *For the Union Dead*, Jutland into Ireland, and so on: all those montage effects of this cinematic poem. It is in short the elaboration of an 'initial forgetting', a forgetting of the violence of origin itself.

NOTES

1. See, for example, Seamus Deane, 'The Timorous and the Bold', in his *Celtic Revivals* (Faber, London, 1985); Elmer Andrews, *The Poetry of Seamus Heaney* (Macmillan, London, 1988); Neil Corcoran, *Seamus Heaney* (Faber, London, 1986). In their 'Introduction' to *The Penguin Book of Contemporary British Poetry* (Penguin, Harmondsworth, 1982), Blake Morrison and Andrew Motion made a polemical claim for Heaney as '[t]he most important new poet of the last fifteen years', one in the forefront of a new 'departure' in poetry 'which may be said to exhibit something of the spirit of postmodernism'. The hesitancies in this final phrase reveal the fact that their notion of postmodernism was extremely underinformed and undertheorised. Antony Easthope trounces their suggestion in his piece, 'Why Most Contemporary Poetry Is So Bad', *PN Review*, 48 (1985), pp. 36–8, where he also argues that 'The Grauballe Man' is, in fact, 'resolutely *pre-modernist*'. Both views miss some essential points of what is at stake in the postmodern, as I'll argue here.
2. Paul Virilio, *L'espace critique* (Christian Bourgois, Paris, 1984). At the simplest level, this corresponds to an organisation of life in terms of 'quality time' or 'labour time' rather than its organisation in terms of the 'metropolis' and the 'suburbs'. Cf. the work of Gilles Deleuze, especially with regard to the idea that social, political and psychological life are all organised around 'lines of flight', making territorialisations and deterritorialisations.
3. Seamus Heaney, *Preoccupations* (Faber, London, 1980), pp. 148–9. For a more detailed explication of this aesthetic in Long, see my *After Theory* (Routledge, London, 1990), pp. 22–4.

4. Heaney, *Preoccupations*, p. 34.
5. Heaney, *Preoccupations*, pp. 54, 132; the latter phrase is attributed to John Montague.
6. See Guy Debord, *La société du spectacle* (Geneva, 1967); Jean Baudrillard, *L'Echange symbolique et la mort* (Gallimard, Paris, 1976); Baudrillard, *Amérique* (Grasset, Paris, 1986). This tendency in poetry is perhaps most marked in the work of John Ashbery. But it has been there in a great deal of modernist writing, where there was a marked interest in the 'interstitial'. Modernist writers did not chart the 'death of the Self': they were interested in the self-in-time, and in the interstitial moments between those significant moments of assured selfhood or supposed self-presence. Hence Proust was interested not in the heartbeat itself but in the 'intermittences du coeur'; Woolf was interested not in actions but in what goes on 'between the acts'; Bergson was interested in the time 'between' marked instants; Eisenstein in the dialectical relation between the images which constituted montage in cinema; Saussure in the relations 'between' signs rather than in signs themselves; Einstein in 'relative' rather than absolute measure; and so on. It is this 'interstitial' area which determines Heaney's writing here.
7. Heaney, *Preoccupations*, p. 56. 'The Presence of the Past' was the title of the 1980 Venice Biennale which initiated the 'postmodern debate' in architecture.
8. Deane, *Celtic Revivals*, p. 179.
9. Jean-François Lyotard, *The Postmodern Condition* (Manchester University Press, Manchester, 1984), p. 79; cf. Fredric Jameson, 'Postmodernism; or, the Cultural Logic of Late Capitalism', *New Left Review*, **146** (1984), 53–92; and Jameson, 'The Politics of Theory', in his *The Ideologies of Theory*, II (Routledge, London, 1988), pp. 103–13.
10. Gilles Deleuze, *Cinéma 1: L'image-mouvement* (Minuit, Paris, 1983), p. 9.
11. Deane, *Celtic Revivals*, p. 179.
12. Sergei M. Eisenstein, *Film Form*, as quoted in Gerald Mast and Marshall Cohen (eds.), *Film Theory and Criticism*, 2nd edn. (Oxford University Press, New York, 1979), p. 104.
13. Deleuze, *Cinéma 1*, p. 47.
14. See Deleuze, *Différence et répétition* (PUF, Paris, 1968), p. 116, especially the passage on Kant and what Deleuze thinks as the 'je fêlé', which marks the becoming of the Subject, its existence in historicity or in the form of time.
15. Virilio, *Espace critique*, p. 15.
16. Virilio, *Espace critique*, p. 77.
17. See, for example, Georges Poulet, *Proustian Space* (Johns Hopkins University Press, Baltimore, 1977).
18. Alain Robbe-Grillet, *Dans le labyrinthe* (Minuit, Paris, 1959), pp. 24–31 *et seq.*
19. Virilio, *Espace critique*, p. 103; cf. Deleuze, *Kant's Critical Philosophy* (University of Minnesota Press, Minneapolis, 1984), pp. vii–viii.
20. Heaney, 'Viking Dublin: Trial Pieces', in *North* (Faber, London, 1975), pp. 21–4.
21. See Heaney, 'Feeling Into Words', in *Preoccupations*; the references here are to Shakespeare's *Hamlet*, 2.2.
22. Deane, *Celtic Revivals*, p. 177.
23. Luce Irigaray, *This Sex Which Is Not One* (Cornell University Press, Ithaca, 1985).
24. Deleuze, *Cinéma 2: L'image-temps* (Minuit, Paris, 1985), p. 132.
25. Heaney, 'Wedding Day', in *Wintering Out* (Faber, London, 1972), p. 57.
26. Heaney, *Preoccupations*, p. 33.
27. See Lyotard, *Rudiments païens* (10/18, Paris, 1977) and *Instructions païennes* (Galilée, Paris, 1977), *Tombeau de l'intellectuel* (Galilée, Paris, 1984), *Le postmoderne expliqué aux enfants* (Galilée, Paris, 1986).
28. Shakespeare, *Hamlet*, 1.2.
29. Robert Lowell, 'Eye and Tooth', in *For the Union Dead* (Faber, London, 1965), pp. 18–19.
30. Seamus Deane, 'Send War in Our Time, O Lord', in *History Lessons* (Gallery Books, Dublin, 1983), p. 12.
31. Lyotard, *Le postmoderne expliqué aux enfants*, p. 126.

Chapter 7

On Ice

Julia Kristeva, Susan Howe and avant garde poetics

Peter Middleton

In her recent book on poetry, *Articulation of Sound Forms in Time*,[1] the American poet Susan Howe offers what appears to be a series of neat rhetorical paradigms for philosophy and theory:

> Algorithms bravadoes jetsam
> All Wisdom's plethora pattern.

Algorithms are the generators of mathematical structures but they are only mechanistic formulae, they are not foundational like axioms. We can read Howe's use of the term algorithms, therefore, as a dismissive name for all kinds of foundationalism. Bravadoes? Is theory no more than men shouting bravely in the face of the unknown, boasting of their power based on a rationality whose masculine rhetoric is all too evident? Jetsam suggests that theory and philosophy are merely wreckage, the hulks of metaphysics and the empty shells of moral discourse, washed up from the sea of knowledge which Isaac Newton imagined, or the ocean of past imperialisms. The designation might accommodate Jacques Derrida or Alasdair MacIntyre[2] or recent theories of colonialism. Susan Howe's enigmatic couplet reflexively offers a direct poetic intervention within the very forms of recent theory that have had most to say about such poetic strategies as this.

Susan Howe is one of the most original and thoughtful American poets to have emerged in the past twenty years.[3] Her work shows an exceptional grasp of the complex intersections of poetry, philosophy, history and sexual politics, manifested in a brilliant attention to the histories of sound and sense in poetic language. Her work appears consciously postmodern in its formal disruption of what she calls the 'visible surface of discourse'[4] but its interest in the possibility of truth and history makes it sit uneasily within that category. Indeed, it is a strength of Susan Howe's work that it is hard to place within any existing category although her poetry would seem to offer itself as a paradigm of that kind of formal literary experiment which uses linguistic disruption to challenge the existing symbolic order. In this essay I want to explore recent claims made on behalf of formal literary experiment, notably by Julia Kristeva, and some Language Poets. (Language Poetry, as it has somewhat misleadingly been called, is a grouping of poets to which Susan Howe is sometimes assumed to belong, although her work has important differences from the main-stream of its practice.) I will directly and indirectly examine the claims that formal poetic experiments with language can lay bare, challenge and rupture the symbolic order, especially ideology. Language poetry seems a paradigm case of formal literary and linguistic experiment and so Kristeva's *Revolution in Poetic Language*[5] ought therefore to provide a satisfactory account of its effects, even if her attention is directed almost entirely to earlier French modernists and symbolists. That her construction of theory begins with a dismissive critique of existing foundational concepts of language, seems especially promis-ing for such a trial of this formalist approach. What I will suggest is that Kristeva's formulation depends upon assumptions about linguistic order which Susan Howe's poetry calls into question.

Kristeva begins her study of avant garde poetics[6] by arguing that existing philosophies of language substitute a fetishised object of study for the partly discursive process they should be engaged with. Such philosophies of language help reproduce the repression of *process* whereby meaning is produced as it traverses the body and the subject, a process which we need to recognise at work within our interpersonal, social experience in order to empower our political struggles, because capitalism has isolated us, in 'islands of discourse' (11–13). Relations between subjectivity and the socio-economic order are not articulated by such accounts of language, because these philosophies are actually dealing with different moments in some translinguistic process which they then identify as language or the subject. According to Kristeva, philosophies of language leave you with mere jetsam, but some literature can weave together the relations of the unconscious, the subject and society, in a manner which both destroys and reconstructs, demonstrating a 'violence positive'(14–16). Such texts could 'explode' phonetically, lexically and syntactically the *object of linguistics* and, by implication, disrupt the cosy arrangements about linguistic reification which philosophies of language practise. This constructive destruction is possible because of the very nature of 'signifiance' or 'cet engendrement illimité'(15–17) which works, via the drives (pulsions) that Freud analysed, 'towards, through and counter to language'(15–17 – my translation), and, therefore, exchange and its protagonists, 'the subject and its sites'(15–17). She deliberately invokes the use of economic metaphors which Saussure used for his account of linguistic 'value', as well as social theories of exchange, as the basis of the symbolic order.

The chora is Kristeva's bold concept for the foundations of the signifying process. It is a way of naming the totality of the drives and primary processes of psychoanalytic theory from the standpoint of their organisation, however limited that organisation might be. The chora 'precedes evidence, verisimilitude, spatiality, and temporality' (23–26). Discourse both depends on the chora, and 'il la repousse' (23–26). The chora can be pointed out, designated and regulated, but not posited, because it cannot be summed up in a proposition. 'One can situate the chora and, if necessary, lend it a topology, but one can never give it axiomatic form'(23–26). The chora has no dependency on truth or any form of representation, has no space or time and so is not subject to contingency. At best the chora can be indicated but not summed up in language. It has a topology but no axioms.

Kristeva's argument about the revolutionary possibility of some avant garde texts founders more on the issue of possibility than revolution. Her analysis never resolves the issue of whether she is arguing that such texts *did* have a revolutionary impact, or that they have a continuing potential to do so. Kristeva avoids having to consider such questions by concentrating her analysis on the means whereby this effect is produced, therefore implying that such texts have a continuing potential for producing revolutionary change. The importance of her argument lies in its claim to give a detailed, instantiated account of both unconscious and political dimensions of formal features of texts. Yet her attention to the subjective process still does not solve the problem. Do avant garde texts keep on disrupting the social order every time they are encountered, produced, or is their effect like that of a political revolution, felt acutely at the time, and then the root of social changes which stem from it and necessarily provide the framework for any subsequent assessment of what occurred? Is our subjectivity the result in part of these texts? If so, they are no longer revolutionary, because they have been successful. Or is this effect somehow endlessly repeated, as if the text were an aspirin or steroids?

To see why Kristeva takes up this position one can begin with her remark that the chora cannot be axiomatised, and consider a surprisingly parallel argument in Wittgenstein's *Tractatus*.[7] Wittgenstein argues that language depends on logic, but that logic itself, although 'transcendental' has no content. It does not represent anything, and it has no truth value (5.552/55). Wittgenstein also says that 'No sentence ['proposition' in the English translation] can make a statement about itself'.(3.332/16) To be able to make a statement about itself the sentence would have to somehow be both inside and outside language at once. That is not possible. This comment about the impossibility of linguistic reflexivity is more than just a comment about sentences (or propositions – the standard translation says that 'no proposition can make a statement about itself' – the German word here is *satz* which can mean both). It has larger consequences:

4   A thought is a proposition with a sense.
4.1 The totality of propositions is language. (19)

And finally: 'the totality of true thoughts is a picture of the world'(3.1/11). Both thought and language are necessarily non-reflexive. Non-reflexivity is a guarantee of this referentiality produced by the totality of propositions.

This leads to the problem with axioms. Mechanics, for example, 'determines one form of description of the world by saying that all propositions used in the description of the world must be obtained in a given way from a given set of propositions – the axioms of mechanics (6.341/68). The trouble is that this is just *one form* of description. Any number of such descriptions are possible, and therefore their use depends on subjective acts of choice. Axioms cannot produce the totality of propositions, and for exactly the same reason that Kristeva's chora cannot be axiomatised. If they could, the chora, or the world, would be able to know itself. It would be able to stand outside itself, or be transparent to itself in a moment of self-reflexivity.

This parallelism of Kristeva's chora and Wittgenstein's logic is not accidental. Both thinkers rely on Frege for their concept of proposition, whatever the divergence in their treatment of it. Kristeva's attempt to formulate a generative matrix for language leads her to make a series of claims remarkably similar to Wittgenstein. Both thinkers share a picture of language as largely shaped by the form of rational propositions, and both recognise that this picture is not sufficient, but then have to provide some form of transcendent Other to language in order to make it work, once they have denied the possibility of reflexivity.

Kristeva actually widens the distinction between theory and text, because her discussions of syntactic disruption do not result in any sort of dialogue with the text concerned, but simply the silencing of any interest the text has in knowledge and truth. Like Wittgenstein's statements about logic, which he offers and at the same time disowns as mere gestures at what cannot be said, her definition of the signifying process results in the generic condition of limits trans-gressed, a condition which effaces any knowledges, truths or even statements made by the text in those areas where breakdown is alleged to occur. Her theory becomes reductive because of its concept of language as the totality of propositions. That is why she needs to found the symbolic on what she calls, following Husserl, the 'thetic phase'.[8] Despite her strictures about philosophies of language, what she does is to take concepts from the analytic philosophical tradition even more literally, or materialistically, than its Anglo-American exponents. Postwar ordinary language philosophy argued that knowing how to use a concept actually meant knowing how to use its particular verbal forms. Kristeva goes further and assumes that philosophemes must be evidence of mental capacities. Husserl's concept of the 'thetic' character of language (which derives from Frege) becomes a phase in psychic development. The problem with this move, even if it is allowed to be legitimate and not some distorted Kantianism, is that it entrenches the authority of the philosophical account of language beyond question in a bodily space which is outside the reach of analysis.

Language poetry as it emerged about 1974 (the same year as *Revolution in Poetic Language*) was characterised by extreme disruption of the linguistic surface[9] often leading to accusations that it was unreadably non-referential writing. Linguistic disruption suggests a link to Kristeva's theory of the literary avant garde, but as we have seen, her theory silences avant garde writing, because it rests on the assumption that language is fundamentally propositional. As a result all the action is supposed to take place on the boundaries or illicitly in the excluded maternal chora, and she cannot allow the possibility of reflexivity in language use, because reflexivity would imply that there were cognitive positions beyond the totality of propositions. Some Language poets have shared such convictions about the linguistic order, but their work has led them to take up other incompatible ideas as well, most notably a preoccupation with reflexivity, which then upsets the initial idea of the symbolic order and its guardianship of referentiality.

Of all the Language Poets Ron Silliman's[10] poetics probably come closest to Kristeva's. He argues that 'when a language moves toward and passes into a capitalist stage of development' there 'is an anaesthetic transformation of the perceived tangibility of the word', and the 'function of reference in language' is 'narrowed into referentiality'(10). Referentiality assumes that it is possible for language to provide a 'depiction' of a reality independent of language, and so defined is another version of Kristeva's implicit picture of language as the totality of propositions. For Silliman it is a historical fact that 'every major Western poetic movement has been an attempt to get beyond the repressing elements of capitalist reality, toward a whole language art'(15). He then goes on to draw certain conclusions about the role of poetry: 'the poem is not only the point of origin for all the language and narrative arts, the poem returns us to the very social function of art as such'(17). Poetry can be 'the philosophy of practice in language', a philosophy which can work out the 'preconditions of a liberated language within the existing social fact'(17) if it recognises the way referentiality has repressed the signifier in favour of the signified, and then relates this to the class struggle. The 'philosophy of practice in language' is a poetry which challenges referentiality and the repression of the signifying process. That programme will justify calling poetry a philosophy, but it also entails a reflexivity which steps outside the bounds of what Kristeva would allow. The consequences can be seen in an essay by another poet who also thinks of poetry as a practical philosophy.

Charles Bernstein, who coedited the magazine *L=A=N=G=U=A=G=E* with Bruce Andrews, speculates directly on the differences between poetry and philosophy in his essay 'Writing and Method',[11] and suggests that 'poetry and philosophy share *the project of investigating the possibilities (nature) and structures of phenomena* . . . As a result, the genre or style of a writing practice becomes centrally a question of method, rather than a transparent given of form'(220). 'For both poetry and philosophy, the order of the elements of a discourse is value constituting and indeed experience engendering, and therefore always at issue, never assumable'(221). In other words, 'all writing is a demonstration of method'(226). Writing is always reflexive, always making a claim about representation and language. The sort of poetry which this stance implies is described by Bernstein as the text 'seen as map, but in the sense of a model, or outline, or legend and not trace'(232–233). In other words it is referential but not transparently so because it includes (as a map does) a theory of its own act of representation. Such a text 'calls upon the reader to be actively involved in the process of constituting its meaning, the reader becoming a neutral observer neither to a described exteriority nor to an enacted interiority'(233). Poetry which unreflectively avows that it is talking about a world out there, or a self in here, is politically reactionary. The radical element in Bernstein's argument is that writing is always a demonstration or claim about method or the conditions of its own validity. This possibility is not allowed by Kristeva, but its admission by Bernstein means that the interruption of referentiality which Silliman describes as the key element in the new poetry can no longer be assumed to be automatically disruptive of the symbolic order since if reflexivity is a possibility then the idea of a thetic boundary between referentiality or propositionality and the fluidities of the semiotic ground, a boundary which linguistic radicalism can shatter, is itself made untenable. The semiotic and the symbolic are revealed as themselves moments of linguistic process.

A passage from Susan Howe's book, *Pythagorean Silence*,[12] seems to gloss this idea of philosophy's association with poetry:

> Intellect idea and (Real) being
> Perpetual swipe of glaciers dividing
>
> pearl (empyrean ocean)
> Text of traces crossing   orient
>
> and occident   Penelope
> who is the image of philosophy
>
> (your wisdom hidden in a mystery)
> what ships I have seen[13]

The sea is text crossed by traces (or composed of traces) while philosophy (or theory) waits faithfully at home (if indeed anyone *can* be the image of philosophy since the line-break poses a question as well as providing an attribute for Penelope), but this is not just any sea, this is an empyrean ocean, sky, heaven and ocean at once. The text itself is an ocean where glaciers divide the pearl, the precious jetsam of the sea, where idea and the Real cut through one another as they melt into one another, while Penelope waits and waits at home to be told by the adventurer 'what ships I have seen'. This at least is one narrative appropriation of these lines. Philosophy stays away from the ocean, the explorations, the orient of texts and the oceans of distance, left with wreckage and the possible return of her spouse. Could that spouse be poetry? And how can philosophy (or theory) be gendered in this way?

The glaciers are made of ice – frozen, closed ocean, or text. What is this ice which swipes (hits, steals) the text? Contemporary poets who write about glaciers and ice ages are usually working across a textual field designated by Charles Olson,[14] for whom ice was a sign of the Pleistocene Era, in which we still live, whose inception was marked by the ice ages which have left behind the geographical conditions that form the ground, literally and figuratively, on which the history of Europe and much of North America depends. The new American economy of the European invaders began with it according to Olson. In several poems he suggests that this America has emerged from the 'sludge'(66) of 'ice wind snow'(88) which one of the first figures to explore the Atlantic, Pytheus, a Greek navigator of the fourth century BC, 'took the water and the air and the sky / all to be one of'(66), in the region of Ulthima Thule, at the boundary of the world. In an even more mythic construction Olson calls the world 'Okeanos' (an empyrean ocean), as a way of naming some 'first figure' (in Susan Howe's phrase) of all. According to George Butterick,[15] Olson's line, 'Deep-swirling Okeanos steers all things through all things', derives from Heraclitus who wrote: 'Wisdom is one thing. It is to know the thought by which all things are steered through all things.'(241) Okeanos is a name for 'wisdom's plethora pattern', and Olson himself is a figure of the male poetic authority which Susan Howe finds it necessary to question. It is an authority which derives in part from its very confidence about its references, its references to official knowledges of history and science.

Further discussion of this tropic space where wisdom, ice and ocean meet can be found in J.H. Prynne's poem, 'The Glacial Question, Unsolved',[16] which has much to say 'in the matter of ice'(64) (echoing the medieval device of naming the history of Britain the 'matter of Britain' and therefore linking history to matter and ice). Most of the poem appears scientifically factual, as it traces the glacial movements during the last ice age across Southern England in terms of isotherms, moraines and striations, but occasionally the poem is suddenly precipitated into a fictional, subjective register incompatible with realist science. We are told that 'the striations are part of the heart's desire'(64). The concluding lines unite us all in a collective which is conditioned by the continuance of the Pleistocene epoch:

> We know where the north
> is, the ice is an evening whiteness.
> We know this, we are what it leaves:
> the Pleistocene is our current sense, and
> what in sentiment we are, we
> are, the coast, a line or sequence, the
> cut back down, to the shore.(65)

To be a reader or writer of this poem is to have good sense and unite on the jetsam of the last ice age: 'We are what it leaves.' Our polity is what the ice both creates and abandons, its sentimental sediment. It is as if this 'we' takes its innermost identity from the feeling the ice leaves this collective with, sure of ourselves in the evening of this epoch, that time when the owl of Minerva takes wing, and theory takes off.

Another poem by Prynne glosses this further. 'On the Matter of Thermal Packing' recalls a country house used during the last war as some kind of temporary school, and then comments on the memory:

> In the days of time now what I have
> is the meltwater constantly round my feet
> and ankles. There the ice is glory to the
> past and the eloquence, the gentility of
> the world's being.(83)

Ice is 'the forms frozen in familiar remoteness'(84), in memories of
this place. Glaciers, war and the eloquence of the 'world's being' are
what leave us to ourselves and our sentiment. We might read this as
sayng that the world's being is a frozen form, a Platonic form of
absolute necessity maintaining a system of transcendental logic,
suddenly melting into the strife of contingency. Or we might read it
as implying that the world's being, the ice, is adequately knowable
through the scientific knowledges that tell us about its composition
and history. Prynne's poem ends:

> the glitter is the war now released,
> I hear the guns for the first time

> Or maybe think so; the eloquence of melt
> is however upon me, the path become a
> stream, and I lay that down
> trusting the ice to withstand the heat; with
> that warmth / ah some modest & gentle
>   competence a man could live
>   with so little
>   more.(85)

The ice is melted by competence, that is to say, by skill and perhaps
by that linguistic competence, the ability to use language, which stays
in the propositional orders of the symbolic, away from the liminal
waters of poetic language. This, the layout of the last lines of the
poem suggests, may not be enough, because the word 'more' sighs
out a wish for something in excess of this mere competence to use
language properly.

Prynne's use of geological data as metaphor poses a question about
the data, the knowledge, itself. Can a geological theory of the ice age
be a means of thinking about otherwise intractable issues concerning
history, memory and language? To what extent does the poem rest
on the authority of this wisdom? The word 'eloquence' implies not
falsity, but certainly a style which ornaments its structures. What
melts here is in a sense the authority of the science which gives us
to ourselves through the removal of the ice. Eloquence is the means
of its transformation, but eloquence is just that, a poetry which is
possibly untrustworthy and certainly lacking the authority and finally
the glory and real eloquence of the world's being, the ice. Eloquence
is that literariness which philosophy has had to acknowledge through

the erosions of theory and which both the world's being and the melt water share. Prynne makes scientific discourses into lyric expression, and in doing so appears not only to disrupt those discourses by making the signifying process and the construction of the subject in language, visible, but to melt their claim to authoritative wisdom. We could say in Kristeva's words, that 'as art, this shattering can display the productive basis of subjective and ideological signifying formations' (13/16). Yet these poems also endorse those scientific discourses as propositional systems which uphold the symbolic, and the poems are thereby made marginal to them. The poems almost entirely relinquish the possibility of becoming a *producer* of knowledge which even Kristeva herself is claiming to be according to the conventions which her book observes.

Susan Howe also begins with such authoritative discourses but proceeds by a different route in order to avoid the rigid divisions between fixed propositions and fluid oceans of linguistic process. Her central materials are deliberately chosen from the ice, the congelation of history in surviving texts, and the alleged foundation of geology, mathematics, philosophy (or theory). Remembering Charles Olson, Susan Howe writes about ice knowing this poetic history as one which great men have written on water. In *Secret History of the Dividing Line*[17] one section begins:

> In its first dumb form
>
> language was gesture
>
> technique of travelling over sea ice
> silent
>
> before great landscapes and glittering processions
>
> vastness of a great white looney north
>
> of our forebeing.(8)

This poem comes close to being a summary of Howe's poetics. The frozen ocean is our 'forebeing', our history, but also Being which we no longer are, and in that sense a form of Being which *is* subject to time. Forebeing is what has made us what we are and language enables us to traverse it. Instead of a call to evolutionary phonology or etymological research, another element takes a swipe at this familiar containable idea. She uses the word 'looney' to grate on the ears of those of us with good 'current sense' (in Prynne's words) as explicitly as possible. This formulation is in the past tense, the language is merely dumb gesture, the landscape or history is frozen, indeed may be insane (or may be just a joke). Its greatness is perhaps more the masquerade and absurd pretension that Nietzsche diagnosed in western culture, than admirable scale. Howe's use of the term 'looney' here is a way of repudiating Charles Olson's bravado about the history of forebeing. Hers is not just a Joycean response to some nightmare of history nor Marx's burden of all the dead generations of the past which weigh on the minds of the living. Also active here is a wariness about such metaphoric authority as is implicit in the very reference to ice as forebeing. Olson's usage, like Prynne's, relies on various forms of archaeological, geological and other scientific authority which takes the form of a knowledge structured as propositions about the world, propositions which belong to specific islands of discourse out in the oceans of signifying practice. This is what prevents Olson from addressing, in his letters from Maximus to Gloucester, the effectively patriarchal authority of these discourses.

Susan Howe's recent book *Articulation of Sound Forms in Time* offers a complex exploration of these issues. Structurally, *Articulation of Sound Forms in Time* explores the tension of its title. To use a definition of poetry which seems to annul poetry by the theoretical authoritarianism of its precise terminology, is to raise from the start the question the book will be preoccupied with. The book consists of two sections divided by a series of formally variable pieces which act as a transition between history and philosophy. The opening section reproduces a seventeenth-century discourse which has been shattered by an almost random reorganisation of phrases in short stanzas. The discourse it so lovingly disarranges is an account of being captured and freed by Indians, a story of the boundaries between civilisation and savagery, reason and irrationality. The final section offers a long series of phrasal units which fall short, but not by much, of being sentences or propositions. They have no assertoric force. When the text says 'Consciousness grasps its subject', not only is there an uncertainty about whether this is an event or a definition, but the substitution of 'subject' for 'object' in the familiar definition of phenomenology, results in the ambiguity which the word 'subject' produces in English. It means both theme and philosophical subject. As the latter there is a strange reflexive moment which takes us back to the issues which Kristeva was concerned with. These lines occupy the thetic boundary which Kristeva locates as the region of avant garde practice, and the linguistic freezing of fluid subjectivity into the reflexivity of the mirror stage.

One section of Part One suggests that this America is a 'myth of beginning' which in the words of the opening of Part Two, has become a 'Corruptible first figure':

Impulsion of a myth of beginning
The figure of a far-off Wanderer

Grail face of bronze of brass
Grass and weeds cover the face

Colonnades of rigorous Americanism
Portents of lonely destructivism

Knowledge narrowly fixed knowledge
Whose bounds in theories slay

Talismanic stepping-stone children
brawl over pebble and shallow

Marching and counter marching
Danger of roaming the woods at random

Men whet their scythes go out to mow
Nets tackle weir birchbark

Mowing salt marshes and sedge meadows

The 'myth of beginning' recurs in Howe's work as the merger of American settlement, paradise, golden age, creation, childhood, and also various poetic figures, most probably here the figure of Wordsworth's Wanderer. Americanism's neo-classical colonnades may conceal a warring culture. Even its narrow knowledge may be deadly. The pastoral origin seems to include fighting children, and the mowers seem especially close to the 'grim reaper' himself.

Howe writes in her book in Emily Dickinson: 'How do I, choosing messages from the code of others in order to participate in the universal theme of Language, pull SHE from all the myriad symbols and sightings of HE. Emily Dickinson constantly asked this question in her poems.'[18] The poet–explorer is a foreigner in this territory. Yet she is also therefore the invader. And, by another twist, the feminine is itself the Other in Western metaphysics and culture. 'But in writing Language advances into remembering that there is no answer imagining Desire.'[19] There is no answer, no algorithm, and bravado will lead to destruction. What we can do is listen attentively to the language, giving it significance even when it comes from the dark side of referentiality. 'In my poetry, time and again, questions of assigning *the cause* of history dictate the sound of what is thought . . . I write to break out into perfect primeval consent. I wish I could tenderly lift from the dark side of history, voices that are anonymous, slighted – inarticulate.'[20]

Julia Kristeva's account of the radicalism of avant garde literary practice seemed to offer authoritative acknowledgement of what many writers have claimed for their work in more poetic terms, but her reasons for calling this work radical depend on a denial of its content in favour of a universalising description of it as a disruption of the symbolic order itself, and therefore a disruption which is literally symbolic. Nothing the texts say matters. Susan Howe's work ought to be a pure example of a Kristevan text. It is preoccupied with almost the same topographies of the symbolic and its others, shares the same criticisms of Hegelian negativity, and takes up the textual materials of specific historical periods and subjects them to various deformations. Howe's poetry doesn't sustain Kristeva's theory because the ice has melted into the history of texts, and there is no other set of authorities which can provide the propositional foundation for the 'eloquence of melt'. Howe's work shows that literary experiment is not necessarily 'destructivism', but can also be an exploration of what is never clearly text nor clearly other, only a history of boundaries, captures, escapes, genocides and glimpses of something 'seen once':

Last line of blue hills

Lost fact dim outline

Little figure of mother

Moss pasture and wild trefoil
meadow-hay and timothy

She is and the way She was

Outline was a point chosen
Outskirts of ordinary

Weather in history and heaven

Skiff feather glide house

Face seen in a landscape once

It is the 'once' that marks this as history remembering its linguistic weather again, without the plethora of structuration by which literary theory has authorised and silenced poetic excursions to the 'outskirts of ordinary'. Whether this is infant narcissism, history or metaphysics is a question which algorithms, bravadoes and jetsam can only reify, freezing the poetic text in the grip of a theory whose definitions of language and rationality are far too narrow. Howe's poetry proposes a new history of such theories.

NOTES

1. Susan Howe, *Articulation of Sound Forms in Time* (Awede, Windsor, Vermont, 1987; Sun & Moon Press, Los Angeles, 1990), no page numbers.
2. See, for example, Jacques Derrida, *Of Grammatology* (Johns Hopkins, Baltimore, 1976), or Alasdair MacIntyre, *After Virtue* (Duckworth, London, 1985).
3. Susan Howe's work has been widely published by the small presses in both magazine and book form. Her books of poetry include: *Hinge Picture* (Telephone, New York, 1974); *Secret History of the Dividing Line* (Telephone, New York, 1978); *Pythagorean Silence* (Montemora, New York, 1982); *Defenestration of Prague* (Kulchur, New York, 1983); *Articulation of Sound Forms in Time* (Awede, Windsor, Vermont, 1987); *The Europe of Trusts* (Sun and Moon, Los Angeles, 1990).
4. In *Articulation of Sound forms in Time.*
5. Julia Kristeva, *La Révolution du langage poétique* (Seuil, Paris, 1974). A portion of the book was translated by Margaret Waller as *Revolution in Poetic Language* (Columbia University Press, New York, 1984). Page references are given to both texts because the English rendition of Kristeva's text is now always reliable.
6. What follows is closely based on the 'préliminaires théoriques', the prefatory material to *La Révolution du langage poétique.*
7. Ludwig Wittgenstein, *Tractatus Logico-Philosophicus*, trans. D.F. Pears and B.F. McGuinness (Routledge, London, 1961). I would like to acknowledge a debt to a reading of part of the manuscript of the sequel to Julian Roberts' study *German Philosophy: An Introduction* (Blackwell, Oxford, 1988). His discussion of Wittgenstein helped me to see the relevance of Wittgenstein to this argument.
8. 'We shall distinguish the semiotic (drives and their articulations) from the realm of signification, which is always that of a proposition or judgement, in other words, a realm of *positions*. This positionality, which Husserlian phenomenology orchestrates through the concepts of *doxa*, *position* and *thesis*, is structured as a break in the signifying process, establishing the *identification* of the subject and object as preconditions of propositionality. We shall call this break, which produces the positing of signification, a *thetic* phase. All enunciation, whether of a word or of a sentence, is thetic' (41–3).
9. The best survey of language poetry is available in Ron Silliman (ed.), *In the American Tree* (National Poetry Foundation, Orono, Maine, 1986).
10. Ron Silliman, 'Disappearance of the Word, Appearance of the World', in *The New Sentence* (Roof, New York, 1987).
11. Charles Bernstein, 'Writing and Method', in *Content's Dream: Essays 1975–1984* (Sun and Moon, Los Angeles, 1986).
12. Susan Howe, *Pythagorean Silence* (Montemora, New York, 1982), no page numbers. The title refers to Aquinas' summary of Pythagoras which Susan Howe discussed in an interview: ' "Pythagoras said that all things were divisible into two genera, good and evil; in the genus of good things he classified all perfect things such as light, males, repose, and so forth, whereas in the genus of evil he classed darkness, females and so forth." In reaction to that, I wrote "Promethean aspiration: To be a Pythagorean and a woman." ' Tom Beckett (ed.), *The Difficulties: Susan Howe Issue* 3, 2. I have been unable in the available space to say much about Susan Howe's treatment of gender, which is an important part of her work. Interested readers should see her brilliant account of Emily Dickinson in *My Emily Dickinson* (North Atlantic Books, Berkeley, California, 1985), as well as her poetry.
13. *Pythagorean Silence* Part 2, Section 11.
14. See Charles Olson, *The Maximus Poems* (University of California Press, Berkeley, California, 1983).
15. George F. Butterick, *A Guide to the Maximus Poems of Charles Olson* (University of California Press, Berkeley, California, 1978).
16. J.H. Prynne, *The White Stones* (1969), in *Poems* (Agneau 2, Edinburgh, 1982). This poem has footnotes which advert to academic articles on geology and geography.

17. Susan Howe, *Secret History of the Dividing Line* (Telephone, New York, 1978).
18. Susan Howe, *My Emily Dickinson* (North Atlantic Books, Berkeley, California, 1985), pp. 17–18.
19. Susan Howe, 'The Captivity and Restoration of Mrs Mary Rowlandson', *Temblor*, 2 (1985), p. 119.
20. Susan Howe, notes on her poetry, *Jimmy and Lucy's House of K*, 5 (1985), pp. 16–17.

Chapter 8

Poetry and Motion

Madonna and Public Enemy

Andrew Ross

Nothing better demonstrates the inadequacy of words-on-the-page criticism than attempts to analyse the lyrics of popular songs. This is criticism as autopsy, reenacting the death of its text, or, at best, criticism as a life support system, bent on clinically preserving whatever vital functions still remain. How can one begin to talk about the meaning of pop lyrics outside the contexts of their performance? Or to put it more frankly, who cares about the lyrics after the music is turned off? Especially if the conversation is going to be about poetics? Whether or not one is concerned with uncovering the kinds of ambiguity that are the characteristic interest of modern critics of poetry, it is clear that the conditions that determine the meaning of lyrics are seldom, if ever, to be found in a reader's engagement with words on a page. In fact, it is not at all obvious to me, as I begin to write this essay, what uses such criticism could serve, unless to point to the futility of this kind of exercise in textual analysis. What follows, then, is not presented as a model example of a 'cultural studies' approach to the practical criticism of popular lyrics as words on the page. The methods and traditional concerns of cultural studies are quite opposed to the socially isolated exercise of practical criticism. This is not to say that cultural studies rejects the 'act of reading'; in fact, its very strength lies in the application of interpretive skills to social and cultural practices. The point of such readings, however, is to analyse the continuity, and discontinuity, between different levels of cultural and social experience, rather than hermeneutically to plumb the meaning of a written text with the aid of a masterable critical method. In this essay, then, I will first consider some of the questions and problems that a cultural studies approach might raise and address for the analysis of popular song lyrics. In proceeding to a discussion of Madonna's 'Papa Don't Preach' and Public Enemy's 'Rebel Without a Pause', I will show how the lyrics of these songs mediate their respective performers' relation to a particular youth audience, acting out and expressively managing that audience's relationship to figures of authority. First of all, then, a few caveats.

Content analysis of pop lyrics has played a role, historically, in the sociological estimate of changing attitudes towards romantic love, sexual pleasure and social fatalism, to cite a few of the staple themes of the pop idiom. It is clear, however, that the relation between the often formulaic messages of the pop lyric and the ideological pressures of the day is not the simple, reflective one that is encouraged by such content analysis. Far from speaking directly about the world at large, most lyrics refer primarily to the recognised conventions of a musical genre – country, R&B, metal, bubblegum, reggae, disco, hip hop – each of which represents a quite different definition of the performer(s)'s relation to his, her or their specific audience, fandom or musical community. These generic conventions embody assumptions about the experience, tastes and desires of their audiences, and require performers to assume self-conscious roles and personae that are appropriate to the genre. It is this set of generic imperatives rather than any independent reference to contemporary social life that will most determine the selection of the lyrics. Even in instances where lyrics are held to have attained the status of 'poetry', the performer's role usually corresponds to his or her audience's conventional notion of what a 'poet' is or does. The 'blues poet' corresponds to a 'folk' notion of the poetic – telling it like it is, in the voice of common (black) folks – while the countercultural (white) version of the bohemian bard is inflected in the poetic mantle bestowed upon sixties rock auteurs like Bob Dylan, Joni Mitchell or Jim Morrison – either through their use of 'timeless' symbolist motifs and imagery or through the anguished medium of confessional sincerity. The 'singer–songwriter' – much less prevalent today – is the case of a sixties rock genre which actually required performers to be 'creative' and 'independent' writers of their own material. Generally speaking, it is true that stars in each genre enjoy a greater degree of control over their material. In large part, however, autonomy of authorship of musical material still depends upon the particular organisation of the music industry with respect to a genre at any point in time.

Many of the same points could be made about formalistic analysis of lyrics. The rhythmic structure of particular generic forms – twelve-bar blues, reggae dub, rapper's boast, pop, soul or country ballad – is a major determinant of features like line length, repetition, rhyming, accent, stress, and diction. So, too, the expressive styling with which the lyrics are performed largely depends upon the repertoire of idiomatic phrasing that is conventionally available to performers within a particular genre. However, while the vocalist's interpretation of a lyric is certainly limited in this way, the varieties of phrasing and inflection are still sufficiently idiosyncratic to compromise seriously any purely formalistic interpretation of the dull syntax of lyrics in print.

Whether one is concerned with content or formal analysis, an audience's familiarity with the distinctive, personal attributes of a well-known performer or star brings many additional levels of meaning into play. What we already know about and have come to expect from a pop or rock star affects our reception of what they sing, how they sing it, and what we use the song for. Far from preexisting, the 'context' of the song is thereby *created*, since knowledge and expectations of this order also determine the kinds of fantasies and emotional responses that fans will invest in the performance of a song. For the most part, these fantasies and structures of feeling are very rarely dictated by the words themselves. In fact, our own experience of the feelings called up by particular songs should tell us that the emotion has little to do with our literal interpretation of the words, or with the message they impart. It has much more to do with the way in which a certain phrase is musically 'turned', or with the felt memories associated with a particular sound at a particular time and place ('summer of 88', Manhattan), and in particular company. In many cases, we mishear the lyrics of pop songs, and when we do hear them correctly, we usually listen selectively, since our attention is more engaged with the 'sound' of the lyrics, interacting with the music, rather than with the meaning of the words themselves. Given the relatively insignificant attention that audiences actually do pay to the meaning of lyrics, it is quite naïve to believe that fans take the words of their idols to heart, as if the star's function as a role model rested upon the authority of the lyrics in their songs; none the less, this is the deluded premise of the current attempts by PMRC (Parents Musical Resources Center) to censor rock lyrics, which the music industry, under conservative political pressure, has agreed to implement. (The premise is part of the hoary old attempt to regulate the behaviour of class cultures, masquerading in the name of protecting those who are easily influenced, i.e. white and black working-class youth, since it is exclusively metal and rap that are the objects of censorship).

Having warned against the overinterpretation or overestimation of the role of pop lyrics, it is important to note that lyrics are none the less an essential component of all popular songs; music that has no lyrics signifies the non-popular, and advertises its appeal to a minority audience with a specific interest in instrumental expertise: folk, classical, jazz, new age, etc. So, too, it is possible, though by no means certain, that the role of lyrics has been augmented by the music video revolution of the last decade. Certain video genres require narrative forms that invite some kind of correlation with the 'story' told by the lyrics of a song. Whether or not these visual narratives do actually *fix* the meaning of a song's lyrics, and thereby limit the listener's freedom to fantasise a song, as some critics fear, or whether they simply provide additional material for fantasy and interpretation, as I am inclined to believe, is a matter for debate. For our purposes here, however, it has become necessary to include the interpretation and affect of the music video in the list of extra-textual features which shape the meaning of lyrics on a page. Anyone, for example, who has seen the video of Madonna's 'Papa Don't Preach' is likely to invoke it in any discussion concerning the lyrics of the song. This is not to say that the video will always function as the final arbiter of the song's meaning; we must, however, recognise that the video is a part of the product, and not just a promotional packaging, if only because it is likely to have been a major element of people's experience of the song.

Bearing in mind the caveats entered above, I will now look at the lyrics of 'Papa Don't Preach' and 'Rebel Without a Pause', and show how they express respective 'attitudes' about authority that are determined by genre, audience and star persona.

TEACHING OR PREACHING?

On the page, the lyrics of Madonna's songs are almost as trite and vapid as anything Tin Pan Alley ever produced. By contrast, her arresting stage and video performance, her blend of bold and sugary vocal phrasing, and the celebrated self-management of her public image often combine to transform brilliantly the idiomatic clichés of her lyrics into a language that her audience can recognise and use. By this I do not mean that Madonna offers lessons culled from 'her' experience to her audience; she makes a set of likely experiences available to her audience in an accessible form. In providing a useful, ordinary language with which people can express and make sense of their experience of a whole range of problems and desires encountered in everyday life, Madonna is exemplary of what pop music does best. In this respect, the lyrics of 'Papa Don't Preach' signify their centrality within the traditional pop mainstream; the song's primary address is to a teen female audience, it deals with the frustrations, desires and responsibilities of romantic adolescent love, and its vocalist dramatises and interprets a role that gives expression to the emotional difficulties that adolescents typically experience around courtship encounters.

No one, however, is likely to conclude from the lyrics alone that the song simply reproduces dominant sexual ideologies. In contrast to the ideal division of pop songs between the romance codes of bliss/discovery/understanding, on the one hand, and desolation/rejection/misunderstood love, on the other, neither of which offers any active control over a romantic situation; 'Papa Don't Preach' dramatises a process of active decision-making in a situation involving a conflict between patriarchal authority and teenage sexuality. The song harbours no illusions about the consequences of the decision; there are no ideal partners, and no happy futures are guaranteed. Armed with this mature sense of realism, the pregnant daughter confronts and respectfully challenges parental authority.

Before we go any further, and overhastily conclude by proclaiming that the song belongs to a list of 'subversive' texts that successfully articulate 'resistance to patriarchy', we need to consider who is singing this song – probably the most well-known woman in the world – and why the song is being sung by this singer. Far from reinforcing the romantic codes of sexual subjugation, Madonna's history as a pop icon and female sex symbol – someone who publicly signifies a set of unofficial attitudes towards female sexuality – cannot be comfortably limited to the category of 'boy toy', the image with which she has consciously flirted, exploited and parodied to the point of generic collapse. Critics have long recognised her success in shaping and controlling a performing identity that exploits good-girl and bad-girl types. The oscillation between chaste purity and sexual invitation is as swiftly and deftly orchestrated as her obligatory change of clothes between numbers on stage. Her exposé of linked iconography from the church and the brothel – white knitwear and black lingerie, crucifix adoration and belly-button fetishism – underpins her commentary on the virgin/whore typology of Judaeo–Christian morality, and has made her a demonised figure in the Vatican's eyes. Some critics have seen, in her manipulation of these images to establish influential control over her teen audience, a conscious commentary on the process of pop's commodification of teenage sexual desire. Others have pointed to the way in which her teenage (and younger) fans use her persona to help fashion an independent identity for themselves. In appropriating and rearticulating images of respect and disrespect for women, Madonna redefines femininity, but she does so by (simply) rearranging the terms set by patriarchy itself.

In 'Papa Don't Preach', Madonna dramatises a role for which she is a credible pop *auteur*, rather than a confessional raconteur – audiences recognise that she has the authority and the credibility to play this dramatic part, although no one has to assume that she has actually lived the part. It is a costumed part that calls for her to play down not only the glamorous trappings of stardom, but also the iconography of the bad girl. This will be Madonna on her best behaviour, and a good deal of the pleasure associated with the song derives from imagining and listening to Madonna play at being a good girl, coyly but insistently challenging 'Papa's' notion of what a good girl ought to be: a daughter who always obeys his word. In other circumstances, we are all aware of Madonna's capacity to play a bad girl, while in this song the only verbal evidence of this capacity lies in the highly eroticised series of moans and throaty sighs that culminate the chorus, and which are rather inadequately signified in the printed text as 'mmm . . .'. On the other hand, the implication of the lyrics about being in an 'awful mess' and 'being in trouble deep' are in fact highly moralistic descriptions of the consequences that are to be equated with behaving like a bad girl.

The song's scenario is that of a dialogue of which we hear only one side, and are left to imagine the father's response. Despite the absence of the father, however, the lyrics focus more on the nature of patriarchal attitudes than on the emergent sensibility of the daughter. Because of the nature of the plea and the emotional manipulation employed by the daughter in arguing her case, we tend to see the song's whole scenario as a problem faced by patriarchy rather than a problem that is being faced and resolved by the self-determining daughter. The appeals are made to paternal wisdom – 'you should know' – and to paternal morality – 'you always taught me right from wrong' – and the plea is for the father to see that her actions are actually in some way continuous with his teachings. Despite the opening suggestion that she may no longer be daddy's 'little girl', the overall argument asks the father to recognise that his daughter is most true to her status as the respectful but strong daughter of her father when she makes a decision to follow a course of action of which he disapproves. In fact, it is the father who is asked to 'be strong' and to live up to the high moral standards of his patriarchal role (while the video suggests that this is a single-parent family, the song takes no account of his 'maternal' functions). As for the daughter's show of mature self-knowledge, her considered willing-ness to 'sacrifice' the joys of unattached youth, her realism about an uncertain future ('maybe we'll be all right'), and her bold self-assertiveness in making her own decisions, all of these qualities are presented as if they were the ultimate result of her father's success at teaching her 'right from wrong' rather than attributes she has developed on her own.

'Papa Don't Preach' is not, then, a simple scenario in which rebellious youth confronts uncomprehending parental authority. It is a scenario in which the patriarchal contract is being affirmed by being all too literally interpreted. The outcome of this interpretation rests upon the distinction between 'teaching' and 'preaching', in which preaching is presented as counter to the teaching of good paternal advice. Patriarchy only works if it can tell the difference between 'good' and 'bad' exercise of its authority: patriarchy must be compassionate rather than dictatorial if it is to maintain its power.

Of course, we can also say that this conciliatory drama is being consciously staged by a daughter who knows how to get around her father; that the beseeching ('please, please'), the assurances that his son-in-law will be a good surrogate, and the arguments for the superiority of his compassion over the peer pressure of her friends, are simply ways of salvaging his love through ritualised emotional blackmail. After all, she has already 'made up her mind', and all that his response will determine is the outcome of the plea upon which the song fades out: 'don't stop loving me, daddy'. But the power of the song's lyrics does not lie in the recognition of her own desires. What the song does is to provide a credible language for the father to recognise her desire as his own desire. For a teenage fan in the same position as Papa's 'Madonna', the song provides a language to negotiate paternal authority without compromising the relation to patriarchy.

There is another set of issues raised by the song, however, and that is its relation to the authority of the Catholic Church and the question of abortion. When Madonna dramatises her role in the song, she necessarily brings along her whole history as a Catholic Italian–American female whose performance engages with and challenges the repressive tradition of Catholic authority over sexual morality. The song's lyrics do not evade this level of meaning; the references to preaching, to the father giving 'his blessing', and the generally confessional tone of the daughter's disclosure openly invite such a reading. In fact, in performances of this song in Italy, Madonna sings 'Papa Don't Preach' against a huge video image of the Pope.

In this respect, some readers might want to extend the song's attack on 'preaching' and its endorsement of 'teaching' to a more articulate critique of the Church itself, for which 'Papa' would then be a metaphorical stand-in. More germane to the drama of the song, however, is the way in which it manages the highly politicised issue of abortion, and not only for women and girls who have been brought up in the Catholic tradition. As a pop star, Madonna is of course precluded, conventionally, from offering explicit political commentary – that is a convention reserved for the rock performer. Her role as a performer of the song, however, dramatises some of the contradictions raised by the act of making choices about teenage pregnancy in a milieu where the wrong kind of choice is often considered immoral.

For the daughter's peers, aborting her pregnancy – 'giving it up' – is juxtaposed with the enjoyment of sexual freedom – 'living it up'. Although this is a rather un-Catholic opposition, it still poses abortion in terms of a sacrifice ('giving it up'). Sacrifice also figures in the dialogue with her father – 'maybe we'll be all right / It's a sacrifice' – where sacrifice is equated with the daughter's willingness to gamble on an unhappy future (or a laborious one, if this choice leads to another broken marriage, and another single-parent family) rather than terminate her pregnancy. From a Catholic anti-abortion point of view, any decision not to 'keep her baby' would put her in the position of 'sacrificing' a life. Although the song makes no explicit reference to this position, 'Madonna's' decision to keep the child, regardless of her reasoning, is ultimately in keeping with Catholic politics and morality. The difference, which may make all the difference dramatically but not politically, is that she has been seen to make a 'choice'. In this respect, the song's politics can be said to be 'pro-choice' – it has a pro-choice feel – while rejecting 'pro-abortion'. This is how the song negotiates and manages the contradictions of dealing with the self-affirmation of teenage identity on the one hand, and with the need to redefine dominant patriarchal ideologies on the other. As a song like 'Papa Don't Preach' shows, there is nothing simple about this process, nor is any ideology simply reproduced.

TEACHING AND PREACHING

To move from 'Papa Don't Preach' to 'Rebel Without a Pause' is to leave behind the (pop) performance codes of artifice and enter a world of music conventionally governed by the performance codes of authenticity. Here, the lyrics are directly addressed to the listener, the audience is assumed to be a 'community', bound together by common experiences and a shared history, and the performers have roots in that community which they draw upon to verify their right to be heard. The genre therefore requires the performer to prove his or her authenticity in the course of a song which comments on the kinds of experiences recognised as appropriate to the genre. This process of 'confirming' the speaker is well established, however, and, for the most part, all the performer has to do is observe the genre's conventions of confirmation.

In contradistinction to the pop codes, the conventions of authenticity govern most 'folk' genres, including blues, rock, soul, reggae, and hip hop. The conventional clichés of authenticity in folk genres are often held to be idiomatic expressions of a collective history, embodying, in sedimented form, the true voice of popular consciousness. Pop, by contrast, is seen as being manufactured from above, and has nothing to do with the vox populi. This view of popular music culture is, I think, deeply flawed, not least by its ritualised inflection of the division pop/folk-rock-blues in gendered terms which reveal a 'masculine' preference for 'tough', 'realistic' music 'with balls' to 'sugary', 'sentimental' pop music.

Rap music is the most recent claimant to the title of 'folk poetry' since it is a genre that comes off the streets, and has a long resonance within African–American cultural traditions. The boasts, threats and arguments that pervade 'Rebel Without a Pause' are rooted in the street-corner jousting talk that became ritually organised in children's word games like 'signifying', 'the dozens', skip-rope rhymes, ring-games, and more adult competitive discourses of boasting, insult and trickster games. The musical form has its heritage in African *griot* songs, and its modern technological antecedent in Jamaican dub reggae, where the DJ 'toasts' and talks over a musical mix or version, cooked up on two turntables in dialogue with each other.

The lyrics of 'Rebel Without a Pause' are sung by Public Enemy's MC, Chuck D, against the turntable mix of Terminator X, which 'speaks' as volubly as the words we have in the written text. His creative technology of scratching, sampling, punch-phasing, and break-beats is the source of another language in the text – 'the noise' – which competes with 'the rhyme' and 'the beat' as hip hop's ruling triumvirate of sound. Consequently, the printed lyrics are only one element of the speaking grammar of rap; Terminator X mixes the 'chorus', Flavor Flav 'supports' the rhyme through a dialogue with Chuck D, and Professor Griff marshals his SIW troops (Security of the First World) in paramilitary manoeuvres in the background. In fact, most people who have heard 'Rebel Without a Pause' will remember it, not for any particular lyric, but for the eerie resonance of the undulating siren-like sound pitched high over the regular time-span of each line, a sound that, when heard in city streets emanating from massive auto sound systems, is a powerful riposte to the aggressive wail of police sirens.

Despite its consistency, the rhythmic regularity of the line does not serve a primarily metronomic function; it is not just a way of keeping or organising time. In the Western musical tradition ('Papa Don't Preach' is an adequate example), the drama of the song is created not by the stable rhythm but by diatonic harmony and melody; in African-based music it is the repetitive rhythm which creates the drama, while harmony is the stable element. This difference explains not only the flatness of the lyrics on the page, but also the futility of discussing this song without invoking the dance riot of animated bodily movement involved in its performance and in its audience reception. The visual rhythm of dancing is another extra-textual element to add to our earlier list of features that determine the meaning of a song. In the case of Public Enemy, we shall also have to add to this list the element of intertextuality, since the lyrics often refer to other PE songs, or to their audience's knowledge about PE's history and public status as activists.

In 'Rebel Without a Pause', it is the relentless, driving rhythm – 'the rebel without a pause' – that is the major actor. The microphonist 'hard rhymer' is like a surfer, not fully in control, and struggling to keep pace: he 'lowers' his 'level' and rides the rhythm of the line, driven on by the siren sound on top. Matching the pace of this rhythm – 'comin' like a rhino' – is already a test of the MC's skill at a verbal pyrotechnics that uses internal rhyming to slice and dice through the line, enjambing one to another to make room for a short breathing pause. The result is a competitive war of the rhymer, who uses every kind of variation, asymmetry, and irregularity, *against* the uniform regularity of the line rhythm. Terminator X, at the turntables, is also working against the beat rhythm. In effect, there are three different 'times' – the beat, the noise, and the rhyme – involved in the making of the song.

The song consistently makes references to other kinds of 'time', however. It invites the listener to learn the lessons of Griff and the SIW (the black nationalist consciousness-raising wing of PE – now defunct as a result of the controversies generated by Griff's anti-Semitism), in order to 'know what time it is'. The reference is to an old metaphor for black educational awareness – Wake up! Don't you know what time it is! – that became common currency in the black power movement of the late sixties. So, too, the rhymer's response in the song to the critics of PE's music is seized as an opportunity to rebut them on his own terms – 'they're on my time' – rather than when 'they're clocking my zone', as in regulating one's speed. In general, 'my time' is defended as a proprietary space (rather than a quarantine space imposed by others) for rappers to be 'loud and proud' – a kind of home turf that can't be taken away or appropriated.

This turf is a highly competitive arena, however, and 'Rebel' is true to the bragging, virility-testing conventions of the rap genre in its swaggering address and put-down of all 'sucker' contenders. For the most part, however, the competition here is not with other rappers but with those in power who cast PE as a 'public enemy' for political reasons, who fear their immense popularity, and who cite their influence on youth as agitators for violence and subversion. In response to this vilification, and in the name of all black male youth branded as 'criminals' and enemies of 'the public', 'Rebel' comes on 'black and strong' in an affirmation of collective power – 'not singular' – and the right to 'voice [their] opinion with volume'. The independence of the black-owned label, Def Jam, the community support of 'Strong Island' (Long Island), the superiority of PE's music – 'suckers burn to learn' – and the righteousness of their 'mission' are all cited as evidence of their success at creating a radical 'voice of power' akin to 'panther power' within a black culture beseiged by police brutality, media defamation, economic exploitation, unofficial segregation, and the spectre of the 'genocide' of young black males, whose life expectancy dramatically decreases year by year.

But it is important to understand that 'Rebel' is not primarily an arena for mounting political arguments; it employs a hit-and-run aesthetic that leaves behind the seeker of rational disputation. The poetry of its critique lies in its economy of rhythmic means – by any necessary – and its presentation of an 'attitude'. In keeping with the African–American musical tradition, in which the musician's function as a community mediator is second only to the preacher, rappers have taken on the role of teaching, and disseminating information and knowledge. 'Rebel' is quite clear about PE's conscious construction of a music that, like the best preaching, delivers knowledge along with pleasure: 'You know the rhythm, the rhyme plus the beat is designed / To enter your mind . . . .' To reach successfully its youthful audience, this 'knowledge' must be attractive. Consequently, it is often presented in a romantic, outlawed form, marked by an open defiance that 'fights the powers that be' by speaking back to socially dominant images of black youth as 'public enemies', and by redefining 'ethnic violence' as 'self-defense'.

For some rappers, whose music has helped to make rap the latest blaxploitation genre, the outlaw mystique takes the form of glorifying gangster machismo, as a way of boldly and bluntly confirming the worst of white fears. The brazen realism of the boasting genre flaunts the codes of 'public decency' (and is subsequently banned in many states), but its romantic tribute to fearless strength and aggressivity also serves to reinforce the militarised climate of social darwinism that has come to prevail over the street culture of North American urban life. 'Rebel' plays a merry tune upon gangster typology, in which the rhyme is the weapon, and the rhythm is the rebel, but the prevailing militant 'attitude' is high machismo, governed by 'hard' masculine braggadochio. 'Rebel' posing 'with attitude' has its own political cogency, shaped by the response to a long history of subordination and persecution. Hip hop, after the fatalism of the blues tradition, and the pride of sixties soul, is the first African–American genre fully to articulate this stylised defiance. More often than not, however, hip hop's masculinism has been an accomplice to high misogyny, and this is the point at which the conventional posing as 'public enemy number one' usually succeeds only at the risk of becoming a 'private enemy' to women. Because 'Rebel''s self-confirmation of the image of a public enemy – 'Smooth – not what I am / Rough – cause I'm a man' – is so exclusively tailored to the hardcore contours of straight masculinity, the empowerment that the song bravely preaches is complicit with those patriarchal privileges that define 'public' and 'private' as more or less exclusively gendered spaces.

In 'Rebel', the strategy of taking the oppressor's terms of calumny like 'public enemy' and converting them into terms of strength of self-determination structurally excludes women from being actors in 'public'. In the same way, we saw how 'Madonna's' role in 'Papa' confirmed the 'private' decision of the daughter only by suggestively reaffirming the father's privilege in being able to certify that decision as a 'public' act. This is why 'Papa Don't Preach' and 'Rebel Without a Pause', for all of their passionate commentary on the contradictions of disempowerment and desire, remain, respectively, a girl's song and a boy's song.

Chapter 9

Signs are Taken for Wonders

On Steve McCaffery's 'Lag'

Marjorie Perloff

Steve McCaffery's new book *The Black Debt* (the title is Hegel's term for writing)[1] is difficult to categorise: its 202 pages contain two continuous blocks of large boldface print (the 119-page 'Lag' and the 80-page 'An Effect of Cellophane'), with justified left and right margins (created by adjusting the spacing of the letters), but no paragraphs or breaks of any kind. 'While the large type', says McCaffery on the dustjacket, 'may be an aid to the visually impaired, it will hopefully bring into play the materiality of reading as a first order physical encounter rendering the negotiation of the lines a highly visceral experience.'

Certainly *The Black Debt* cannot be read 'normally' as a 'lyric poem' or 'narrative' or 'critical prose', or even as a set of aphorisms or headlines – a kind of postmodern commonplace book. The physical appearance of the text calls to mind billboards, tickertape, and electronic mail: one all but expects the text to go off screen even as one is looking at it. As for the succession of phrases and sentences, grammatical as each one is at the level of microstructure, the individual units refuse to cohere, no phrase seeming to connect to that which precedes or follows it. To call this text 'prose' rather than 'verse' is thus not, strictly speaking, accurate, the text being made up of equal line lengths.

'In vain', says Samuel Johnson in the epigraph from Boswell's *Life*, 'shall we look for the *lucidus ordo*, where there is neither end or object, design or moral, *nec certa recurrit imago*.'[2] For Johnson, such absence of the Horatian *lucidus ordo* (he is talking to Boswell about the 'tiresome repetition of the same images' in Macpherson's pseudo-epic *Fingal*) is of course a fault; a poem without design or moral, where no definite image recurs, cannot be good. But for a poet living in the late twentieth century, like Steve McCaffery, *lucidus ordo* and *certa imago* belong to the world of billboards and TV commercials, poetry now positioning itself, so McCaffery's practice implies, as that discourse that defers reading. Thus McCaffery's first text, appropriately called 'Lag', consistently resists the reader's attempts to overcome its partition and segmentation and to make the individual phrases cohere into some sort of 'meaningful' narrative. Here, for example, is the opening page:

SENTENCE NOT SENTENCE, A
RED envelope, the rain stood up, the
prolonged cosseting or a silhouette
the customer knows, dead drunks
arriving at a gate, these enormous
movements of soap intact and called
a breakdown on the road, winter-
thorn but a floating crow in flight, as
secondary systems round the kitchen,
a list of old socks, independent with
dessert then pushing a chair to the
left, setting this down well in advance
of the middle limp before the brat,
dawning night waned, a way of doing
coke, binoculous interior on inspected
coffee, when an ashtray's cracked, an
evanescent need to fill and putty tra-
vails on a tray, waking at eight to an
echo, three means a half inch width,
nine seven four two five, the cracking
of spokes codes this distance, whis-
pered vowels due to laxity, whole
lengths of paragraphs in prose, passions building sounds, them and the
name of Howson on a truck, all the

The only punctuation mark used in 'Lag' is the comma, that politest and weakest of breaks in continuity, whose traditional function, the *OED* tells us, is to 'separate the smallest members of a sentence', so as to 'make clear the grammatical structure, and hence the sense of the passage'. Ironically, the phrasal syntax of 'Lag' is indeed quite clear – 'a red envelope' is a noun modified by an indefinite article and an adjective; 'the rain stood up' has a subject noun modified by a definite article followed by an intransitive verb, and so on – but semantically, the segments often make no sense individually, and even less when they are related to one another. Indeed, each phrase acts to restrain the larger flow of which it is a part, only to call attention to itself as a conundrum to be solved.

On the opening page (and this pattern will remain consistent throughout), the poet's phrasing ranges from simple statements of negation, $a \neq a$ ('SENTENCE NOT SENTENCE' or, in its more complex punning variant on subsequent pages, 'absinthe not absence', 'miasma not my asthma', and so on); definition ('three means a half-inch width'); and the listing of numbers (nine seven four two five, evidently the digits of a phone number, or an address, IBM barcode, or even a social security or insurance policy number); to simple declarative sentences with past-tense verbs ('the rain stood up'; 'dawning night waned'); to noun phrases ('a red envelope', 'a list of old socks', 'a way of doing coke', 'the lengths of paragraphs in prose') and gerunds ('waking at eight to an echo'); 'when' clauses ('when an ashtray's cracked'), 'as' clauses ('as secondary systems round the kitchen'), and clauses of discrimination ('the prolonged cosseting or a silhouette the customer knows'; 'winterthorn but a floating crow in flight'), in which the second term is regularly missing.

On first inspection, the reader is likely to take this page as a kind of Chomskyan exercise in non-sensicality, a phrase like 'waking at eight to an echo' violating, as I said a moment ago, not grammatical but semantic convention. One wakes at eight to an alarm or a phone call or a pat on the head or a kiss, but not to an echo. Or would it after all be possible? Certainly, if one were asleep in, say, a ravine. What makes the phrasing of 'Lag' so strange is that the more these 'meaningless' phrases are probed, the less nonsensical they turn out to be.

Consider the five opening phrases of 'Lag', 1. 'SENTENCE; NOT SENTENCE': the text begins with a statement of aesthetic; what you read, McCaffery suggests, will be written in sentences but they will not be the sentences you are used to reading, even though you are now sentenced to do so. 2. Red envelopes are not common (except for valentines, Christmas cards, and so on), but every envelope we send or receive in the mail is 'read'. 3. Rain doesn't 'stand up'; it falls; then again, when it rains very heavily, it looks as if the drops are standing up on the windshield or the window pane. In the next phrasal unit, 4, the word 'cosseting' stands out, a literary word common enough in the Victorian novel, but now nearly obsolete, especially in American English. Like Beckett, McCaffery is fond of interjecting the odd archaism or obscure learned word into what is otherwise highly contemporary idiom. 'Prolonged cosseting' (being petted, indulged, caressed) is just what takes place in elegant clothing boutiques, when the seasoned 'customer' hits upon a 'silhouette' (perhaps her own?) she 'knows' and likes. Is the customer envious of someone else's silhouette? Or does the dress, cossetting the customer's own body, produce the desired 'silhouette'? 5. 'Dead drunks arriving at a gate' initially sounds like a contradiction in terms: to be 'dead drunk' means to be out cold and hence not 'arriving' anywhere – at least not on one's own steam. Perhaps the dead drunks are in the paddy wagon, arriving at the hospital or prison gate. On the other hand, if we take the phrase literally, the reference may be to drunks who are dead, corpses being carted through the cemetery gate. And, finally, if we take a matter-of-fact view of the situation, it is not at all impossible for even those who are 'dead drunk' to stumble somehow to the gate, say, of a shelter.

Such 'language games' immediately bring to mind the Wittgenstein of *Philosophical Investigations*: for example, 'When we say: "Every word in language signifies something" we have so far said *nothing whatever*; unless we have explained exactly *what* distinction we wish to make.'[3] McCaffery, one of whose previous books of poetry is called *Evoba: The Investigation Meditations 1976–78* (Toronto: Coach House Press, 1987), takes the Wittgenstein theorem that 'the meaning of a word is its use in the language' (43) to its absurdist extreme. For what does 'use' mean in the public space of billboards, and TV discourse? Consider, for example, a Philadelphia billboard that bears the following message:

> O. R. LUMPKIN BODY-
> BUILDERS, FENDERS
> STRAIGHTENED.
> WRECKS OUR SPECIAL-
> TY. WE TAKE THE DENT
> OUT OF ACCIDENT.[4]

To whom is this text addressed? Hardly to those who have just been involved in a wreck (and hence are hardly in a billboard-reading frame of mind) but rather to those who are experiencing normal traffic conditions and can appreciate the lineation that cleverly relates 'lumpkin' to 'body', 'builders to fenders', and juxtaposes 'dent' to 'accident'. 'Wrecks' are thus not really O. R. Lumpkin's 'special-ty'. Rather, the body shop's aim is literally to 'take the dent out of accident' and put it in the driver's subconscious so that, if a wreck occurs, O. R. Lumpkin will come to mind.

It is such a sleight-of-hand (or should I say sleight-of-sign) that McCaffery is parodying in 'Lag'. Watch out, the text seems to be saying, when you read those headlines, those cigarette ads or road signs: the 'message' may not be what you think it is. Or, conversely, a seemingly obscure statement may be the bearer of a perfectly ordinary message. In reading the sixth phrase on page 1, for example, one's first reaction is likely to be that there is no reason why 'these enormous movements of soap intact' should be 'called a breakdown on the road', or why these two phrases are connected by 'and'. But the 'breakdown' makes perfect sense if we think of the 'movements of soap' as a van shipment, the cartons of soap evidently remaining intact despite the breakdown. The use of 'but' in the next phrase is similar: we need only supply a phrase like '[I thought it was] winter-thorn but [what I saw was] a floating crow in flight.' And that would make good sense except for the fact that 'winter-thorn' is not in the *OED* (does it refer to a dark thorn, seen against a wintry sky or perhaps against white snow?) and that it has, at the literary level, the inescapable connotation of 'Winterbourne' (the hero of Henry James's *Daisy Miller*). And further: look at the sound structure of this phrase:

  winter- / thorn but a *floating crow in flight* –

with its elaborate alliteration and assonance.

But, the sceptical reader may say at this point, even if what you say is true: so what? Why should McCaffery expect us to play along while he spins out his little riddles and word games, especially since the individual phrases seem to be purely arbitrary and have no connection to one another? And even if such phrases as 'a way of doing coke' parodise such familiar phrases as 'Things go better with coke' or 'a way of doing dishes', can such word play really be considered poetry? Where, after all, is the imaginative transformation of this ordinary material? And where is the response of the lyric self?

Here again I turn to Wittgenstein. 'The aspects of things that are most important for us are hidden because of their simplicity and familiarity. (One is unable to notice something because it is always before one's eyes)' (129, p.50e). Perhaps the best way to read 'Lag' is as one poet's lyric roadmap whereby the all-too-familiar is made strange. Its strategy is to place the reader, along with the author, in the position that we are now actually in as we drive the freeways, shop on the mall, push our carts through the supermarket, or watch the evening news. To give just one example: shortly after I had read 'Lag', I was listening, on the car radio, to a call-in political programme on KPFK (Pacifica). An irritated caller was complaining that whites don't give credit to the achievements of black people. 'For instance', he said, 'Richard Stokes invented the stop watch'. 'Yes', said the host. The caller corrected himself: 'I mean the stop light.' The host said 'yes' again as if it made no difference, the issue being, of course, not the fact of the particular invention but the question of white racism. Stop light, stop watch – they're all 'inventions', aren't they? Or, in McCaffery's parodic version: 'absinthe not absence' (12), 'Hanoi not annoy' (24), 'commerce not commas' (35), 'theodicy not the Odyssey' (50), 'letters spray not let us pray' (81).

In 'Lag', puns, palindromes, and anagrams alternate with stock phrases to present a world whose seeming 'normalcy' regularly gives way to short-circuits. What could be simpler, for example, than 'a list of old socks' (11)? Any child can understand what the words mean. But – and here is the 'lag' – what *is* a list of old socks? Even if anyone wanted to make one, how would one do it, socks being so limited in colour and material. We might say 'three pairs of navy blue ski socks', but then how would we further specify the items in this category? By referring to the pair of navy blue ski socks that has a hole in the heel? Or again, a phrase like 'continuing to have a nice day' sounds almost like the injunction we hear at every supermarket check-out counter or bank teller's window, except that no one ever raises the issue of 'continuing' to 'have a nice day', since *having* a nice day means you're going to *have* one – or does it? One thing is sure: the person who tells you to 'Have a nice day' won't be around to find out whether indeed you are having it. And this is why 'continuing to have a nice day' is so absurd.

'In vain', the Johnson epigraph tells us, 'shall we look for the *lucidus ordo*, where there is neither end or object, design or moral, *nec certa recurrit imago*.' In 'Lag', each phrase is no sooner articulated than it gives way to the next, usually quite unrelated phrase. There is no 'clear image', no master narrative, no expository pattern, not even an autobiographical thread to provide a constant. Yet once we get the hang of McCaffery's 'prose', its *ordonnance* is seen to be quite reasonable. 'Impersonal' as this text is, it is by no means unemotional or uninvolved. We learn nothing – at least nothing direct – about McCaffery's (or his narrator's) personal life, his opinions or ruminations. None the less I would posit that 'Lag' projects a highly particularised way of looking at things – of processing the most diversified information fields – geology and genetics, archaeology and advertising, classics and commercials – that is finally as recognisable in its particular ways of negotiating with knowledge as is the more personal lyric consciousness we expect to find in poetry. Indeed, the poem gives the lie to the *nec certa recurrit imago*, for items do have a way of reappearing: the 'red envelope' of p. 11 turns up on p. 16 in the 'letter falling from its reader's hands', the 'list of old socks' (11) in the recognition that 'this foot is a sock', and so on. On the last page of 'Lag' we read, 'how does one reach the end of language', and the answer, of course, is that one doesn't, since 'being is the word that writing shatters' (119). Thus the poem can end only with negation – 'Nature not Nietzsche' – followed by a final comma, which is followed by white space. The comma suggests continuity: the 'black debt' continues to be paid.

The mode of 'Lag', and of its companion piece 'An Effect of Cellophane', owes more, I think, to eighteenth-century satire, especially to Swift, than to the Romantic poetry we still take as normative. The poet appears here as cultural critic, but a critic who must fictionalise his materials so that they will appear in their true horror and absurdity. The visual dimension plays a key role here: as we open *The Black Debt*, perhaps at random, we are confronted by the seemingly endless print block of contemporary writing and try to make out the words and phrases. On p. 35, for example, I caught the words 'come back for martinis'. Then my eye moved up a line and I realised that it's 'a come back for martinis' – a total shift in meaning. Read the print block up or down, forwards or backwards, McCaffery suggests, and you will come to see how vulnerable we are to prefabricated messages, bogus claims to authority, and endless dubious prescriptions like 'going up in a plane and not coming down until wet'. The hermeneutic 'lag' is thus the forced delay that makes us see what is really happening, that, for example, 'not coming down until wet' implies that the plane is making a crash-landing in the ocean.

About a third of the way into 'Lag', we read:

    . . . by the letters big we announce a
    giant,   the   cite   of   myopia   snapping
    this   thread,   grammatical,   grief,   ground,
    guessing . . . (37)

The 'letters big' of billboard land are always announcing giants – whether the GIANT FOODS Supermarket or BIG MAC or the PEP BOYS – such signs are the site as well as the 'cite' of 'myopia snapping this thread'. But the alliterative sequence 'grammatical' – 'grief' – 'ground' – 'guessing' suggests that finally we can undo such 'grammatical, grief', that it can prepare the 'ground' for our 'guessing', a guessing that provides the potential for change.

There are readers who will find 'Lag' and its companion piece 'An Effect of Cellophane' too eccentric, who will complain that what McCaffery himself calls the 'rhizomatic writing' of such texts is too random, too unstructured to function as poetry. Yet if we accept Ezra Pound's definition of poetry as 'news that stays news', as 'language charged with meaning', I think McCaffery's *Black Debt* takes its place in the evolution of twentieth-century poetic as a particularly challenging 'long poem'. Indeed, such recent works as Clark Coolidge's *The Long Prose* and Steve Benson's *Back*, as well as Carla Harriman and Lyn Hejinian's collaboration on *The Wide Road*,[5] suggest that we will be seeing a good deal more 'poetry' that, far from escaping from the media landscape into some pastoral realm or into a private visionary space, takes the electronic world head on and challenges some of its assumptions. The resultant dialectic is one that bears watching.

NOTES

1. Steve McCaffery, *The Black Debt* (Roof Books, New York and Nightwood Editions, Toronto, 1989). All page references are to this copublished edition.
2. Samuel Johnson, cited by James Boswell in the *Life of Johnson* (Oxford University Press, London and New York, 1961), p. 443 (December 1770; *Aetat* 61). The phrase *lucidus ordo* (clearness of order) comes from Horace, *Ars Poetica*, line 41.
3. Ludwig Wittgenstein, *Philosophical Investigations*, 3rd edn, trans. G.E.M. Anscombe (Macmillan, New York, 1968), number 13 (p. 7e). Subsequently cited in the text as PI.
4. Cited in Robert Venturi, Denise Scott-Brown, and Steven Izenour, *Learning from Las Vegas* (MIT Press, Cambridge, MA, 1977), p. 52.
5. Clark Coolidge, 'From *The Long Prose*', *Talisman* **4** (Spring 1990), pp. 92–106; Steve Benson, 'From *Back*', *Raddle Moon* **7** (March 1989), pp. 5–19; Carla Harriman and Lyn Hejinian, 'From *The Wide Road*', *Aerial* **5** (1989), pp. 27–53.

Chapter 10

Difference Spreading

From Gertrude Stein to L=A=N=G=U=A=G=E poetry

Peter Nicholls

In 1978, a new magazine appeared on the American poetry scene. The magazine, strangely titled *L=A=N=G=U=A=G=E*, became during its four years of publication a main forum for a group of young writers keen to engage in theoretical speculation and debate about their medium. *L=A=N=G=U=A=G=E* disappeared in 1981, but its name has lingered on, mainly as a means of designating a highly varied body of work which was shaped by the emerging protocols of the magazine. The names of writers involved will not necessarily be familiar to the British reader (some are discussed elsewhere in the present volume): Bruce Andrews, Charles Bernstein (the editors of *L=A=N=G=U=A=G=E*), Lyn Hejinian, Michael Davidson, Hannah Weiner, Ron Silliman, Barrett Watten, Clark Coolidge, Bob Perelman, Tina Darragh, Michael Palmer, Steve McCaffery, Carla Harriman, Ray DiPalma, ...[1] The list could easily be extended, for the magazine's project of a writing which is 'language-centred' and which works in terms of 'diminished reference' has offered an attractive experimental format for those concerned with breaking the hold of a more conventional, modernist-derived poetics. Are we dealing, then, with a definitive *post*modernism? The *L=A=N=G=U=A=G=E* theorists rarely use that word, but it suggests itself for two reasons: first, because this new poetics is closely enmeshed in contemporary Marxist and post-structuralist thought; and second, because the *L=A=N=G=U=A=G=E* project has strong connections with an 'alternative' line of American writing which prefigures aspects of postmodernism in a way that the more conventionally mainstream modernism does not.

The literary line which counts here is one which includes Gertrude Stein and William Carlos Williams, Louis Zukofsky, Laura Riding, John Ashbery (the Ashbery of *The Tennis Court Oath*) and Jackson Mac Low. Given Stein's privileged place in this line it isn't especially surprising that it was her work on which several writers were asked to comment in a special issue of *L=A=N=G=U=A=G=E*. Responses were invited to three pieces from *Tender Buttons* (1914): 'A Carafe, That Is A Blind Glass', 'Glazed Glitter', and 'Roastbeef'. The Toronto poet Steve McCaffery provided the following poem:

TRANSLATIONAL RESPONSE TO A STEIN SINGLE

a carafe that is a blind glass

she types clarity
relations to a scene
a seen in
zero

queer ones in the pain
of pattern
wheeled directions to
a fullness

that negated more to
more what chaos enters in

no one same article
unlike a wide.[2]

Gertrude Stein's 'single' reads as follows:

A CARAFE, THAT IS A BLIND GLASS

A kind in glass and a cousin, a spectacle and nothing strange a single hurt color and an arrangement in a system to pointing. All this and not ordinary, not unordered in not resembling. The difference is spreading.[3]

McCaffery's 'translational response' to Stein's text will help us trace the passage from modernism to a form of postmodernism, but since his poem engages so closely with its original, something must first be said about the technique of 'A Carafe'.

The first thing we notice about Stein's text is that it is difficult – and difficult mainly because its way of referring to a carafe seems abstract and obscure. There are problems at every turn: the grammar is unsystematic, terms are unclear (what is 'a system to pointing'?) and propositions are opaque ('The difference is spreading'). With a second reading, though, we may begin to suspect that the periphrasis of Stein's text, its way of circling around the object so confidently announced in the title, is not so much a failure of reference as a problematising of reference itself. As the poet Michael Davidson observes in his contribution to the same *L=A=N=G=U=A=G=E* forum, 'The objects themselves are commonplace – as common as the carafes, bowls and guitars of Cubist still lifes – but Stein's disjunctive prose removes them from their commonality and accentuates the gap between object and description.' (*LB*, p. 197) The strangeness of Stein's language, then – its way of 'leaping free of the gravity of the familiar', as Bob Perelman puts it (*LB*, p. 199) – makes us aware of the *difference* between language and its objects, producing a verbal artefact which is related to the real (it is 'a cousin' to the actual carafe) while not literally 'resembling' it. Davidson concludes that

> What this implies for the act of reading is that there are no longer any privileged semantic centers by which we can reach through the language to a self-sufficient, permanent world of objects, foodstuffs or rooms. We must learn to read *writing*, not read *meanings*; we must learn to interrogate the spaces around words as much as the words themselves; we must discover language as an active 'exchange' of meaning rather than a static paradigm of rules and features. (*LB*, p. 198).

Davidson's distinction between 'writing' and 'meaning' points up the extent to which Stein's work diverges from what is often considered to be the main line of Anglo–American modernism. Think, for example, of Pound's criteria for imagism: 'direct treatment', a strict regimen of verbal economy (an economy with often distinctly moral implications), and a fundamental commitment to the natural object as 'always the *adequate* symbol'.[4] The image gave Pound the means to assert the rights of 'absolute metaphor' against what he saw in the early phase of his career as the self-indulgent vagaries of associative metonymy.[5] Like Eliot's related concept of an 'objective correlative', imagism aimed to produce a balance between internal and external worlds, using a model of visual perception to instigate desired formal constraints. In this sense, the visual offered an index of intelligibility, a guarantee of language's power to detach emotion from the purely associative and 'occult' flux of psychic process.[6] In his early criticism, Pound liked to speak of the poem as a sort of 'equation' for a state of mind, thereby suggesting that poetic language entailed symbolisation of an originally inchoate experience.

When we look back at Stein's piece about the carafe it is striking how much at odds it is with these ideas of 'objectification' and 'direct treatment'. In fact, Stein seems to imply that words do not evoke concepts of things so much as things generate patterns of words.[7] We begin with the idea of a carafe but the words which follow are often produced by associative contexts which are triggered by the words themselves ('blind' sets up an echo for 'kind', for example). The progression of the carafe text, then, the manner in which 'The difference is spreading', assumes that it is only by a sort of *indirect* treatment that we can hope to grasp the object – 'indirect', because as soon as we name it, call it a 'carafe', our sense of a vital particularity is eclipsed in the generic blankness of the noun. As Stein puts it in 'Poetry and Grammar', 'A noun is a name of anything, why after a thing is named write about it.' (*LMN*, p. 125) Stein's great discovery, as she recalls in another essay called 'Portraits and Repetition', was that writing and description are two very different things:

> And the thing that excited me so very much at that time and still does is that the words or words that make what I looked at be itself were always words that to me very exactly related themselves to that thing the thing at which I was looking, but as often as not had nothing I say nothing whatever to do with what any words would do that described that thing. (*LMN*, p. 115)

This passage shows very clearly how *Tender Buttons*, like the Cubist painting to which it is often compared, tends to situate itself midway between representation and abstraction. While her search for words is motivated by a desire to express what made 'what I looked at be itself', her discipline of 'looking' entails a freeing of perception from memory and that 'dead' language of description by which memory makes the past familiar ('looking was not to mix itself up with remembering' [*LMN*, p. 113]).

Stein's idiom may seem coy at times, but her reference to 'excitement' is more than whimsical hyperbole: for the fact that non-descriptive terms suggest themselves to her produces pleasure in precisely the degree that it frees the mind from the obligations of reference and conventional repetition. This particular freedom is the objective of a form of modernism which is quite different from the one we associate with Eliot; compare, for example, his view of 'naming':

> Try to think of what anything would be if you refrained from naming it altogether, and it will dissolve into sensations which are not objects; and it will not be that particular object which it is, until you have found the right name for it.[8]

For Stein, though, the domain of writing is precisely that of 'sensations which are not objects': once released from the instrumental duties of 'naming', language begins to take on a polymorphous life of its own, generating 'excitement' as it becomes a thing to be enjoyed for itself. It's perhaps not surprising that so many of the pieces in Stein's *Tender Buttons* are concerned with food, for eating epitomises that fundamental association of linguistic materiality with oral pleasure (locutionary and sexual) which runs throughout her work. I am reminded here of a passage in Freud's *Jokes and Their Relations to the Unconscious*. Freud is discussing cases of jokes which depend upon wordplay, cases where, he says, 'the (acoustic) word-presentation itself take the place of its significance as given by its relations to thing-presentations'. We experience a particular pleasure on such occasions, and Freud concludes that

> It may really be suspected that in doing so we are bringing about a great relief in psychical work and that when we make serious use of words we are obliged to hold ourselves back with a certain effort from this comfortable procedure.[9]

'Hold ourselves back': Freud implies that a 'serious use of words' always entails a kind of repression, that if words are savoured in the mouth rather than being put swiftly to work, meaningful tasks will never be accomplished. To lift this repression, to abolish the lack on which a descriptive language is founded, is to disclose what Stein calls a 'continuous present' of language in which desire might seem to engage its object. Instead of Pound's imagistic 'instant of time' – an instant accorded immediacy by being lifted out of time and fixed, as an object to be perceived – the 'present' of Stein's texts is the unrepressed 'now' of writing and reading.

This idea of the poem as 'process' overcoming the exigencies of reference gives one key to Stein's importance for the $L=A=N=G=U=A=G=E$ poets – for if, as McCaffery puts it, 'Reference in language is a strategy of promise and postponement' (*LB*, p. 189), the authentic time of the poem should be, in the words of Charles Bernstein, 'a series of substitutions or replacements that don't *stand for* or in *place of* but themselves embody that moment of time'.[10] If $L=A=N=G=U=A=G=E$ poetry sees itself as distinctively new (postmodern, perhaps), it is because such ideas repudiate a whole tradition of writing about remembered experiences of the lyric self, turning attention instead to the 'tense-less' condition of language as medium.[11] Hence the view of Robert Grenier, another respondent to the $L=A=N=G=U=A=G=E$ forum, that *Tender Buttons* entails

> the realization of new nominatives – (not neologism but) *whole text, in process*, 'replaces' worn-out, now-merely-conventional name offered up (in title, commonly) to be melted down in crucible of language process attention forging other access to the ongoing of what's what. (*LB*, p. 205; my emphases)

Grenier goes on to observe, however, that Stein cannot be fully assimilated to contemporary 'language-oriented writing' because much of her work 'show[s] her thinking language not as object-in-itself, but as composition functioning in the composition of the world' (*LB*, p. 206).

Grenier's qualification may now help us to read McCaffery's poem, for here we evidently *are* dealing with language as 'an object in itself', with the difficulties of Stein's text not only intensified but raised, as it were, to a higher power. In 'A Carafe', the spreading of 'difference' (the gap between language and its object) also carries the trace of an actual thing which the text parodically 'describes' ('A kind of glass . . .'). And like many of the pieces in *Tender Buttons*, this one sometimes shadows the form of the declarative sentence not merely to heighten the effect of 'not resembling', but also perhaps to inhibit the emergence of a purely sound-based writing.[12] It is as if the 'process' of the text does not abolish the referent so much as enact the suspension of its materiality. So, for example, 'a single hurt color' is at once a phrase generated within the text (as part of a very loosely determined complex of terms expressing relationship, 'kind', 'cousin', etc.) and a fairly easily 'translated' reference to red wine. Stein wants us to see that there is an 'order' which is not dependent on 'resemblance', but her practice is almost dialectical in its retention of the trace which is our point of departure.

By way of contrast, the 'translational response' in McCaffery's poem is such as to make the process of linguistic composition completely sufficient to itself. 'Translation' here is a deliberately adopted strategy which, like the 'procedural' writings of Jackson Mac Low, Ron Silliman, Tina Darragh, and others, substitutes an arbitrary but usually systematic structure for the conventionally authenticating forms of 'voice' and sensibility. Stein's text is handled as a linguistic object, a collection of words rather than of expressive items whose meanings must be respected. McCaffery's way of 'centering language within itself' (*LB*, p. 189) can best be seen by following line by line his negotiation with Stein's text (her words are given in italic):

> [she] types/*kind* clarity/*in glass*
> relations/*a cousin* to a scene/*a spectacle*
> /a seen in
> zero/*nothing*
> queer/*strange* ones/*single* in the pain/*hurt* [*color*]
> of pattern/*an arrangement*
> wheeled directions to/*in a system to pointing*
> a fullness/*All*
> that/*this* negated/*and not* more to/*not*
> more what chaos/*unordered* enters in/*in*
> no one same/*not resembling* article
> unlike/*The difference* a wide/*spreading*.

Some of McCaffery's 'translations' are simply synonyms which provoke modifications of meaning ('cousin' becomes 'relations', for example).

In other cases, the synonym allows a shift to a different part of speech (the noun 'kind' becomes the verb 'types'). Other forms of wordplay are designed to make us focus on the opacity of the language: the pun on 'scene'/'seen', for example, or the contorted phrasing of 'more to/more what chaos enters in', which seems to be triggered by the literal positioning in Stein's text of 'unordered' ('chaos') between 'not ordinary' and 'not resembling'. McCaffery 'translates', then, by synonym and wordplay, but with a quite deliberate inattention to semantic continuities, so that, for example, the phrase 'queer ones' is produced from two words ('strange' and 'single') which occur in different clauses (Stein, of course, has prepared the ground for this fluent conjunction by dropping any punctuation between the clauses).

Most of McCaffery's substitutions are intended to break down the surrounding contexts of particular words and prevent their integration into higher grammatical levels.[13] So 'wheeled directions' is produced by the deliberate removal of the translational context which, presumably, read 'pointing' as '*wield*ing directions'. With the last line of the poem – 'unlike a wide' – McCaffery completes his destruction of the trace of the carafe in Stein's text. Here we are firmly within the domain of what Barrett Watten calls 'the self-sufficiency of the sign',[14] as the 'translation' forces an adjective to do the work of a noun. This is the (degree) zero 'scene' of writing[15] which restructures meaning by abolishing reference. If Stein's text represents an extreme pitch of modernism in its desire to somehow suspend or bracket the referent, McCaffery's 'translation', with its rather portentously illogical phrases, insists on that loss of the real which we associate with current theories of postmodernism. (Jean Baudrillard's concept of the 'simulacrum' is perhaps the most influential example.)[16]

Yet there is no pathos here about the recession of the 'real'. On the contrary, McCaffery's poem fully endorses the priorities of a well-known essay by Ron Silliman, 'Disappearance of the Word, Appearance of the World'. As that title suggests, Silliman's main contention is that the ideological production of a natural, commonsense 'world' (the world of an unproblematic realism) depends on the illusion of the 'blank' page, on the transparency of language (*LB*, p. 127). The 'disappearance' of the medium is, in Silliman's view, an effect governed by those processes of exchange and reification which define commodity fetishism: the text is 'exchanged' for a world which is always given in advance. The task of an oppositional writing, then, is to efface the world in order that language might 'appear' in all its insistent materiality, constituting thereby 'a *barrier* to actuality' (*NS*, p. 179). This idea has, of course, little novelty in itself, and can be traced in its more extreme modernist versions from Mallarmé through the sound poetry of futurism and dada. Yet it is not simply a technical insistence on the medium which is important here: beyond the foregrounding of artifice there is a concept of writing's *origin* as lying within language itself (not, that is, within that discipline of 'looking' which generates the texts of *Tender Buttons*).[17] McCaffery observes, for example, that the 'unavoidable presence of words within words contests the notion of writing as a creativity, proposing instead the notion of an indeterminate, extra-intentional, differential production'.[18] Language is, as it were, mined for the ideas it may produce: as Lyn Hejinian puts it, in terms which recall the formalist theories of Roman Jakobson, 'where once one sought a vocabulary for ideas, now one seeks ideas for vocabularies' (*LB*, p. 29). This way of thinking implies a certain diffuseness and indeterminacy of meaning – or meanings, because semantic integration is obstructed in the service of a highly localised production. McCaffery's 'translation' provides a 'jamming of the message', as he puts it elsewhere,[19] allowing the reader to grasp meaning not as something transcendent but as a sequence of local intensities. Whereas language subordinated to representation is 'a huge mechanism for suppressing libidinal flow', McCaffery's preferred form of writing is committed to what Georges Bataille called a 'General Economy', 'an economy of loss and expenditure without reserve'.[20] Such 'expenditure' is primarily on those non-semantic aspects of language (phonemic and graphemic) which cannot be recuperated at the level of the signified. The results are clear in the poem we are examining: there is a deliberate 'viscosity of thought', to borrow a phrase of Charles Bernstein,[21] a materiality which should produce quasi-erotic pleasure as we hear 'the sound *come into* meaning rather than a play with already existing meanings by way of metre'.[22]

'. . . unlike a wide'. – that phrase, with its triumphant period aping closure, trails in its wake at least one difficult question: is this artificial and mannered language simply decadent, or does it respond to the challenge of a distinctively postmodern period?[23] Of course, the highly developed theoretical matrix of this poetry prevents any naïve equation of the postmodern with the authentically 'new'; not only are these writers keen to acknowledge their own lineage, through Russian futurism, dada and surrealism, but they would assume, too, the truth of Jakobson's observation that 'virtually any poetic message is a quasi-quoted discourse'.[24] The issue of 'decadence' turns rather, I think, on the question of artifice and the extent to which a practice of 'writing' (as textuality) can be seen to direct attention away from not only the lyric sensibility but from social discourse generally. It was the loss of a social horizon which the nineteenth-century critic Paul Bourget saw as the consequence of a decadent atomisation in his own time (hence his criticism of the Goncourts' style on the grounds that 'It delights in witticisms and couplings of terms which make the reader jump, while classical prose tries [to ensure] that no word of the phrase comes loose from the securely woven web of the style as a whole.'[25] Bourget's anxiety, that this disruption of syntax would lead to language being valued for itself rather than as a means of articulation, reappears in Eliot's critique of Swinburne's verse, where meaning 'is merely the hallucination of meaning, because language, uprooted, has adapted itself to an independent life of atmospheric nourishment'.[26] 'Hallucination of meaning' might seem an apt description of the effect of McCaffery's poem, but from the perspective of $L=A=N=G=U=A=G=E$, the idea of 'hallucination' erroneously assumes a fixed ('reified') meaning in the first place (*LB*, p. 162). In contrast, these writers are keen to bring about that very 'uprooting' of language which Eliot laments, and to ensure the writer's *failure* to 'digest and express new objects, new groups of objects, new feelings, new aspects'.[27] By a striking reversal of terms, the linguistic effects marked as 'decadent' by Bourget and Eliot now become the condition of a social horizon: as McCaffery puts it, 'The referent no longer looms as a promissary [*sic*] value and the text is proposed as the communal space of a human engagement.'[28] In fact, for the $L=A=N=G=U=A=G=E$ writers, the aim is precisely to create what Bruce Andrews calls (in terms curiously akin to Eliot's) 'A semantic atmosphere, or milieu, rather than the possessive individualism of reference' (*LB*, p. 36).

That characteristic leap from the linguistic to the socio-economic should make us pause. Andrews's way of opposing a disarticulated conception of 'meaning' to 'reference' as appropriation (a reaching through language to grasp or 'digest' the real) epitomises one main strand of $L=A=N=G=U=A=G=E$ thinking which adduces systematic connections between structures of discourse and those of capital (conventional 'meaning' is equated with surplus value, for example).[29] This seems to me the most tendentious aspect of the whole theoretical project, backed though it is by an impressive array of marxist and post-structuralist sources.[30] Let us consider instead Andrews's critique of 'individualism', for $L=A=N=G=U=A=G=E$ writing is most assimilable to the broad outlines of the postmodernism debate when it mounts a sceptical interrogation of the subject. The main ideas here are familiar from recent continental theory: the subject is constituted in language and is excentric to the language s/he speaks (Lacan); the subject is unstable or 'in process' (Kristeva); the subject is 'interpellated' by ideology, hence subjectivity is an ideological effect (Althusser). In terms of poetic writing, this network of ideas has two main results; first L=A=N=G=U=A=G=E writing aims to break with what Bernstein calls 'the modernist assumption': 'the impulse to record or transcribe the movements and make-up of one's consciousness' (*LB*, p. 42); second, L=A=N=G=U=A=G=E largely repudiates a poetics based, like that of Charles Olson, on the voice and breath, with its attendant 'heroic stance' and 'will to dominate language'.[31]

This attack on the voice epitomises the main aspects of L=A=N=G=U=A=G=E which we have already examined, and it certainly seems to accord with the 'disappearance of the subject' and the fading of 'depth' and history which Fredric Jameson discerns in postmodernity.[32] Perhaps, though, it is misleading to describe L=A=N=G=U=A=G=E poetry, as Jameson does, as having 'adopted schizophrenic fragmentation as its fundamental aesthetic'.[33] Jameson means to draw attention to the breakdown of the signifying chain in this writing which produces 'a rubble of distinct and unrelated signifiers', a 'linguistic malfunction' which prevents us from unifying 'the past, present and future of the sentence' and of our own experience.[34] The poem which elicits this analysis – Bob Perelman's 'China' – is, however, hardly as atomised as Jameson suggests, and indeed its formal discontinuities remind us that the erasure of 'voice' may lead, not to the schizophrenic production of the 'isolated Signifier', but to a cross-cutting of different tonal registers. This is the 'dialogical' quality which Michael Davidson has in mind when he remarks upon 'the various registers and tones, generic markers and rhetorical devices by which even the most hermeneutically intransigent poem is made'.[35] McCaffery says something similar when, in response to an interviewer's question about the uniformity of tone in some L=A=N=G=U=A=G=E poetry, he refers to 'the orchestration of several discourses and a violent centripetality of contexts'.[36] But does McCaffery's own traffic with Stein's text produce 'a communal space of human engagement'? If our answer is in the negative it is perhaps because of a felt discrepancy between the reader's required 'productivity' at the local level and the concept of a 'communal space' which is induced from an externally elaborated body of theory. As it 'translates' us from modern to postmodern, McCaffery's poem in fact suggests that to reject the 'voice' is not only to deny the imperial claims of the lyric self, but also to court an extreme of tonelessness which effaces social discourse in 'style' (as Davidson remarks in another context, 'What may begin as a desire to expose language as system may result in an avoidance of the socially-coded nature of larger linguistic units').[37] While McCaffery observes that 'The fight for language is a political fight. The fight for language is also a fight inside language' (*LB*, pp. 159–61), his poem may serve to remind us not only that the postmodern is that contradictory space in which 'our' language (whose?) is always in the balance, but also that the spreading of 'difference' opens the possibility of both repossession and expropriation.

NOTES

1. The two main anthologies of this writing are *The L=A=N=G=U=A=G=E Book*, Bruce Andrews and Charles Bernstein (eds.), (Southern Illinois University Press, Carbondale and Edwardsville, 1984) and *'Language' Poetries: An Anthology*, Douglas Messerli (ed.) (New Directions, New York, 1987). For a fuller length study, see George Hartley, *Textual Politics and the Language Poets* (Indiana University Press, Bloomington and Indianapolis, 1989).
2. *The L=A=N=G=U=A=G=E Book*, pp. 200–1 (hereafter cited in the text as *LB*).
3. *LB*, 195. The full text of *Tender Buttons* is reprinted in Gertrude Stein, *Look at Me Now and Here I Am: Writings and Lectures 1909–45*, Patricia Meyerowitz (ed.) (Penguin Books, Harmondsworth, 1971), pp. 161–206 (hereafter cited in the text as *LMN*).
4. *Literary Essays of Ezra Pound*, ed. T.S. Eliot (Faber, London, 1960), pp. 3, 5.
5. See *Gaudier-Brzeska: A Memoir* (1916; rpt. The Marvell Press, Hessle, 1960), p. 84 on the Symbolists: 'They degraded the symbol to the status of a word. They made it a form of metonymy.' There is a brief but suggestive discussion of Pound's shift from metaphor to metonymy in J.H. Prynne, 'China Figures', in *New Songs from a Jade Terrace*, trans. Anne Birrell (Penguin Books, Harmondsworth, 1986), pp. 367–9.
6. Eliot remarks of Joyce and Milton, for example, that 'a dislocation takes place through the hypertrophy of the auditory imagination at the expense of the visual and the tactile, so that the inner meaning is separated from the surface and tends to become something occult' (quoted in Andrew Ross, *The Failure of Modernism* (Columbia University Press, New York, 1986) where there is a useful discussion of related issues).
7. See, for example, Randa Dubnick, *The Structure of Obscurity: Gertrude Stein, Language, and Cubism* (University of Illinois Press, Urbana and Chicago, 1984), p. 33.
8. *Knowledge and Experience in the Philosophy of F.H. Bradley* (Faber, New York, 1964), p. 134.
9. *The Pelican Freud Library*, Vol. 6 (Penguin Books, Harmondsworth, 1983), pp. 167–8.
10. *Content's Dream: Essays 1975–1984* (Sun & Moon Press, Los Angeles, 1986), p. 362.
11. See, for example, Bruce Andrews, *LB*, p. 37: 'Language-centering seems to capture some of the more exploratory aspects of the consequences of itself, without referential guidance, without parental guidance, without tense.'
12. See, for example, *LMN*, p. 119: '. . . I was getting drunk with melody and I do not like to be drunk I like to be sober and so I began again.' Stein concludes here (p. 120) that 'Melody should always be a by-product it should never be an end in itself . . . .'
13. For an influential discussion of the 'new sentence' as a means of inhibiting 'integration' and 'keep[ing] the reader's attention at or very close to the level of language', see Ron Silliman, *The New Sentence* (Roof, New York, 1987), pp. 63–93 (hereafter cited in the text as *NS*).
14. *Total Syntax* (Southern Illinois University Press, Carbondale and Edwardsville, 1985), p. 8.
15. The 'zero' in McCaffery's poem certainly seems to allude to Roland Barthes's

concept of 'Writing Degree Zero'; compare McCaffery's remarks on 'zero-semantic sound poetry' in *LB*, p. 161.

16. See, for example, Jean Baudrillard, 'The Precession of Simulacra', in *Simulations* (Semiotext(e), New York, 1983).
17. See Bernstein, 'Words and Pictures', in *Content's Dream*, for an expanded critique of 'the poetry of sight' in modern American writing.
18. *North of Intention: Critical Writings 1973–1986* (Roof, New York, 1986), p. 208.
19. *North of Intention*, p. 105. Cf. Charles Bernstein, 'Language Sampler', *Paris Review*, **86** (1982), p. 78, 'The trouble with the conduit theory of communication (me→you) is that it presupposes individuals to exist as separate entities outside language and to be communicated at by language.'
20. *North of Intention*, p. 64.
21. *Content's Dream*, p. 67; Bernstein also speaks of 'a gooeyness and gumminess . . . resistant to easy assimilation' in the work of Clark Coolidge (ibid., p. 263).
22. Ibid., p. 391.
23. Marjorie Perloff, *Dance of the Intellect* (Cambridge University Press, Cambridge, 1985), p. 217, comments on the *fin de siècle* quality of this writing with 'its renewed emphasis, after decades of seemingly "natural" free verse, on prominent sound patterning and arcane, or at least "unnatural" diction'.
24. Quoted in Watten, *Total Syntax*, p. 141.
25. Paul Bourget, *Essais de psychologie contemporaine*, 2 vols. (1883, 1885; Plon, Paris, 1924), II.173 (my translation).
26. *Selected Essays* (Faber, London, 1972), p. 327.
27. Ibid.
28. *North of Intention*, p. 20.
29. See, for example, McCaffery, 'From the Notebooks', *LB*, pp. 159–62.
30. See also Rod Mengham, Review, *Textual Practice*, (Spring, 1989), pp. 115–25; cf. Andrew Ross, 'The New Sentence and the Commodity Form: Recent American Writing', in Cary Nelson and Lawrence Grossberg (eds.), *Marxism and the Interpretation of Culture* (Macmillan, Basingstoke, 1988), pp. 361–80.
31. Bernstein, *Content's Dream*, p. 329. The 'phallocentric' entailments of the voice are also proposed here.
32. See especially 'Postmodernism, or the Cultural Logic of Late Capitalism', *New Left Review*, **146** (July/August 1984), pp. 53–92.
33. Ibid., p. 73. For an extended critique of Jameson's reading of Perelman's poem, see Hartley, *Textual Politics*, pp. 42–52.
34. 'Postmodernism', p. 72.
35. 'Hey Man, My Wave!: The Authority of Private Language', *Poetics Journal*, **6** (1986), p. 42.
36. *North of Intention*, p. 115.
37. 'Discourse in Poetry: Bakhtin and Extensions of the Dialogical', in Michael Palmer, ed., *Code of Signals: Recent Writings in Poetics* (North Atlantic Books, Berkeley, 1983), p. 144.

Chapter 11

Pat Parker

Feminism in postmodernity

Dympna Callaghan

> The first thing you do is to forget that i'm Black.
> Second, you must never forget that i'm Black.
> > Pat Parker, *Movement in Black*, p. 68[1]

'Women of colour', a name contested at its origins by those whom it would incorporate, as well as a historical consciousness marking the systematic breakdown of all the signs of Man in Western tradition, constructs a kind of postmodern identity out of otherness, difference, and specificity. This postmodernist identity is fully political, whatever might be said about other possible postmodernisms. (Donna Haraway, 'A Manifesto for Cyborgs', p. 197)[2]

Pat Parker, poet, health care worker, and activist, tragically died of cancer in June of 1989. Audre Lorde described Parker's visionary political poetics as 'womanly and uncompromising'.[3] Indeed, what is most remarkable about her work is the multiplicity of its resistances – resistances to all forms of oppression, and its multiplicity of poetic voices, which range from a humorous treatment of butch/femme role play ('My lady ain't no lady'), to anguished grieving on the murder of a sister, and a tender rendering of lesbian parenting. Her work, however, for all its resistances, is not just a litany of complaints. Rather, it is a vigorous condemnation of current injustices and a vigilant critique of feminist strategies for change, balanced by a constant affirmation of transformative possibilities. These characteristics make her poetry entirely appropriate to a consideration of 'poetry for the nineties'. In particular, Parker's poems address issues crucial to the viability of a feminism striving to relinquish its humanist, essentialist understandings of 'woman' as well as the racism, classism, and homophobia on which that understanding fed.

The epigraph with which I begin this essay represents the converging and conflicting formulations of identity and the subject I wish to explore here. These formulations are characteristic of both feminism in postmodernity and Parker's poetry. Since such an exploration entails that delicate balance between forgetting and remembering various aspects of Pat Parker's identity, I am particularly concerned to engage with the poem 'as an act of language, first and foremost', as Toni Cade Bambara puts it, but as a 'fully political' one by asking 'What might poetry be able to say about such things as race and gender that is distinctive to poetry?'[4]

The above epigraphs present the nexus of this problematic of reading and interpreting the poetry of Pat Parker. The first, Parker's own statement, enjoins any white interpreter to at once confront and dispel her ethnic identity. It provokes an awareness about reading African–American, lesbian 'otherness' without colonising it by ignoring, dispensing with, or overemphasising the poet's gender, sexual preference and ethnicity.[5] The second epigraph, a theoretical formulation very current in contemporary feminist theory, suggests the radical constitution of the writerly identity of the woman of colour as the paradigmatic postmodern 'cyborgian' identity which defies essentialist and monolithic conceptions of the subject and escapes the categories used to describe hegemonic culture.[6] Indeed, Parker's poetry articulates the political problematic of unlocatable identity, the impossible subject position from which she must speak – from a radical identity 'marked' by white racism, but not purely constituted by it: 'I am a feminist. I am neither white nor middle class. And the women that I've worked with were like me. Yet I'm told that we don't exist and that we didn't exist.'[7] Response to this predicament requires a definitively postmodern manoeuvre, what bell hooks calls bridging the gap between subject and object in a voice that is 'not unilateral, monologist, or static but rather multi dimensional.'[8] Yet, Parker insists on the situatedness of her politicised identity in feminism and on the material reality of the lives of women of colour despite all hegemonic endeavours to erase them.[9]

This impossible subjectivity, 'woman of colour', is itself part of the struggle to locate counterhegemonic resistance, particularly that around the designation 'Third World'. 'Third World' describes diverse literatures that have been shaped by the experience of imperialism, but includes that of people of colour writing in the West, and the writing of a number of countries on the capitalist periphery.[10] On the one hand, the term disrupts the transnational gestures of late capitalism, but on the other, it deprives cultures of autonomy in always situating them in relation to the West and to dominant white culture. Parker's work intersects with this debate in important ways. While it stages the radical restructuring of boundaries and the reconfiguration of identity and identity politics, from individual to collective identity, which Donna Haraway sees as the hallmark of the postmodern, a break-down of the 'distinctions structuring the Western self',[11] it can be understood neither as a response to oppressive white, heterosexual cultural imperatives nor as an apolitical dislocation and diffusion of identity. That is, the specificity of difference cannot be reduced to the obverse of the dominant, the shadow, or the negative. Further, the dispersal occurs at specific nodal points, rather than in a social vacuum. In this sense, Parker's poetry both exemplifies and resists the concerns of contemporary postcolonial writing where the subject, the i/I of Parker's poem, is a nexus of complex power relations produced by social and institutional formations.

1

My lover is a woman
  & when i hold her -
    feel her warmth -
    i feel good - feel safe

then/ i never think of
  my families' voices -
  never hear my sisters say -
  bulldaggers, queers, funny -
  come see us, but don't
  bring your friends -
  it's okay with us,
  but don't tell mama
    it'd break her heart
  never feel my father
  turn in his grave
  never hear my mother cry
  Lord, what kind of child is this?

2

My lover's hair is blonde
  & when it rubs across my face
    it feels soft -
  feels like a thousand fingers
  touch my skin & hold me
  and i feel good.

then/ i never think of the little boy
  who spat & called me nigger
  never think of the policemen
  who kicked my body and said crawl
  never think of Black bodies
  hanging in trees or filled
  with bullet holes
  never hear my sisters say
  white folks hair stinks
  don't trust any of them
  never feel my father
  turn in his grave

never hear my mother talk
of her back ache after scrubbing floors
never hear her cry -
Lord, what kind of child is this?

3

My lover's eyes are blue
& when she looks at me
i float in a warm lake
    feel my muscles go weak with want
        feel good - feel safe

Then/ i never think of the blue
    eyes that have glared at me -
    moved three stools away from me
        in a bar
never hear my sisters rage
of syphilitic Black men as
        guinea pigs -
rage of sterilized children -
watch them just stop in an
intersection to scare *the old*
        white bitch.
never feel my father turn
in his grave
never remember my mother
teaching me the yes sirs & mams
        to keep me alive -
never hear my mother cry,
Lord, what kind of child is this?

4

And when we go to a gay bar
    & my people shun me because i crossed
        the line
    & her people look to see what's
    wrong with her - what defect
    drove her to me -

And when we walk the streets
    of this city - forget and touch
    or hold hands and the people
    stare, glare, frown, & taunt
    at those queers -

I remember -
    Every word taught me
    Every word said to me
    Every deed done to me
    & then i hate -
    i look at my lover

> & for an instance - doubt -
> Then/ i hold her hand tighter
> And i can hear my mother cry.
> Lord, what kind of child is this.

'My Lover is a Woman' typically begins with an open, declaratory statement, the straightforwardness of which is complicated by the fact that it is the assertion of a transgressive, counterhegemonic identity. Emily Erwin Culpepper reports that Pat Parker used to wonder wryly, 'Was it racism or classism, or sexism . . . that led folks to sometimes think that the plain speech in her poems meant they weren't hard to write.'[12] This initial declaration insists on the integrity of the lesbian couple, independent of homophobia, and the censoriousness of family and society. There is, in the smooth certainty of relationship, a single voice with an unfaltering rhythm:

> My lover is a woman
>   & when i hold her -
>   feel her warmth -
> i feel good - feel safe

If the words are simple, the position through which the poet chooses to locate herself, as the poem goes on to show, is inscrutably complex, to the point that this initial moment of 'clarity' becomes not a means of subjecting the reader to a regime of ideologically constructed 'intelligibility'[13] but the articulation of a contradiction. What is presented as transparent and accessible for the reader is nothing less than the insoluble problem of difference. Further, this lack of opacity forestalls any simple paraphrase of the poem's overt, political statements in the act of interpretation. Amitai Avi-Ram remarks of the poets of the Harlem Renaissance, 'one cannot simply read the political position of a poem by noting its explicit avowals alone'.[14] The directness of Parker's assertion of sexual identity permeates the boundary between the personal and political to produce both a political and an aesthetic effect. In Parker's stunning performances of her own work (not always solo), she was palpably 'an activist thinker'.[15] Thus, 'plain speech' enunciation becomes action.

As the first line indicates, this poem, like many Pat Parker wrote, is autobiographical without being a confessional revelation of authentic identity fostered by liberal humanism. Judy Grahn writes that Parker's poetry is 'speaking on behalf of numberless other people, doing it in the first person'.[16] This is an affirmation rather than an appropriation of identity, but it is countered by dissonances and disruptions integral to it in the form of the voices of the poet's family and their disdain for 'bulldaggers, queers'. There is a cacophony of multiple disapproving female voices which reach a crescendo in the stanza's final couplet, the cry of the poet's mother, which becomes the poem's refrain, 'Lord, what kind of child is this?'

The reproving voices of the Black community are temporarily suppressed by the poet in the physicality of love evoked by the repetition of 'feel' three times in the first stanza, a physicality echoed in the chilling lines

> never feel my father
> turn in his grave

The dead father's imagined torment and the back-breaking pain of menial work endured by the poet's mother undercut the poet's sexual bliss.

The nature of the poet's sexual 'transgression' becomes clearer in the opening of the poem's second section: 'My lover's hair is blonde.' This stanza follows the verse pattern and tone of the opening one in a way that renders difference palpable and pleasurable in the sensuous repetition of 'feel' – the tactile perception of difference inscribed lovingly on the poet's body by her lover:

> My lover's hair is blonde
> & when it rubs across my face
>   it feels soft -
> feels like a thousand fingers
> touch my skin & hold me
> and i feel good.

The caress of the poet's lover erases the sting of past encounters with racism, and of the brutality historically inflicted on Black bodies – spat upon, kicked, lynched, perforated with bullets, objects of violent desecration:

> Black bodies
> hanging in trees or filled
> with bullet holes

Similarly, the choral poem from which the volume takes its title 'Movement in Black' is a chronicle of Black history, of the lives and collectivity of those who have been denied a history. It functions as an inscription of their contribution which has been so systematically erased since the first moment of its enactment. For Parker, events always entail historical consequences at the level of the collective, as in her analyses of crimes – the Atlanta child murders, the Jonestown 'suicides', the domestic violence which led to the murder of Parker's sister, Shirley Jones. Thus the Black community is not simply castigated for its homophobia or its dislike of white folks, but rather this is simultaneously complicated and rendered intelligible through this historicisation, which the poem contains and expresses in terms of a repression and a negation:

> never hear my sisters say
> white folks hair stinks
> don't trust any of them

Such hatred is at once the reflex response to oppression and one of the conditions of its endurance. The poet's individual, specifically lesbian identity is evoked again through the refrain 'Lord, what kind of child is this?' It sets the poet's identity in the context of her family, her community and her history even as it signals her difference from that collectivity.

There is nothing here, however, that signals the dispersal of identity as a free-floating utopian condition. Rather, there is a desire for coherence, even a fictional one, that would offer a place from which to speak, and it gets translated into a specific political goal. Judy Grahn writes:

> I asked her once about her personal idea of a revolution. What would she want to see happen? She said, 'If I could take all my parts with me when I go somewhere, and not have to say to one of them, "No, you stay home tonight, you won't be welcome", because I'm going to an all-white party where I can be gay, but not Black. Or I'm going to a Black poetry reading, and half the poets there are anti-homosexual, or thousands of situations where something of what I am cannot come with me. The day all the different parts of me can come along, we would have what I would call a revolution.'[17]

The diffusion of identity is as historicisable as the African diaspora; it is a strategy by which to negotiate social reality. In order to participate in the pleasures of sensuality with her lover, the poet must render mute the voices which have shaped her identity as a woman of African descent, and must forget, 'never think', refuse to remember the brutal forces which have shaped her family's reaction to her white lover. The negatives here are significant. Chela Sandoval has pointed out that there is no essential criterion for identifying a woman of colour because 'the definition of the group has been by conscious appropriation of negation . . . a U.S. black woman has not been able to speak as a woman or as a black person. . . . Thus she was at the bottom of a cascade of negative identities, left out of even the "privileged" oppressed authorial categories called "women and blacks"'.[18] Identity is at once constituted by affirmation and negation.

The next stanza juxtaposes the history of Black oppression with the body of the poet's lover, and the joy she produces in the body of the poet:

> feel my muscles go weak with want
>   feel good - feel safe

The blue eyes of the beloved are set against the racist stares of the poet's personal experience, and the poet's sisters' fury at their treatment by white society. The separation from whites has been, the poet acknowledges, in the interests of survival, but it has also entailed a certain compliance with whites, a response to the excoriating social divisions they have imposed:

> . . . my mother
> teaching me the yes sirs & mams
>   to keep me alive -
> never hear my mother cry,
> Lord, what kind of child is this?

However, Parker's poetry never assumes that being a lesbian, working-class woman of African descent means that she is absolved of all the sins of oppression. Even those subject positions – of oppressor and oppressed – are interrelated, as in the poem 'there is a woman in this town' where stanza after stanza relates the lives of ideologically unacceptable women, the dope-head, the capitalist, the lunatic, the housewife, the fat woman, the butch, and with each stanza comes the refrain 'Is she our sister?'[19] Crossing the threshold of the gay bar becomes a transgressive act. The bar, however, is another arena of conflict, not a utopian arena of 'safe space'. While 'forgetting' their transgressive status will provoke the censure of the wider community ('. . . the people / stare, glare, frown, & taunt / at those queers -'), they will not be permitted to forget it either in the confines of the 'liberated' bar:

> & my people shun me because i crossed
>   the line
> & her people look to see what's
> wrong with her - what defect
> drove her to me -

Here Parker affirms her feminism via a rigorous and vigilant critique of the movement's racism, just as elsewhere she has reproved its antipathy towards gay men, its structure of exclusions, and the dangerous fads and advertising angles (e.g. 'revolutionary tampons') it seems to have spawned. Parker is absolutely clear-sighted about what is liberatory and what is not – ever aware of the dangers of falling back into the old oppressions under new names, particularly of a coopted feminism which 'offers women not liberation but the right to act as surrogate men'.[20] Hence Parker's poem on sado-masochism:

> Is this why we did it?
> Did we take to the streets
> so women can carve swastikas on their bodies?[21]

Feminist commitment in Parker's poetry is commitment to the collective rather than to the individual, as in white bourgeois feminism, which is where an untheorised, reactionary rendition of the subject has proved most damaging. bell hooks writes: 'Although the contemporary feminist movement was initially motivated by the sincere desire of women to eliminate sexist oppression, it takes place within the framework of a larger, more powerful cultural system that encourages women and men to place the fulfilment of the individual aspirations above their desire for collective change.'[22] For Parker, positive transformation or 'revolution' is an ongoing process figured in the recurring references to boundaries, lines of demarcation, thresholds, points of transgression, and definitions of self-identity.[23] 'The reality is that revolution is not a one step process: you fight, you win – it's over. It takes years. Long after the smoke of the last gun has faded away the struggle to build a society that is classless, that has no traces of sexism and racism in it, will still be going on. We have many examples of societies in our time that have had successful armed revolution. And we have no examples of any country that has completed the revolutionary process.'[24] There is no more refuge in espousing a monolithic uncritical feminist identity than in any of the other possible single identities with which Parker engages.

The penultimate stanza of the poem becomes a metonymy of racism and the way it can be simultaneously remembered and dismembered in this transgressive, lesbian love, so that the end of the poem's

> And i can hear my mother cry.
> Lord, what kind of child is this?

becomes now an affirmation. The mother's cry and her utterance are now separated by a period, unlike every prior use of these words in the poem. The utterance now takes a non-interrogative form, an uncharacterisable identity, in excess of all previous identities and yet built from them. The child here is the new race (akin to Haraway's cyborg, a creature of transition and transgression) rather than the aberrant offspring (the 'goat Child' of Parker's long autobiographical poem) – she is to be wondered at, admired, having transgressed rather than transcended the boundaries of sexual and racial propriety.

Via poetic renderings of imbricated subjugated identities, Parker is able 'to shake poetry out of a kaleidoscope of overlapping oppressions'.[25] This ostensibly postmodern identity is symbolised by the 'Aya', fern symbol of defiance, and 'Nkyimkyim', 'a twisted pattern meaning changing oneself or playing many parts', which respectively begin and end each of the poems in the volume *Movement in Black*. Such symbols, of resistance, transformation, survival, are synonymous with the life of an African–American lesbian in a racist and homophobic society rather than with the 'freely chosen' consumer selection of hyper-technologised late capitalism. It is in this sense that the poem functions as an instance of an atypically political post-modernity, and it is precisely its politicisation that causes it to interrogate and problematise Haraway's formulation of woman of colour as the paradigmatic postmodern identity. That is, 'My Lover is a Woman' brings the contradiction of politics and postmodernity to a crisis. In the poem, the subject never arrives at a utopian identity but commits to a struggle for it. There is, then, a double movement in the poem because identities are deeply imbricated with one another, but the 'complex' subject is always firmly located in a recognition of the spaces closed to her by sexism, racism, and homophobia, and firmly located in an array of spaces, or 'liberation fronts' as Parker titles one of the sections in *Movement in Black*, from which to resist. Identity is not multifarious 'ludic' postmodernity, but a history of pain and joy that has its origins in the structures of oppression and resistance.

NOTES

1. Pat Parker's work includes *Child of Herself* (Diana Press, n.p., 1972), *Pit Stop* (Diana Press, 1973), *Womanslaughter* (Diana Press, 1978), *Jonestown and Other Madness* (Firebrand Press, Ithaca, 1985), and *Movement in Black: The Collected Poetry of Pat Parker 1961–78*, Foreword by Audre Lord, Introduction by Judy Grahn (Crossing Press, Trumansburg, NY, 1983).
2. Donna Haraway, 'A Manifesto for Cyborgs', in Linda Nicholson (ed.), *Feminism and Postmodernism* (Routledge, New York, 1989).
3. *Movement in Black*, p. 9.
4. See Trinh T. Minh-ha, *Woman, Native, Other: Writing, Postcoloniality, and Feminism* (Indiana University Press, Bloomington, 1989), p. 17, and Henry Louis Gates Jr, 'Tell Me, Sir, . . . What Is "Black" Literature?', *PMLA* **105**, 1 (1990), pp. 19–20. Gates argues that in these circumstances, formalist readings of literature were often the most radical ones: 'Virtually no one, it seems clear, believes that the texts written by black authors cohere into a tradition because the authors share certain innate characteristics. Opposing the essentialism of European "universality" with a black essentialism – an approach that in various ways characterised a large component of black literary criticism since the black arts movement has given way to more subtle questions. What is following the critique of the essentialist notions that cloaked the text in a mantle of "blackness", replete with all the accretions of all

sorts of sociological cliches, is a "postformal" resituation of texts, accounting for the social dynamism of subjection, incorporation, and marginalisation in relation to the cultural dominant.

Black literature, recent critics seem to be saying, can no longer simply name "the margin". Close readings . . . are increasingly naming the specificity of black texts, revealing the depth and range of cultural details far beyond the economic exploitation of blacks by whites.'

5. 'Imputing race or sex to the creative act has long been a means by which the literary establishment cheapens and discredits the achievements of non-mainstream women writers. She who "happens to be" a (non-White) Third World member, a woman, and a writer who is bound to go through the ordeal of exposing her work to the abuse of praises and criticism that either ignore, dispense with, or overemphasise her racial and sexual attributes. Yet the time has passed when she can confidently identify herself with a profession or artistic vocation without questioning it and relating it to her woman of colour condition. Today, the growing ethnic-feminist consciousness has made it increasingly difficult for her to turn a blind eye not only to the specification of the writer as historical subject . . . but also writing itself as a practice located at the intersection of the subject and history. . . .' Trinh T. Minh-ha, *Woman, Native, Other*, p. 6.

6. Fredric Jameson, 'A Brief Response', to Aijaz Ahmad's 'Jameson's Rhetoric of Otherness and the "National Allegory"', *Social Text*, **16** (1986), p. 26.

7. Cherri Morraga and Gloria Anzaldua (eds.), *This Bridge Called My Back: Writings by Radical Women of Colour* (Persephone, Watertown, MA, 1981), p. 241.

8. bell hooks, *Talking Back: Thinking Feminist, Thinking Black* (South End Press, Boston, 1989), p. 12.

9. See Hazel V. Carby, *Reconstructing Womanhood: The Emergence of the Afro-American Woman Novelist* (Oxford University Press, New York, 1987), pp. 3–19, for a discussion of various critical understandings of Black feminism in literary theory.

10. Fredric Jameson (note 6 above) describes such elements of US literature as 'third world' – a category which is, as he recognises, at once useful and problematic.

11. Haraway, 'A Manifesto for Cyborgs', p. 217.

12. Emily E. Culpepper, 'A Genius for Putting the Emphasis Where It Belongs', *Gay Community News*, 3–9 Sept. 1989, p. 12.

13. Trinh, *Woman, Native, Other*, p. 16.

14. see Gates.

15. Culpepper, p. 12.

16. *Movement in Black*, p. 13.

17. *Movement in Black*, p. 11.

18. Haraway, 'A Manifesto for Cyborgs', p. 197.

19. *Movement in Black*, pp. 154–7.

20. bell hooks, *Ain't I a Woman* (South End Press, Boston, 1981), p. 192.

21. 'Bar Conversation', *Jonestown and Other Madness*, p. 13.

22. hooks, *Ain't I a Woman* (South End Press, Boston, 1981), p. 191.

23. A similar preoccupation with borders as symptomatic of reconceptualised subjectivity and national identity is to be found in Gloria Anzaldua's *Borderlands / La Frontera: The New Mestiza* (spinsters / aunt lute, San Francisco, 1987).

24. Morraga and Anzaldua, *This Bridge Called My Back*, p. 241.

25. *Movement in Black*, p. 11.

Chapter 12

Nothing but Mortality

Prynne and Celan

Geoffrey Ward

From Dadaist shenanigans in the Cabaret Voltaire, or André Breton's 'La beauté sera CONVULSIVE, ou ne sera pas', to Olson's 'What does not change / is the will to change', or Steve Benson's improvising poems during readings, it might be concluded that the only common factor in the avant gardes of twentieth-century poetry has been a pleasure in disruption.[1] But the site of disturbance is not only to be located on the reading platform. Modern and postmodern poetry return obsessively to phenomenological disruption and ambiguity, to questions of what constitutes Inner and what Outer event. If this could be seen in the Surrealist conflation of dream and revolution, it has continued to animate more recent poetry: witness the puns in Robert Duncan's title *The Opening of the Field*, or a motto such as 'The inside real / and the outsidereal' from Ed Dorn's freewheeling epic *Gunslinger*.[2] I shall be looking at two poets, Paul Celan and J.H. Prynne, to whom public performance is irrelevant, and whose rare interventions in debate about poetry have been of the most wry or elliptical kind.[3] Yet textual disruption, often trained on the border between internal and external event, is pushed by each of these poets to a new extreme. The influence of both has been great: much current writing in France, from the poetry of Jean Daive or André Du Bouchet to the prose of Maurice Blanchot or Edmond Jabès, bears the marks of a deep engagement with Celan's practice. In America Michael Palmer, perhaps the most generally respected of the poets published under the Language banner, writes explicitly in relation to Celan. Meanwhile, Derridean theory has found Celan to be an important precursor of its own methods.[4] In crucial respects a rootless figure, Celan is without doubt the most influential poet to write in German since Rilke. Nevertheless, the bone of contention for detractors from the work of both Celan and J.H. Prynne has been the issue of semantic (and other) difficulty. To the poets included in the recent

139

Carcanet anthology *A Various Art*; Prynne has clearly provided a various stimulus, while remaining largely inimitable: yet Peter Porter has complained that 'Prynne is hermetic and priestly: he wants disciples not readers.'[5] To my eyes the undoubted difficulty of Prynne's poetry is not at all a manner with which one is asked to collude, nor a matter of such unresponsive density that reading is doomed. As with Celan, his difficulty is *vital*: the poetry has its own life, and is only to a limited extent a use of language. Instead, its explorations, and the reader's tapping and testing different lines of meaning, are instances of the larger life to which poetry gives access. Perhaps more contentiously, this essay draws attention to an emphasis shared by these two poets that cuts bleakly across current orthodoxies. In the rush to attack as outmoded any theory of the subject that would free it from social determinants, marxian, feminist and other contemporary modes of theory have tended to empty the subject of interiority altogether. No poetry has been more affected by historical determinants than that of Celan, who experienced the Holocaust. And Prynne's *Word Order* denies absolutely any conception of the subject as autonomous. But the work of both shows a deep and consistent engagement with pain, and recalls us to a form of writing, the lyric poem, whose dark and ambiguous terrain has been that of interiority.

Celan (b. 1920) drowned himself in the Seine in 1970. However much his suicide was the culmination of private despair, it may also have been determined by the Final Solution that shadowed both his poetry and historical lifetime. Celan was Romanian by birth: both his parents were deported and perished in the death-camps.[6] Exiled in Paris from 1948 until his death, 'a Jew with an unpronounceable name' (Celan being an anagrammatisation of Anczel, the 'cz' sound unavailable in French) the poet was, in Benjamin Hollander's words, 'forced to occupy his estrangement deeply'.[7] From the time of his schooldays Celan translated poetry across several languages, frequently taking on the impossible: Emily Dickinson, Shakespeare's sonnets; Valéry's 'Le Jeune Parque', rejected by Rilke as too difficult. Yves Bonnefoy recalls Celan saying '*you* (meaning French or Western poets) *are at home, inside your reference points and language. But I'm outside* . . . .'[8] To Celan, all poetry may therefore be seen as an act of translation, never at home with expression. In his later years he worked on pieces that seem to be talking about him: by the suicide, Sergei Esenin; or by Robert Desnos, a Surrealist who died in the camps; and Marianne Moore's 'A Grave'.

For a Jewish poet to compose in German after the Holocaust is an irony so dark as not merely to shadow but inhabit the substance of

Celan's poetry. The *Muttersprache* had been totally, perhaps irredeemably, contaminated by Nazi ideology. In reply to a 1958 questionnaire concerning work in progress, Celan spoke with an uncharacteristic directness to this crux:

> German poetry is going in a very different direction from French poetry. No matter how alive its traditions, with most sinister events in its memory, most questionable developments around it, it can no longer speak the language which many willing ears seem to expect. Its language has become more sober, more factual. It distrusts 'beauty'. It tries to be truthful . . . a 'greyer' language, a language which wants to locate even its 'musicality' in such a way that it has nothing in common with the 'euphony' which more or less blithely continued to sound alongside the greatest horrors.
>
> This language, notwithstanding its inalienable complexity of expression, is concerned with precision . . . it names, it posits . . . .[9]

This direct comment does consort with the work he was about to publish as *Sprachgitter* (1959). The poems in his first two collections, *Mohn und Gedächtnis* (1952) and *Von Schwelle zu Schwelle* (1955), tolling or severe as they may strike the ear, are still deeply involved in an engagement with French poetry of the 1920s and 1930s and Surrealism in particular. The imagery is often powerfully exotic, and reminds us of the mixed cargo of sensuousness, occultism and prophetic irony carried over by Rimbaud from Baudelaire to Breton. Although the most famous of Celan's early poems, 'Todesfuge' and 'Espenbaum . . .' deal graphically with the Holocaust, they do so partly through a poetic inheritance that predates the 1940s. Only fourteen years after the war, with *Sprachgitter*, does the Holocaust become a dominant *hic et nunc* reality in the poetry. Henceforth Celan's decontamination of German would be twofold; a stripping down, a scrupulous baring of poetic material as essential, but essentially ambiguous, matter – and a tendency to neologism around the building-blocks of the German syllable. The word 'Sprachgitter' is a case in point: speech-grid? word-mesh? A grid by which poetry can be mapped and made; or a mesh that confines, like barbed wire fencing? Here, Celan's writing anticipates deconstruction, not by destroying language but baring its roots, revealing ambiguities in words rather than serving what the deposed architects of 'the greatest horrors' wanted them to say. Nevertheless, some linguistic material was too contaminated and had to be abandoned. Translating, Celan would never convert 'la race' into 'die Rasse', for example.

To adapt a phrase of Jean Daive's, the poetry of Paul Celan keeps watch over the annihilated. It has no faith in humanism: instead it tries to conjure life in what the poet called 'a realm which is turned toward the human, but uncanny . . . '.[10] Moving beyond humanity does not put the poet in contact with actual landscapes, or even the nature-in-mind explored by Hölderlin. Rather, we hear a series of key words, chanted repeatedly as from a space beyond the human, and so *unheimlich*, but from the home of poetry: *Schnee, Ferne, Nacht, Asche, Mund*. They can be directly symbolic, even referential: 'Asche' (ash) for example, is given an appallingly direct meaning by the death-camps, but even this does not give a full account of what these key words can do. They operate in ways not dissimilar to Prynne's repeated use of words such as 'snow', 'window', 'water', 'mirror', in his *The Oval Window* (1983) – words which are at hand in their familiarity, signs of the faraway in their calmly non-human associations; welcoming yet distanced yet magnetic in a recognisable but elusive configuration. That the things they signal are mysterious takes nothing away from their articulation of fundamental human experience; quite the reverse. At a more literary and perhaps superficial level, a close reading of Rilke may have played an enabling part, for the work of both Celan and Prynne. The Ninth and the Tenth *Duino Elegies* (1923) are those most explicitly concerned with the means by which this fleeting world seems to keep calling to us: us, *die Schwindendsten*, the most fleeting of all:

> Sind wir vielleicht *hier*, um zu sagen: Haus,
> Brücke, Brunnen, Tor, Krug, Obstbaum, Fenster, –
> höchstens: Säule, Turm . . . aber zu *sagen*, verstehs,
> oh zu sagen *so*, wie selber die Dinge niemals
> innig meinten zu sein.[11]

> (Are we perhaps *here*, in order to say: House / Bridge, Fountain, Gate, Pitcher, Fruit-tree, Window – / at most: Column, Tower . . . but to *say*, don't you see, / oh to say them *so*, as the Things in themselves would never dream to mean to be.)

And in the Tenth Elegy, the speaking Lament names 'Die Sterne des Leidlands' (the stars of the Land of Pain) '*Wiege; Weg; Das Brennende Buch; Puppe; Fenster*'.[12] (Cradle, Path, The Burning Book, Doll, Window.) Of course this is the same and not at all the same as Celan's and Prynne's acts of naming: Rilke is more interested than either in an extra-linguistic reality of Things; but still there seems something shared.[13] What is happening with all three is the attempt to figure in poetry a fundamental encounter between the inner self and the outer world that is *an sich* an act of figuration. There is an awareness of a spectrum of experience through which the inner and outer are not separate, ranging from unity with Nature, to the self as conduit for social forces and signs. The first draws on an immersion in the European Romantic tradition shared by these writers, the second on the transition of Romantic phenomenology to an urban and secular realm. Yet there is also an awareness of separation between self and not-self: the fact of naming draws attention to the lack of unity between namer and named. Language, that always misses its mark, both spells the creative difference of man from the animals and other presences, but signs his estrangement. Yet the stars seem to look at us. Things often seem to be waiting for something. Water, that can kill or sustain, resonates as an image in the mind somehow more than itself. The mirror is man-made and everyday, but magical. And we all know this. Even the experience of turning away – of the self from the world, of one person from another, of parts of the mind from other parts – is shared. The key words – mirror, window, snow, night – are not at all pointers to a simplified or an avidly poeticised world, but are *condensations* in poetry of human encounter: with the world outside the single self or species, through the verbal order outside which no encounter may be thinkable, but which is itself encountered as other, and yet into which we are born. What constitutes home and what estrangement seem to move like a Möbius strip. The consequences for poetic meaning can be radical, as with this poem from *Sprachgitter*, 'Tenebrae'. The multiplication of points of reference for what is 'near' or 'there', 'yours' or 'ours' is as ironised and destabilising as in any postmodernist offering, but what is at stake is more nakedly of life and death importance:

> Nah sind wir, Herr,
> nahe und greifbar.
>
> Gegriffen schon, Herr,
> ineinander verkrallt, als wär
> der Leib eines jeden von uns
> dein Leib, Herr.
>
> Bete, Herr,
> bete zu uns,
> wir sind nah.
>
> Windschief gingen wir hin,
> gingen wir hin, uns zu bücken
> nach Mulde und Maar.
>
> Zur Tränke gingen wir, Herr.
>
> Es war Blut, es war,
> was du vergossen, Herr.
>
> Es glänzte.

Es warf uns dein Bild in die Augen, Herr.
Augen und Mund stehn so offen und leer, Herr.
Wir haben getrunken, Herr.
Das Blut und das Bild, das im Blut war, Herr.

Bete, Herr.
Wir sind nah.

(We are near, Lord, / near and at hand. // Handled already, Lord, / clawed and clawing us though / the body of each of us were / your body, Lord. // Pray, Lord, / pray to us, / we are near. // Wind-awry we went there, / went there to bend / over hollow and ditch. // To be watered we went there, Lord. // It was blood, it was / what you shed, Lord. // It gleamed. // It cast your image into our eyes, Lord. / Our eyes and our mouths are so open and empty, Lord. / We have drunk, Lord. / The blood and the image that was in the blood, Lord. // Pray, Lord, / We are near.)[14]

I first read this harsh and horrific poem in my mid-teens, about twenty years ago, and can recall quite clearly the steps by which I made some sense of it. The poem appeared – and in some respects still seems – to be based in an image of Communion, ghastly and travestied. Rather than bread and wine being turned through transubstantiation into the body and blood of the Lord, here the act of ingesting has turned into a monstrous and cannibal ('ineinander') thirst for more. The use of the Communion structure has been fused with elements of Genesis, so that ingestion of the blood, and the image gleaming in the blood, resemble eating from the Tree of Knowledge, a terrible maturation. As the roving pack close in on the kill, the positions of Master and supplicant are about to be reversed: *Bete, Herr. / Wir sind nah.* It was with a jolt, then, that I read these incidental comments by John Felstiner, who urges an interpretation that seems at first to be massively more obvious. Speaking of the prayer-like rhetoric of the poem's opening, Felstiner notes, ' "*Tenebrae*" moves quickly from this prayer or psalm-like invocation into the human toils of a gas chamber . . .'[15]. By this view, the alliteration of the opening lines evokes the instinctive clawing of the victims herded into the sheds as the nature of what was being done to them became clear. No murderous pack, these are the murdered, voices speaking from the far side of their death: 'a realm which is turned toward the human, but uncanny . . .'. Celan's formulation of the place of art is here literally the subject of the poem's dead voices. Words such as *Windschief, Mulde, Maar* would then be intended to describe the kind of grey and unforgiving landscape to be seen around Auschwitz–Birkenau. Evidently, my initial reading was conditioned by the Christian associations of the poem's repeated nouns, Felstiner's by the general importance of Judaism and the Holocaust to Celan's work. I read my own background into the poem. On the other hand, there is much in the poem that still remains unaccounted for, if its images are located too firmly in either the experience of the extermination camp, or the kind of rewriting of Judaeo–Christian myth I initially felt underpinned the poem. *It was blood, it was / what you shed, Lord*: this still seems to me to refer ineluctably to the central Christian image of the Crucifixion. Does the poem imply that the image of the *individuality* of suffering as the pathway to redemption, so fundamental to Christianity, is now entirely consumed, devoured, in the genocidal flame of the Holocaust? Could these voices beyond the grave articulate a *revenge* on the God whose face was turned away while the furnaces burned? A hovering shadow of irony is not to be excluded from the ambiguities of 'Tenebrae'. In sum, one might want to say that by inscribing speech from beyond the human realm, by including possible reference to Jewry in the Holocaust but conveyed in the German language of the oppressor, the poem exerts a biting revenge on the master-order into which any poetic utterance is born, substituting its own tenebrous realm, *unheimlich* home.[16]

To Celan the world is mysterious, but not a mystery that might be solved; the Holocaust monstrous, but not an aberration: the poem is exploratory without asking for location. Interruption becomes, as Budick and Iser observe, 'the very condition of sense-making' in Celan.[17] Maurice Blanchot writes of the 'white space, these arrests, these silences' of Celan's work as being not pauses or intervals, but the positive, indeed rigorous, registration of a void: 'less a lack than a saturation, a void saturated with void'.[18] This may be similar to what Celan himself once spoke of, rather mordantly, as his poetry's 'strong tendency towards silence'.[19]

Like his near-contemporary Beckett, Celan was an essentialist, believing in art – notwithstanding a great show of reluctance and irony – as a meditation on the *condition humaine*. Consequently, both utilise a deliberately limited lexicon. By contrast, Prynne's poetry includes the widest range of discourse and vocabulary since Pound. Prynne, like Celan and like Beckett, is a writer willing to take on everything. But where the other two burrow for essentials, Prynne does the polis in its different voices, passing from satire to a Romantic multiplication of meanings. Here is a body of writing that is not merely different from, but in important ways conceptually *larger* than the cultural consensus which up to now has regarded it with suspicion and alarm. It is an intuition of Prynne's work that language may not only shape the world it enables us to name, but also inhabits it organically, as new human subjects find themselves already inscribed within its codes and cells. To that extent poetic language is there in order to reveal what was already pursuing an unseen life. This view gives sequences such as *Into The Day* (1972) a textural beauty partly in keeping with Romantic traditions of lyrical prophecy. 'It is the rarest thing, the compounded blood / and light makes lustre swerve in the dream.'[20] But Prynne's writing has always carried anxieties of a political order, and it tackles head-on the dispersal of orders of language into specialist 'disciplines', especially the scientific, supposedly inaccessible to what the cultural norms outside his poetry would define as the ordinary reader. As a result Prynne's work entails a massive act of restitution, or a new constitution, of all language as open to use. But if the prodigious lexical array of these poems is in one sense Utopian, conjuring a new Sublime, it is also acidly satirical and mounted in the present. (Consider the way Prynne's writing of the 1980s makes such productive use of stockmarket and Treasury buzzwords.) As a result of this multiplicity of perspectives the poems are at once descriptive and non-referential, which gives a range and complication unique in contemporary poetry to lines such as 'Above the night sky the atrophy continues, / costing just what it says on the ticket.'[21] Or at least, such has been the case since *Brass* (1971). Prynne's work prior to that time was far less radical in its strategies and would in some ways sit alongside the phenomenological poetry of landscape composed by Charles Tomlinson or Donald Davie, an early mentor.

The pleasures and complexities typical of Prynne's writing in the 1970s are shown in these, the opening lines from 'Treatment in the Field', the first poem from *Wound Response* (1974):

> Through the window the sky clears
> and in sedate order stands the order of battle,
>   quiet as a colour chart and bathed
>   by threads of hyaline and gold leaf.
> The brietal perfusion makes a controlled
>   amazement and trustingly we walk there, speak
>   fluently on that same level of sound;
> white murmur ferries the clauses to the true
>   centre of the sleep forum.[22]

Prynne's poetry has been coupled with Ashbery's, though they have little in common beyond a shared liking for the sentence which proceeds calmly as if it made perfectly conventional sense, while resisting it thoroughly. The lines quoted are 'fluently on that same level' occupied by normal discourse: syntactically controlled, grammatically cohesive. Despite this, the reader is drawn into an elegantly phrased and an exacting but an outrageously perverse use of words such as 'clear', 'order', 'trustingly' and 'true': it is far from clear what truths are enunciated, what might or might not be trustworthy and to what orders we might be asked to pay attention. The phrase 'white murmur' is disconcerting, but its derivation from the more familiar phrase 'white noise' is quite logical; and so if this poetry subverts conventional usage, we are given notice that there is method in its madness, no ludic free-for-all.

The ambiguities of the word 'hyaline' are characteristic of the passage as a whole. Meaning 'glassy', it connotes transparency and opacity at the same time, reminding that a view of the sky is both facilitated and limited by being visible 'Through the window'. The titles 'Treatment in the Field' and *Wound Response* announce a medical context confirmed by the reference to Brietal, a short-acting anaesthetic. Consequently a technical usage of 'hyaline', as in hyaline degeneration of the cartilage, can't be excluded from the poem's possible meanings. Yet the word is also a conspicuous poeticism, traditionally apostrophising the smoothness of water, the clarity of sky, as in Milton's 'From heaven gate not far, founded in view / On the clear hyaline, the glassy sea'.[23] (In much the same way, the title of Prynne's sequence *The Oval Window* (1983) uses its Romantic connotations and its anatomical meaning as part of the ear.) The ambiguities of 'hyaline' spread like the patterns frost makes across a window, so that even 'gold leaf' now begins to shimmer; the previously used 'colour chart' makes it look like a flat strip from a catalogue, yet a reading of these lines as an autumn scene makes the 'leaf' literal. One could go on: I have scratched the surface. The poem, like all of Prynne's writing, is crystalline, and although the refraction of meaning and dazzling multiplication of surfaces are what strike the eye first, it has a definite structure.

Coleridge, in 'Frost at Midnight' (1798), had offered a Romantic meditation in which the voyaging consciousness delved ever deeper into its own memories and thoughts to be eventually returned, in one sense to the same place, but to a place and as a consciousness changed by having made that exploration. In the meantime the 'secret ministry' of frost has continued its silent work, the construction of votive icicles now, at the poem's close, 'Quietly shining to the quiet Moon'.[24] Frost and consciousness are not the same things, but to Coleridge the first is not simply a metaphor for the creativity of the second. The human and the supposedly inanimate are independently but analogously creative, and reading the poem is exploratory in a like way. By the time of Baudelaire's 'Correspondances' (1845?), the world could be presented as 'une ténébreuse et profonde unité', an echo-system of creativity and analogy, but one of '*confuses* paroles' (my emphasis), dangerous explorations.[25] Synaesthesia, the mutual translation of the senses, is undeniably a dislocation as much as a promise of an ultimate 'unité'. To Prynne, a lyric poet in the era of late capitalism, the composition of poems is even more than to Baudelaire an involvement in a culturally marginal activity. Any claim to prophecy or the revelation of *correspondances* from such a quarter would look vulnerably bardic in 1974, and the poetry builds sardonic acknowledgement of this into its every utterance. Synaesthesia has been replaced by anaesthesia: yet understanding 'flits cross-wise from branch to branch' of living knowledge, like the wren mentioned later in the poem. Perhaps the possibility of knowledge is all in the *like*, as if with each trusting movement we make in the world the preceding step vanished. The poem is amnesiac, every twist of image turning it elsewhere, and yet begins – by metaphor and analogy – to build a new, overarching fusion of discourses; this endeavour, while not remotely Coleridgean in a nostalgic sense, returns to the same breadth of intellectual agenda, and with a strenuousness all the more breathtaking given the multiple pressures applied to poetry since the nineteenth century to make it withdraw from any such ambitiousness. The bribe offered was a becomingly modest melancholy, which poetry could keep as its own province.

Those pressures are not overcome in Prynne's poetry. Nor have they all come from outside. *Down where changed*, written at the end of the 1970s, had all the bleakness of a last book. Prynne's writing since that point has frequently seemed provisional, a surprised return, and most powerful in fact when this seems most the case, as in the final pieces from *The Oval Window* or the new *Word Order* (1989), more gripping than the controlled satires of *Bands Around the Throat* (1987).[26] Indeed, *Word Order* is about being gripped, 'right hard by the crop', to quote from the poem by Wyatt, itself a half-translation from Seneca, deployed by Prynne in the lines 'overtly dazed with dreadful face, eyes / turning back to the closed window'.[27] Prynne's poetry retains a proximity to the modernism of Pound and Eliot in its overt literary allusiveness, but is much closer to Eliot in its repeated discovery that private distress is echoed rather than assuaged by entry into the network of past records.

> the free the offer repeatedly, hit as he lay on
>   the ground stroked no struck to put
> words into the mouth the truth the life
>   and take the ethereal vapour
>   like a chance
> crossing the street. For anyone could . . .[28]

An unnamed man is hit, attacked, and the blows echo and ricochet through these shocked and painful lyrics. 'anyone' could end up in the same position, assaulted or struck down by illness, accident, other men. Even the medical assistance brought to the stricken man, perhaps a cardiac resuscitator, can look like an act of violence: 'quickly / stand back he said, stand clear'.[29] The word 'chance' returns obsessively, no mantra, Rilkean mnemonic or laral sign, but a dismayed registration of human frailty. Chance hovers ambiguously, pointing to the triumph of the random, a world without meaning, and to the possibility of a hidden order underpinning our ceaseless collisions and accidents. Surrealist writing was acutely aware of this doubleness in Chance, particularly Breton through his emphasis on 'le hasard objectif'. But Surrealism retained enough Dadaist *je m'en foutisme* to draw creative energy from the random, turning it into an aesthetic of the aleatory; and the other chance, the possibility of hidden order, was equally seductive to neo-Rimbaudian dream-artists with an opportunist interest in magic and the occult. None of these Romantic positions is remotely available to Prynne, whose Chance has more in common with the poem from Tottel's *Songes and Sonnettes* beginning 'I see that chance hath chosen me / Thus secretly to live in pain' – except that the 'woeful case' diagnosed by Prynne appears to be a universal malady.[30] I dwell on the self-severance from avant garde causes because it seems an important tendency in Prynne's recent work: just so, a poem of 1987 offers a savage and politically despondent parody of Olson's most quoted motto: 'Nothing / changes the will to change nothing.'[31]

We are struck into life, words put into our mouths. Fundamentally, Prynne's recent writing enacts, rather than comments on, the shock of mortality; it is a shock *at* life felt *in* life, not limited to horror at its abrupt or cruel termination. The poetry now articulates from inside what was dealt with in a more measured way by the early and satirical *Kitchen Poems* (1968) where death, 'biologic collapse', was described as 'violence reversed, / like untying a knot'.[32] Somewhere between the two stands Prynne's only elegy for a named person, the 1970 poem 'Es Lebe Der König: (*for Paul Celan, 1920–1970*)'. The poem is too long, intricate, and dependent on cumulative effect to be dealt with in brief, but this is its close:

> Give us this love of murder and
> sacred boredom, you walk in the shade of
> the technical house. Take it away and set up
> the table ready for white honey, choking the
> white cloth spread openly for the most worthless
> accident. The whiteness is a patchwork of
> revenge too, open the window and white fleecy
> clouds sail over the azure;

                                              it is true. Over and
        over it is so, calm or vehement. You know
        the plum is a nick of pain, is so and is also
        certainly loved. Forbearance comes into the
        stormy sky and the water is not quiet.[33]

The apparent repetition of images of whiteness is no repetition; in
each case it is a different whiteness, but one with equal potential to
turn from bland attractiveness to destruction – 'choking' – in an
instant. Anything, any instant attaching to our rituals of home and
food and shelter can become an instrument of murder or sudden
'accident'. The 'flag' that has become 'technical' at an earlier point in
the text, might like the German flag take on sudden, new associations
of homicide, as the hand that is 'stroked' at one point comes near to
being burned several lines later. But if we inhabit a dangerous and
unreliable world where what did exist is transformed or gone the next
moment, there follow positive as well as negative consequences, even
if the chance they offer is subject to absurdity. The 'water' into which
Celan threw himself is 'not quiet', and if storms can develop out of
nowhere, so can 'Forbearance'. The King is dead – Long Live the
King, to give the poem's title in English. 'Es Lebe Der König' is also
a phrase drawn from Georg Büchner's play *Dantons Tod* (1835), and
one of which Celan spoke in 'The Meridian', an address given in 1960
on accepting the Büchner Prize. At the end of the play Lucile is left
alone, her lover Camille and his friends having gone to the guillotine.
A citizens' patrol passes, and in response to their automatic 'Who
goes there?', she answers, deliberately, 'Long Live the King!', signing
her own death-warrant.[34] Celan argues that this utterance, an apparent statement of fealty to the *ancien régime*, is in reality 'an act of
freedom . . . a step . . . . It is homage to the majesty of the absurd
which bespeaks the presence of human beings.'[35] It is 'poetry', he
goes on: yet in the same address poetry is termed 'an externalization
of nothing but mortality, and in vain'.[36] In the era of postmodernism,
disruption of the textual surface and a compound fracture of the
meaning and the subject all gain positive and even playful connotations.
However, texts by Prynne and Celan can be implicated in the general
post-structuralist fallout only through culpable inattention to the
irony, interiority and dark stoicism which marks the shared ground
of their poetry.

                                      The years
        jostle and burn up as a trust plasma.
        Beyond help it is joy at death itself:
        a toy hard to bear, laughing all night.[37]

NOTES

1. André Breton, *Oeuvres Complètes* I, eds. Marguerite Bonnet *et al.* (Gallimard, Paris, 1988), p. 753. Charles Olson, 'The Kingfishers', *Archaeologist of Morning* (Cape Goliard Press, London, 1970), unpaginated.
2. Edward Dorn, *Slinger* (Wingbow Press, Berkeley, 1975), Book III, unpaginated.
3. Given pressures of space, I was unable to give consideration to two prose pieces by J.H. Prynne that bear on the themes of this article: his Worton Lecture 'English Poetry and Emphatical Language', in *Proceedings of the British Academy*, Vol. LXXIV; 1988, (Oxford University Press, 1989) and 'Reader's Lockjaw', in *Perfect Bound*, 5 (Cambridge, 1978), pp. 73–8.
4. See Stéphane Moses, 'Patterns of Negativity in Paul Celan's "The Trumpet Place"', in *Languages of the Unsayable: The Play of Negativity in Literature and Literary Theory*, Sanford Budick and Wolfgang Iser (eds.), (Columbia University Press, New York, 1989), pp. 209–25.
5. *A Various Art*, Andrew Crozier and Tim Longville (eds.), (Carcanet Press, Manchester, 1987). Porter's comment on Prynne's volume *Poems* is as given by James Keery, 'Nature, Flowers and the Night Sky: a Review of *A Various Art*', *Bête Noire*, 8/9 (Hull, 1989/90), p. 51.
6. Some information regarding Celan's life and background may be gleaned from *Translating Tradition: Paul Celan in France*, Benjamin Hollander (ed.), *Acts*, 8/9, (San Francisco, 1989).
7. Ibid., p. 1.
8. Ibid., p. 11.
9. Paul Celan, *Collected Poems*, trans. Rosmarie Waldrop (P.N. Review/Carcanet Press, Manchester, 1986), pp. 15–16.
10. Ibid., pp. 42–3.
11. Rainer Maria Rilke, *Sämtliche Werke*, Erster Band (Insel Verlag, Frankfurt am Main, 1955), p. 718. All translations from Rilke's German in this essay are my own.
12. Ibid., p. 725.
13. The importance of naming in the philosophy of Martin Heidegger, and its likely influence on both Celan and Prynne, may also be relevant here.
14. *Poems of Paul Celan*, trans. Michael Hamburger (Anvil Press, London, 1988), pp. 112–13.
15. John Felstiner, 'Translating Celan/Celan Translating', *Translating Tradition*, p. 117.
16. The two poems by David Gascoyne entitled 'Tenebrae' may usefully be read alongside Celan's. See Gascoyne, *Collected Poems* (Oxford University Press, 1988).
17. *Languages of the Unsayable*, p. xviii.
18. *Translating Tradition*, p. 228.
19. Celan, *Collected Prose*, p. 48.
20. J.H. Prynne, *Poems* (Agneau 2, Edinburgh/London, 1982), p. 203.
21. Ibid., p. 255.
22. Ibid., p. 214.
23. John Milton, *Paradise Lost*, Alastair Fowler (ed.) (Longman, London, 1971 rept.), p. 393. The lines quoted are from Book VII, 11, pp. 618–19.
24. *The Complete Poetical Works of Samuel Taylor Coleridge*, E.H. Coleridge (ed.) (The Clarendon Press, Oxford, 1912), pp. 240–2.
25. Charles Baudelaire, *Oeuvres Complètes*, Yves-Gerard Le Dantec (ed.) (Gallimard, Paris, 1954), p. 87.
26. J.H. Prynne, *The Oval Window* (privately printed, Cambridge, 1983); *Bands Around the Throat* (privately printed, Cambridge, 1987); *Word Order*, (Prest Roots Press, Kenilworth, 1989).
27. Sir Thomas Wyatt, 'Stand whoso list upon the slipper top', *Collected Poems*, Joost Daalder (ed.) (Oxford University Press, 1975), p. 205. J.H. Prynne, *Word Order*, p. 15.
28. Ibid., p. 7.
29. Ibid., p. 19.

30. Wyatt, *Collected Poems*, p. 229.
31. Prynne, 'Punishment Routines', *Bands Around the Throat*, p. 13.
32. Prynne, 'A Gold Ring Called Reluctance', *Poems*, p. 20.
33. Prynne, 'Es Lebe Der König', ibid., pp. 168–9.
34. The connexion between Büchner's play, Celan's address and Prynne's poem was noted first by David Trotter. See his *The Making of the Reader: Language and Subjectivity in Modern American, English and Irish Poetry* (Macmillan, London and Basingstoke, 1984), esp. pp. 218–20.
35. Celan, *Collected Prose*, p. 40.
36. Ibid., p. 52.
37. Prynne, *The Oval Window*, p. 34.

Chapter 13

Postmodern Postpoetry

Tom Raworth's 'tottering state'

Peter Brooker

Since the first uses of the term in the late 1950s and early 1960s, 'postmodernism' has acquired an amoebic range of attributions and meanings, in academic debate and in journalism. In general terms it can be said to describe a mood or condition of radical indeterminacy, and a tone of self-conscious, parodic scepticism towards previous certainties in personal, intellectual and political life. Thus in its two most influential arguments, associated with J-F. Lyotard and Jean Baudrillard, it is felt that the 'grand narratives' of human progress and liberation, rooted especially in Enlightenment thought, have lost credibility; and that a culture of detached media images have come to suffocate and out-clone the 'real world', ousting old-fashioned worries about the relationship of the image to the real. This wide and double crisis of legitimacy and representation has thrown everything in the air. And, not surprisingly, the term 'postmodernism' itself has become airborne. Loosened from the fixed categories and hierarchies which held art and culture still, yet full of a lack of confidence in rational thought and consensus, it goes slaloming across the forms, media, and discourses it means to survey. It is difficult, consequently, to pin down.

What is more, 'postmodernism' is used both as a descriptive and an evaluative term, and not always of the same phenomena. The trio of terms postmodern, postmodernity and postmodernism are thus all used as a way of periodising (usually postwar) developments in capitalist economies and societies; to describe developments across or within the arts (which do not necessarily synchronise with the first set of developments or with each other), but also to signal an attitude or position on these developments; and these can settle anywhere between fervid evangelicalism or faddish knowingness to resignation or resistance. Furthermore, as a relational term, *post*modernism is seen either as a continuation of, or break with, dominant features in modernism or the avant garde, about which there is also naturally much debate.

Whatever else, these earlier terms are inescapable in any discussion of postmodernism, and are a place to start in discussing a poet like Tom Raworth. The first thing we ought to appreciate, then, is that modernism has been culturally specific; or rather that the term has been employed far more regularly in discussions of Anglo-American than of European art movements. In England and America, modernism came to designate a particular set of authors: T.S. Eliot, Ezra Pound, Joyce, Woolf, Faulkner, Wallace Stevens, ringed by minor, that is to say, awkward and hence marginalised, figures such as W.C. Williams, Wyndham Lewis, Gertrude Stein, H.D. and many others. In the face of the experience of modernity (technological and economic change, political dissent, the fractured subjective experience of the modern metropolis) the arch-modernist Eliot sought to inscribe both this anomie and a new unity of consciousness and culture through the overarching controls of myth and tradition. This radical conservatism then hardened through its representative figures into the hegemony of a self-encorporated modernism. By 1950 (the beginning of the decade which was to announce postmodernism) Eliot was, said F.R. Leavis, 'a public institution'.[1]

One needs to see clearly, therefore, that Anglo-American modernism was a cultural construction, around selective aesthetic and ideological values, and not a thing in itself. Accordingly, many individual writers and achieved bodies of work outside the paradigm (and outside England and America) were distorted, diminished, or simply went unnoticed. This hegemonic modernism needs, then, to be distinguished from the historical avant garde: an unquestionably diverse set of movements (in Futurism, Dada, Cubism and Surrealism) but which shared an opposition to the institution of art, and sought under anarchist or communist or fascist inspiration to establish a new productive engagement between art and the world. It is then this tendency, the avant garde assault on artistic autonomy; a dehierarchisation of received relations between high and popular culture; an intermingling of genres and media, which it is argued has rematerialised as a feature of postmodern culture, made general now by the information explosion, global TV and film networks, the ubiquities of rock and pop and fashion styles. Art and literature (themselves conceptually unstable) are integrated into the world of social praxis, free at last of the prison house of high culture. The price, say some, is that the political project of the historical avant garde has receded; for art is free now only to join the circulation of commodities, a further product and prop of a triumphant consumer capitalism.

Across its spinning glassy surfaces of free choice and rapid turnover, single-minded political strategies can gain no hold. Yet another position would see postmodernism as straddling cultural and intellectual systems; a transitional mentality and condition, hooked to the fixities it unravels, by turns and by degrees, complicit and critical.

If it is true that Eliot (with Yeats, Pound, Joyce, Woolf and Lawrence in close attendance) stood, in England especially, as a model of modernist literature, it is true to say, too, that the first reaction to this model was not postmodernism, but the low key 'realism' of the Movement poets and novelists. In other words the relative autonomies of poem and signifier in postsymbolist modernism did not give way as a necessary next stage to their full liberation from wordly reference, since they were met instead by an attempt to reattach signifier to signified (though this is the last way it would have been put) in the self-ironic, anti-mythologising, anti-intellectual, feet-on-the-ground parochialism of Philip Larkin and other writers of the 1950s. We need to appreciate this 'negative feedback', as it has been called, to appreciate the further reaction of a generation of writers, including Raworth, who then emerged in the 1960s.

In Raworth's case some of the actual subtleties and exceptions to these alignments can be established anecdotally. Raworth was a mature student at Essex University where Donald Davie was first Professor of Comparative Literature. Not only was Davie a contributor to the Movement anthologies and the author of its key manifesto, he was also a major interpreter of Pound and of Eliot, an early advocate of the American Black Mountain poets. Ed Dorn, for example, was, at Davie's invitation, writer in residence at the University when Raworth was a student there and already himself a writer and small publisher. Black Mountain poetics, centrally Charles Olson's essay 'Projective Verse' (1950) and with it a counter-hegemonic reading of Ezra Pound and a preference for W.C. Williams over Eliot, could therefore provide a strong alternative tradition to Eliotic modernism and to Movement poetry for a younger English poet.

All this occurred in one sense in the postmodern(ist) period, but the upshot for a poet taking an alternative 'American-Anglo' route might also more strictly be termed postmodernist, since Olson had been one of the first to use, if not closely to theorise the term in the 1950s. In one significant example he writes in *The Special View of History* of the relevance of John Keats's 'negative capability' ('when a man is capable of being in uncertainties, mysteries, doubts without any irritable reaching after fact and reason') for an age 'post the Modern'.[2] This and other attributions are consistent with Olson's call to scale down and demote the ego in 'Projective Verse' and his criticism of Pound's egoism ('the ego as beak') in the *Cantos*. Elsewhere in an essay titled 'The Present is Prologue' Olson delivers a series of appeals and assertions ('Down with causation . . . all hierarchies, like dualities, are dead ducks . . . I am of the heterogeneous present') in a presentation that rejects the 'boring and evolutionary laws of the past' in anticipation of a new civilisation, projecting into 'the post-modern, the posthumanist, the posthistoric, the going live present.'[3] Olson's thinking runs at an eccentric tangent to what have become prominent postmodern debates, but ideas such as the above do, quite evidently, stake out some of its leading deconstructionist positions.

I think this rather lengthy prologue to a discussion of postmodern textuality is necessary for two reasons. First, because postmodernism as a possible tendency within the era of postmodernity will be differently nuanced in different cultures and arts, and without some attention to this we will paint with a very broad or formalist brush; and second because it is important to establish that the context of postmodern poetics to which Raworth relates emerges as a double protest against the protocols and exclusions of high modernism and low-level Movement empiricism. Marjorie Perloff has argued similarly that postmodern American poetry 'in the Pound tradition' challenged the exclusions of material and discourse and the desired unities of culture and subjectivity in modernist poetics. She sees postsymbolist modernism, moreover, as sharing the Romantic and still pervasive common sense view that poetry is a lyric discourse of traditionally shaped meditation and epiphany. The accessible tones, regular pace and predictable contours of Movement verse have more obviously reinforced this same assumption. Postmodernist poetry will therefore be constituted by its reaction to these orthodoxies: a decentred, dehierarchised exploration in 'writing', moving beyond the 'impasse of lyric' to accommodate different discursive forms, including theory and narrative, ethical and political argument and so, says Perloff' 'make contact with the *world* as well as the *word*'. Her prime example of such work is the American $L=A=N=G=U=A=G=E$ poets to whom Raworth stands, it is said, as 'a kind of elder statesman'.[4]

I cannot comment on this connection, or as I see it divergence, between postmodernist poetrys. Perloff's discussion does, however, confirm the view of postmodernist verse as counterhegemonic and deconstructionist, both of establishment forms and established 'popular' attitudes, and so in addition raises the question of its relation to its readers as well as to the word and the world. To rephrase these terms and some of the discussion above, I want to suggest four rough topics with which to gauge postmodernist poetic texts: intertextuality (beyond self-reflexive autonomy and the organicism of the 'well

made' poem); subjectivity (beyond the centred, unifying consciousness of the lyric and 'egoism' of the modernist long poem); narrative
(the (im?)possibilities of a long postmodern poem, and its relation to
the world); and politics (the above, including the question of a poem's
readers and readings). Since it would contradict the force of these
topics to *isolate* a poem, what follows is a way of *situating* one poem
by Raworth titled 'Mirror Mirror on the Wheel' in these terms.

'Mirror Mirror on the Wheel' appears, undated, in the volume
tottering state. Selected Poems 1963–1987, first published, significantly,
in an earlier version in the United States in 1984, but in 1988
published by Paladin in tandem with the volume *The New British
Poetry 1968–88*. In the same year new volumes by Allen Fisher, Roy
Fisher and Andrew Crozier also appeared, as did the collection *A
Various Art*, edited by Crozier and Tim Longville. In *The New British
Poetry* Eric Mottram groups Raworth, Crozier, John James, Barry
MacSweeney, Wendy Mulford and others under the title 'A treacherous
assault on British Poetry'. He describes their earlier appearance in
Poetry Review and in little magazines and presses (including Goliard
Press founded by Raworth and Barry Hall), and characterises them
as anti-Movement and as internationalist yet regionally based. These
poets appear in the anthology alongside other sections of poetry by
black and women poets and poetry by younger writers. Raworth's
volume was further proof, then, that a closely networked but differently
inflected challenge to traditional conceptions of English poetry and
to a unified, white and patriarchal 'Englishness' was belatedly coming
to notice.

The front cover of *tottering state* features a lithograph in grey and
flaming red and yellow by Anthony Davies which shows scenes of
destitution, domestic and state violence, counterposed (if it is counterposed at all) by the image in a corner window of a black mother breast
feeding a child. In the square of window above there is a scene of
attempted strangulation and next to the apartment building where
these events take place – sandwiched between it and an American
style traffic light signalling 'No/Go' – a policeman in riot gear runs
across the hollow shell of the Chrysler Building. Both this skyscraper
(a modernist icon), the apartment building and traffic light are
leaning. One can interpret the lithograph, then, as indeed it appears
to be titled, as a 'tottering state' of both person and nation (noting
that this is not the rhetoric of 'smashing the state' and nor is
the state 'fallen'). Rather, the picture is of a major city – a beacon and
inspiration for many early modernists – as now a picture of hell, as
almost any city, in a process of collapse, its people strung out across
the jangled emotions of hate, power, succour and despair.

The frontispiece to the volume shows a drawing by Arthur Okamura of Raworth reading at Bolinas, California. The figure leans back without apparent physical support, his head and shoulders slightly forward above a lectern. In front of this figure, level with his head, is a second head and shoulders, brought more forward. As with the cover illustration, this drawing can also be read as an intertextual analogue for the book's title: the figure is tottering or rocking between positions, in motion and in a sense decentred, becoming two in one, or one in two.

The drawing is followed by a dedication to four people 'as their selection' with below it the (to me) untranslatable script ﻛﺒﺭﺩﻩ ﻋﺎ ﻭﺓ ﺣ . On the next page there is an expression of thanks to a list of those who first published some of the poems, the declaration that they appear in order of writing rather than publication and that four poems are from a series of 'retranslations' of poems in Hungarian; 'a language', write Raworth, 'I neither speak nor read'. The vectors of intertextuality for poet and reader are therefore set very wide, and include visual representation and analogue as well as the utterly foreign but graphically apprehendable (the word as marks or design) or 'retranslatable' (language as marks and heard sound). At the same time the poetry is set, in advance, in a quadruple narrative of its fugitive publications (named as much, or more, as a sustaining human network of editors and fellow writers as of publications), in the list of Raworth's published works (given with dates but which it is impossible to relate accurately to individual poems), in the preferred chronology in which they appear (the process of writing set above the moment of achieved publication), and finally as a selection made by (four) others.

The poet 'Tom Raworth' is thus constructed in a set of representations, relations and processes: via the public themes of the cover illustration, the drawing of the act of reading and through the angled selections of others. Personal identity is devolved into the career of the writing and its possible contexts, already unfixed and decentred (the personal pronoun is held permanently at lower case in the volume), and this writing is set swinging between the personal and the political, the familiar and the foreign, and across time.

MIRROR MIRROR ON THE WHEEL

what is my frame?
dry hot handkerchief
pressed to my eyes

unreal
i am examining
my love for this child

who looks so like me
i am inside
his movements

now he drops my keys
and stares
at the tapedeck

'all your sea-sick sailors
they are rowing home'
we hear

time, i love you
you are the way
i see the same anew[5]

This poem contains two immediate intertextual references, from the children's fairy tale *Snow White* and from a commercially produced ballad 'Its all over now Baby Blue' by the folk/rock anti-establishment star Bob Dylan. It rewrites and resituates these snatches from 'popular' sources (itself a feature of postmodern writing) but in so doing indirectly questions the supposed homogeneity of 'low' popular discourse which 'higher' literary forms have required to sustain this hierarchy.

The title rephrases the step-mother and 'evil' queen's question to her mirror ('Mirror, mirror on the wall, who is the fairest of them all?'): a question prompted by recurring anxiety and the fear of rivalry. In the tale it is the question of a woman who requires confirmation of her self in her beauty (as the 'fairest' – when she is black haired, white faced but not 'snow white'). By extrapolation we might say this is the question of a woman in an image driven, mirror-ridden consumer culture, who in John Berger's distinction is constrained 'to appear' while men 'act'.[6] Here the gendered significance the question and tale might carry are transferred from a female step-mother to a male speaker and father. Whether this is a controlled or unconsidered appropriation the reader will decide (Raworth writes elsewhere that 'intentions count for nothing', p. 184), producing a meaning for, or across, the gap between 'original' female and present male speaker. In addition, in the tale of *Snow White*, the mirror speaks the truth. More than reflection this imaged second-self and oracle confirms a languishing identity, only then to splinter this unity (as the mirror is itself then splintered) by revealing the truth that the self is no longer sovereign and unrivalled but bested by the other (Snow White, the husband's daughter).

Further 'mirror relations' are presented in the poem's early stanzas, particularly between the adult (father?), who is unsighted, but examines (looks into) his own love and the child (a son?) who looks like and is inhabited by the father figure. A psychoanalytic narrative seems not far behind, and a reader might choose to make this silent intertextual relation between poem and theory explicit by introducing Jacques Lacan's poststructuralist concept of 'the mirror phase'. Briefly, this describes the moment of transition from the unity of the 'imaginary' stage when I (the seeing eye) and me (the eye reflected in a mirror) appear identical, to the 'symbolic' stage when, at the moment of the acquisition of language and the felt authority of the father, the child *misrecognises* itself in the mirror and sees that 'I' and 'me' are at a slant. Individual subjectivity is henceforth constructed in language out of this sense of non-equivalence and difference, installing a sense of lack and of unfulfilled desire, associated with the power of the father as model and rival. One could make something along these lines (a joke as much as a theoretical point) of the moment in the poem when the child *stares* at the tapedeck and drops the father's *keys*. (The idea of a castrated *father* might suggest the joke is on an all too predictable 'symbolic interpretation'.) Whatever its tone, the relevance of gender could be once more pressed here, through feminist critiques of the construction of an exclusively male subject in psychoanalytic theory, which would further 'frame' the poem.

For the reader the process of reading therefore becomes one of producing possible meanings, or, rather, problematics for the poem. One might therefore go on to adduce a further set of 'unintended' intertextual relations having to do with arguments (from a host of sources) on the mimetic function of art (art as a mirror to nature), and of its critique. Thus one might arrive at Derrida's concept of 'mise en abyme', describing the doubling and redoubling effect, mirror image in mirror image, consequent on the deconstruction of assumptions of a stable point of origin and reference on which realist representation, and much else, depends.

Is Raworth's poem 'realist'? In this connection we might note that the mirror in its title is on 'the wheel' not the wall; a rewriting which suggests that questions of identity and representation are an unstoppable, ever-rotating source of anxiety, or pain; so that the individual in reflecting, in looking in and looking out to seek 'my frame' (body/boundary/frame of reference) must constantly consult and resecure itself. Or accept a doubleness (at least): not the self's fixed singularity or simple repetition, but its spinning and relational mobility across a personal life-time and across ages, as between father and son.

Along these lines the tapedeck is a further revolving mirror which the child stares at (possibly learns language from, imitates, quotes, 'retranslates') but which adult and child join in hearing. Bob Dylan's words from a recording in 1965 on the album *Bringing it all Back Home* are heard again or for the first time, but by both listeners in a moment of what might be called settled unlikeness, when 'the same' (the song heard again, the child who looks like the father) and the different are collocated but not compounded ('i see the same anew'). 'Misrecognition', one might say (of the present self mirrored in the past, the adult in the child), is acknowledged and accepted, sensed as a rhyme not a repeat.

These thoughts suggest how we might begin to produce Raworth's poem as a postmodernist text: one which encorporates and rewrites 'non-poetic' popular idioms, which explores the making and unmaking of the self, which raises questions of realism and representation. It is a poem, one could say, which problematises the experiential base and assumptions of the lyric, while retaining its characteristic shape and reflective mode (from an opening question to a final resolution), its referential language and concern with subjectivity. I have suggested, too, in a cursory way how we might gloss and interweave these concerns with readings in literary and poststructuralist theory.

There is the obvious danger of course of suggesting that this poem is typical. Certainly other poems in *tottering state* are in a now close, now distant dialogue with this text: in image; in the volume's persistent concern with self-division, the 'dopple effect' as one poem terms it, and the allied process of composition and decomposition, whether of subjectivity, sound, picture, or book; and in the frequently enacted workings and failings of memory. Other later poems particularly, however, ('Ace', 'Writing', 'West Wind', 'Making Marks') are longer, swifter, less experiential and less 'lyric'. One perception moves instantly onto another, as Olson insisted; pulling the reader (if the reader is willing) through a tunnel where words flicker and flash in and out of assonance and sense, where phrases clip and abandon syntax, voices weave in and out of atomised and prosaic statement, the whole structure 'falling forward forever' (212). There is plenitude and thinness all at once as the poems speed by in blocks, wispy fragments and tight columns, driven by Olson's ideas for 'projective verse' ('make it fast', 112), but as much, one feels, by a Rimbaudian distortion of the senses ('all / senses / gone / could go / on for ever', 153), and a Surrealist aesthetics of chance: an avant garde cocktail, coloured finally by the wit and jaunty quips Raworth draws (I think) from generational and class styles in English speech.

Most of all, however, where many poems rock and spin like time machines, 'looking back, looking forward' (130), throwing off ideas, objects and events, or accelerate away from each other, 'Mirror Mirror on the Wheel' comes to a point of relative stability. The immediately previous poem in the volume, 'Patch Patch Patch' ends '"fuck it, finger, this poem *leaks*"' (117), and in the long poem 'Writing' one 'poem' does manifestly leak into so as to generate another, to produce a rhythm and process ('to start a line') along which a leaking, disjointed, tottering narrative can be balanced. This self-generating production does not create the walled-in humming object of symbolist dreams, but a precarious, questing structure set precisely against closure; against the 'fused image' at which the imagination beats (226–7); against 'an unlimited / closed system / a flooded market' (206). Nor does this concerted and contestatory openness on a number of fronts simply confirm Raworth's poetry as postmodernist; it shows us rather what a particular kind of postmodernist text will be like.

'Mirror Mirror on the Wheel' is therefore something of an exception. Its opening question finds an answer though this is not an affirmation of personal love or the unified self, but of time, the dimension through which the self discovers its relational, differentiated identity. The poem's final line 'i see the same anew' also gives a particular, again affirmative, inflection to the key modernist dictum of 'making strange' or defamiliarisation. Indeed, the formalist or more worldly orientations of different modernist and avant garde tendencies could be mapped through the theory and practice of this device. It is sometimes argued also that estrangement has become exploited and itself familiarised in postmodern culture, to the point when anything, however 'strange', can be absorbed, and recycled, made new now. On this reckoning, modernism and the avant garde have been robbed of their central aesthetic/political device and any oppositional cultural politics in the postmodern period is exposed to compromise.

'how i see / is alien' writes Raworth (194). His 'endless words' present an apparently frictionless verbal anarchy and disorienting, indulgent incompleteness in tune and in time with this world. Yet the speed and attack of his verse, as it beats against the doors of closed verse and the closed system of a flooded market, suggests something else. His work moves along a double dimension, fittingly, of political implication and engagement. Firstly, along an 'interior' course, it runs the risk of decreated subjectivity, of the links and lapses between word and thought and object, memory and perception, enacting a politics of representation. Secondly, it gathers what speed and power it can to rival and outpace the spinning but closed circuits of finance capital and conformity; the money [that] circulates / too fast to see' (236), 'the state as / the status / quo' (213). Unlike the American $L=A=N=G=U=A=G=E$ poets, Raworth's verse does not shy away from reference but touches down, to pick up, reshuffle and push against the world of dominant forms and meanings. Like a saw mill his spinning wheels have teeth.

In another, equally political, but apparently 'unpostmodern' aspect, Raworth's later verse also attempts to reinvent and reshape narrative. In the essay 'Projective Verse', Charles Olson was interested in the methods and energies of 'composition by field' and in the 'stance towards the reality outside a poem', 'what that stance does, both to the poet and to his reader', and in the possibilities it held for 'larger forms', for an epic verse which would 'carry much larger material'.[7] In the poem 'Tracking (notes)' Raworth raises this question again in a full awareness of changed narrative conventions and possibilities:

> the connections (or connectives) no longer work – so how to build the long poem everyone is straining for? (the synopsis is enough for a quick mind now (result of film?) you can't pad out the book) (a feature film with multiple branches: you'd never know which version you were going to see (91)

After thoughts on the dialectic of past and present, injunctions to 'stay open / to your time . . . follow life / stay on the wheel' this poem ends with the drawing of a moving circle whose arrowed circumference labelled 'inside' and 'outside' contains at its centre the words 'image/blur'.

This sketch of the moving and therefore blurred image (of the self?), alternating inside and out (the poem and poet and his times); in short a drawing of the mirror on the wheel, is an image of Raworth's verse and of his solution, I suggest, to the question of the long poem. The fruits of this appear under a new narrative dispensation, employing cuts, flash backs and flash forwards, montage, synopsis, and multiple branches of the inner 'personal' and the outer 'public' worlds, in the poem 'West Wind'.

In 'West Wind', 'considering time / as two dimensions' memories move along the channel that brings a mother to hospital, and athwart the condemned public spectacle of a 'colourless nation' at war (the Falklands). The pain and failing connections of the first are set against the 'false tears' and false unities of the second; 'a nation with no pain' wrapped in the ideology of 'our former glory'. The political attitudes here are unmistakable, if fleeting: 'a president / with an autocue / "the book stops here" / pronounces / the ability / to use money / to effect a legal bribe' and 'the poor / said handbag / are lucky to be alive / breathing my air / contributing nothing to profit'. Worldly reference and narrative are obvious. Nor does this – though I hinted it above – make the poem 'unpostmodern', for neither Derrida nor Lyotard suggest that reference or narrative are expunged in the present. Rather, that older assumptions and forms are in crisis and therefore problematised. Lyotard's argument is that a leading feature of the postmodern era will be the supersession of the delegitimised 'grand narratives' of bourgeois society by 'petit narratives', and that these will be local, fragile, temporary and unsure of their ground. Raworth's longer poems not only bear this out but show how such mini-narratives may be montaged together, in a reversible rather than linear sequence, in the same gesture that time's disjunctures and uncertainties are inscribed rather than smoothed away. As a result there are (will be) moments in individual poems and in the broken and branched, disjointed, narratives of *tottering state* when things, memories, selves and others are joined. 'Mirror Mirror on the Wheel' I think presents one such moment.

It remains to confirm that the above is a reading of Raworth and of postmodernism, a double construction which sees both as problematising rather than holding to set positions; as having moved beyond the unities of subject, art and culture, and beyond the binaries which have characterised descriptions of both modernism and postmodernism. Opposed terms (self and other, signifier and signified, narrative and anti-narrative, etc., etc.) are precisely what are negotiated and sometimes directly politicised (i.e. power/poverty) in Raworth's poems as the very condition of their risks and discoveries. And losses, for the later poems chance both their materials and readers. If we in general accept such an account, however, one which sees the postmodernism of Raworth's verse as lying in its explorations 'midway between stations / fading in and out' (227), then we see too that the reader must risk him/herself in the production of meanings, however scattered and provisional.

Other readers would read Raworth and postmodernism differently. Of course. It might also be thought that the deconstructive aspect of postmodernism should be applied directly to criticism itself. Thus the arguments I have made above could be presented differently; in a collage of quotations and citations from the poems and elsewhere, with or without comment, so as to unsettle distinctions between criticism, theory and poetry in a more open and less directive text (without its conventional invocations of 'the reader', 'I', 'one', 'we'). And this might be thought to be more postmodernist because more internal to postmodernism's procedures. To be 'inside', however (and there is the profound complication that postmodernism itself occurs inside the developments of postmodern, late capitalist society), is not to be 'mid-way', a position which I believe finally gives (this) postmodernism the political purchase it has. For criticism, as for theory and art, this is the politics of problematisation, of self-conscious demonstration, of 'putting into crisis'.

NOTES

1. F.R. Leavis, *New Bearings in English Poetry* (Penguin, London, 1963), p. 177.
2. Charles Olson, *The Special View of History*, edited and introduced by Ann Charters (Oyez, Berkeley, California, 1970), pp. 33, 47.
3. Charles Olson 'The Present Is Prologue' in George F. Butterick (ed.), *Additional Prose* (Four Seasons Foundation, Bolinas, California, 1974), pp. 39–40.
4. Marjorie Perloff, *The Dance of the Intellect. Studies in the Poetry of the Pound Tradition* (Cambridge University Press, Cambridge, 1985), pp. 181, 234.
5. Tom Raworth, *tottering state* (Paladin, London, 1988), p. 118. Further references to Raworth's verse are given by page numbers to this volume.
6. John Berger, *Ways of Seeing* (Penguin, London, 1972), p. 47.
7. Charles Olson 'Projective Verse' in James Scully (ed.), *Modern Poets on Modern Poetry* (Collins, London, 1966), pp. 280, 271, 282.

Chapter 14

'In the Wake of Home'

Adrienne Rich's politics and poetics of location

Harriet Davidson

> the best world is the body's world
> filled with creatures   filled with dread
> misshapen so   yet the best we have
> our raft among the abstract worlds
> Adrienne Rich, 'Contradictions: Tracking Poems'

The title of Adrienne Rich's 1986 collection of poetry *Your Native Land, Your Life*[1] seems an oddly conservative one for this radical feminist, known more for her fierce deconstruction of the domestic than for her embrace of the native land. But the echo of writings on colonialism and imperialism, particularly Aimé Césaire's *Return to My Native Land* (1938),[2] indicates a turn and a return of her own in Rich's thought. While feminism has been a primary force in Rich's writings, at least since her 1961 'Snapshots of a Daughter-in-Law', Rich has also written with passion about other political issues, especially the violence of imperialism during the Vietnam era. Her feminism has always been driven by issues of power and politics more than female essentialism, though she is widely misinterpreted as an essentialist and 'ideologue' by those wanting to dismiss her disturbing and accusatory work.

Only in the 1980s has feminism broadened to embrace the concerns about imperialism that Rich signals in her powerful poems of the late 1960s such as 'The Burning of Paper Instead of Children', 'Shooting Script', or 'Ghazals: Homage to Galib'. Rich's work now joins that of other feminist theorists in trying to understand the subject not only in terms of gender, but also in terms of race, class, ethnicity, and sexual preference. Under the critique of post-structuralism and of those women who felt excluded by feminism in the 1970s – third world women, women of colour, lesbian women, working class women – the international and universalist claims of feminism have come to seem one more argument in the logic of dominance, an imperialism of its own. Rich now turns to an examination of her own roots, to the vision circumscribed by her life as an upper middle-class white American, a southerner, a Jew, and, of course, a woman, to find the points of her own complicity with and resistance to oppression.

The move away from what Lyotard labels the meta-narrative to the local narrative is common to much postmodern as well as feminist thought. The subject as complexly contextual, positioned, and inescapably located challenges the possibility of the subject's critical stance of outsider. But this situation seemingly enmeshes the subject in webs of determinism that present a dilemma about the efficacy of personal agency and collective action, a dilemma that feminism as a political movement must address. Many feminists have responded by deepening the materialist analysis, finding that the situated subject is necessarily a complex, changing, and non-unified one, thus perhaps loosening determinism's grip. As Chantal Mouffe writes: 'It is not a question of moving from a "unitary unencumbered self" to a "unitary situated self"; the problem is with the very idea of the unitary subject. . . . But we are in fact always multiple and contradictory subjects, inhabitants of a diversity of communities . . ., constructed by a variety of discourses and precariously and temporarily sutured at the intersection of those subject positions.'[3] Returning agency to a subject both situated and contradictory, as well as rethinking the binary oppositions of community and difference, the proper and the improper, the inside and the outside, are the key issues at work in a series of feminist and postmodern theoretical works, such as Judith Butler's *Gender Trouble*, Paul Smith's *Discerning the Subject*, the essays in the collection *Feminism/Postmodernism* and the work of Biddy Martin and Chandra Mohanty, especially their joint essay 'Feminist Politics: What's Home Got to Do With It'.[4]

Rich's recent poetry and prose engages these philosophical debates, making the feminist gesture of bringing these debates back home, so to speak, to the material instance of this country, this family, this historical moment, this particular place where one is from. As Rich writes in the 1984 essay 'Notes Toward a Politics of Location' from *Blood, Bread and Poetry*,[5] her meditations on her roots and her home are part of a larger project of, '[r]ecognizing our location, having to name the ground we're coming from, the conditions we have taken for granted' (219). Location, for Rich, involves more than a merely physical spot; a ground is also discursive, so that, for instance, she must understand 'the meaning of my whiteness as a point of location for which I needed to take responsibility' (219). But if location implies discursive communities, it also implies difference and contradiction in its emphasis on the material particularity of life; this place and this time are always singular, always changing. Location, for Rich, becomes a way to think community and difference simultaneously.

This rethinking of location has significant consequences for feminism. Rich reorients her politics away from a 'form of feminism so focused on male evil and female victimization that it, too, allows for no differences among women, men, places, times, cultures, conditions, classes, movements' (221). The recognition of 'difference', so charged in current theoretical debates, becomes for Rich a primary goal, disrupting the simple binary male/female that she now compares to a cold war mentality: 'Living in the climate of an enormous either/or, we absorb some of it unless we actively take heed' (221). Rich's admonition to 'actively take heed' is a firm assertion of consciousness and agency, which sits uncomfortably with her desire to deconstruct the either/or, the difficulty of which is indicated by her meteorological metaphor. Can we escape the climate? The deconstruction of the binary has, for many theorists, a perilous effect on our understanding of consciousness itself, shaped as it is by that climate of binary oppositions. If there is one debate now uniting much theoretical inquiry in feminism and postmodernism about the subject, it is just this one: how can we undo our climate, unweave the very fabric of our consciousness without giving up the human agency it carries? In spite of the clear political intent of Rich's work, her position entails a certain amount of contradiction, ambivalence, and even confusion. Difference threatens to disrupt the political basis for action: 'You cannot speak for me. I cannot speak for us. Two thoughts: there is no liberation that only knows how to say "I"; there is no collective movement that speaks for each of us all the way through' (224). The unanswerable question with which she ends her essay (as she uses questions to end so many poems) is 'Who is *we*?' (231).

Rich's poetic analysis of home finds her, as she says in the title of a 1983 poem from *Your Native Land, Your Life*, 'In the Wake of Home': neither at home, nor free from it. This poem takes the very literal notion of home, the family house, as a physical and psychic presence as well as absence and works toward an analysis of home as a politically defined place. Rich's poem maintains a finely balanced ambivalence about home – about what it is versus what we imagine it to be, about how it both is and is not what we are, about home as a private and public space. Home becomes the site of a complicated struggle between the desire to return to a place of sheltered belonging and the desire to leave oppressive social structures. Rich would find a middle way between the determined home and indeterminate flight, challenging not only her own early images of escape from home (as in her 1961 'The Roofwalker' or 1965 'Orion'), but also a complacent acceptance of and security in the world. This project affects her poetics as she struggles with an old problem of art and politics: the choice between formal disruption (non-participation in discourse) and normative communication. Her choice has always been for the latter, even when she was convinced of the modernist premises of the former: 'this is the oppressor's language // yet I need it to talk to you', she writes in 1968 (*Fact*, 117). Now, she is less willing to give the house of language over to the oppressor, just as she is less willing to imagine female utopias. Her poetry engages a complex task – to indicate the sense belonging to a certain culture and also to disrupt the sense of that culture or that self as unitary, all the while maintaining her sense of political and ethical purpose.

As the poem begins, Rich introduces the idea of home as narrative coherence only to undermine it with disjunction and absence, the loss of the plenitude of meaning in the material particularity of life and language. The first section of eleven numbered sections sets out the simplest of visions:

> You sleep in a room with bluegreen curtains
> poster   a pile of animals on the bed
> A woman and man who love you
> and each other   slip the door ajar
> you are almost asleep   they crouch in turn
> to stroke your hair   you never wake
>
> This happens every night for years.
> This never happened. (section 1)

Rich's evocation of 'normality', the happy nuclear family, is disturbed both narratively and typographically. The jarring narrative contradiction of the final couplet is shadowed by the slight disjunction between 'you are almost asleep' and 'you never wake', making the vision waver between reality and dream. The night-time quiet of the scene, almost motionless as a repeated act, shifts under the pressure of the last line into a death-like stillness. The voice slips uneasily from an indirect first-person 'you' to an objective second-person, a slippage that occurs throughout the poem until the firm assertion of the speaking 'I' in the penultimate section.

The disturbance is reinforced by the material aspects of the verse. The poem begins with an irregular pentameter line, which shifts from an opening iamb into a trochaic beat. Institutionally trained ears settle into this rhythm comfortably – it is a familiar room – and the predominance of muted speech rhythms foregrounds the narrative and descriptive aspects of language. But in subsequent lines the excessive spacing between some grammatical units disturbs the standardised narrative flow, much as line-breaks do, dislodging the images from a secure metonymic world, adding to a sense of unreality, of the non-referential, disturbing the coherence of narrative stories. The spacing introduces what we might call additional moments of production into the consumable surface of the poem: like free verse line-breaks, the spaces point to Rich's production of the poem and require of us that we produce meaning, apart from the narrative meaning so easily available, to justify those gaps. The gaps emphasise the material nature of the poem, its typographical construction on the page, gently undermining the plenitude and easy reference of narrative. Rich's low-keyed way of drawing attention to the constructed nature of an ideal vision will escalate as the poem progressively implicates the historical and political forces surrounding this vision, as well as the forces of accident and chance which disturb any form of wholeness.

The mirroring of 'This' in the final couplet also draws attention to the thinginess of the word, further confusing the already ambiguous reference of 'this'. How much is gathered into the net of 'this'? Only the final not waking? The actions of the woman and man? Or the particular bluegreen curtains themselves? Without clear contextual cues, the reference of the ostensive 'this' blurs and the material nature of the word is foregrounded. The material rather than the meaning of language is also reinforced by the use of the homonyms of 'wake', used as a noun in the title to indicate a path or track made by something, as in the wake of a boat, but used in this section as the verb, to wake up. A third use of 'wake' is suggested as the poem dwells more and more on what is not there, what is absent, abandoned, or lost, as the poem becomes home's funereal 'wake'. The scandal of the homonym for Aristotle is that it disturbs referential meaning, pointing to the accidental, faulty nature of language, and making it necessary to rely on context for meaning. But contexts are unstable and incomplete; Rich would give us both a larger range of determining context and also the unstable field of indeterminate meaning.

Thus, the homonym 'wake' combines the meanings of after-effect, mourning, and coming to consciousness, all of which cluster around and decentre the idea of 'home' by calling our conscious attention to the sources of our nostalgia and loss. 'Nostalgia is only amnesia turned around', Rich writes in 'Turning the Wheel' (*Fact*, 306); it is not a forgetting of the past but an illusory memory. 'Home' in this poem becomes a trace figure, the longing for a plenitude never there, which leaves us despairing, unsatisfied and unable to see the political forces shaping our life.

But the middle-class scene which opens the poem is never fully undermined or erased by the poem. Indeed, many readers have felt uncomfortable with how little Rich disrupts the ground on which middle-class, bourgeois values are built, wishing she would choose a more radical poetics to complement her radical politics. Certainly, Rich has experimented extensively with poetic form throughout her career, fracturing her text by intercutting it with other texts, relying heavily on visual and sound effects to draw her verse forward, and undermining the coherence of her own voice. But she also uses a straightforward discursive voice and eloquently defends the need for communication, even while she reveals this voice to be chosen, constructed, and finally quite tenuous given the fragility of any communal effort: 'Who is we?' The voice of this poem undergoes questioning with the rhetorical moves in section 10. And yet finally the poem does not violently disrupt language, voice, or a shared ground of value. In fact, as the poem moves from adult memories of home to the wrenching image of the homeless child, the opening image of the room as a safe haven from violence counters the more middle-class anger about the repression caused by those middle-class values.

In section two Rich expresses that anger and sense of the repression of home, returning to an old feminist theme of escaping home by echoing one of her Vietnam-era images:

    The family coil   so twisted, tight and loose
    anyone trying to leave
    has to strafe the field
    burn the premises down

The dual meaning of 'premises' again emphasises the physical and psychic doubling of home: home as a place and as a ground for our thinking, both of which we may want to leave. But the desire to 'burn the premises' vies with her need to take responsibility for what goes on within those premises. And the shift to memory in section three indicates the impossibility of leaving home behind.

In sections 3 and 4 the anger toward home is counterpointed with a nostalgic sense of personal loss and existential angst. Yet the personal is quickly dispersed into an historical view, shifting the target of anger:

    The voice that used to call you home
    has gone off on the wind
    . . .
    or maybe the mouth was burnt to ash
    maybe the tongue was torn out
    brownlung has stolen the breath
    or fear has stolen the breath
    maybe under another name
    it sings on AM radio
    And if you knew, what would you know? (section 4)

The voice of the parent and all that the parent may metaphorically represent is taken away from the child's limited perspective and placed in a larger culture with its history of violence and uncaring. And what has been a 'secure' knowledge of personal loss becomes an uncertain knowledge of the many webs of history and society around us, webs too complex, perhaps, to know. The strange transposition of the voice into the popular song on the radio is one more dispersion of a unitary personal voice into a fragmented cultural one, but this voice of popular culture warns against the too easy answers of either a personal or a structural epistemology.

Still, Rich acknowledges the will to home, as a safe haven, a plenitude where 'fathers mothers and children / the ones you were promised would all be there' (section 9), where 'once at least it was all in order / and nobody came to grief' (section 5). But this rage for order reveals itself as Thanatos:

> But you will be drawn to places
> where generations lie
> side by side with each other:
> fathers, mothers and children
> in the family prayerbook
> or the country burying-ground
> You will hack your way through the bush
> to the *Jodensavanne*
> where the gravestones are black with mould (section 5)

Again, the safe haven is revealed as a deceptive memory, an erasing of difference and struggle in the graveyard. The curious journey to the Jodensavanne deepens and historicises her analysis once again. As in so many Rich poems, an endnote fills in the historical fact: 'The Jodensavanne is an abandoned Jewish settlement in Surinam whose ruins exist in a jungle on the Casipoera River.' Rich's search for her own partially erased Jewish roots turns up a failed community venture, one connected with the colonising of South America (Surinam is Dutch Guinea) and also eerily connected by its proximity to Guyana to a contemporary site of community and death, Jonestown. The search for community and order melds uncomfortably with the homes we want to deny:

> you will want to believe that nobody
> wandered off   became strange
> no woman dropped her baby and ran
> no father took off for the hills
> no axe splintered the door (section 5)

These histories underlie the stories we want to tell; they are also, inevitably, a result of those grand narrative drives for wholeness, coherence, and order.

The narratives of order are disrupted by both existential loss in time and the historical uncaring visited by society upon the fragile home. But the disruption is also something less easily defined, something that retreats from understanding. The sense of loss is intensified by an absence of conceptual wholeness caused by the singularity of your location. The self as an identity or an idea is shaken by the reminder – as the colloquial phrase puts it – of how much of us is there. Our material being and the webs of culture and society which ensnare us interfere with our ability to see ourselves as self-made or transcendent: material difference must disrupt the community of home. In section 6, the centre of eleven sections, Rich turns to that material particularity and finds the ambiguity of presence and absence. Absence remains an undefined disturbance in the knowledge of belonging that home suggests:

> Anytime you go back
> where absence began
> the kitchen faucet sticks in a way you know
> you have to pull the basement door
> in before drawing the bolt
> the last porch-step is still loose
> the water from the tap
> is the old drink of water
> Anytime you go back
> the familiar underpulse
> will start its throbbing: *Home, home!*
> and the hole torn and patched over
> will gape unseen again (section 6)

Home is both the wonderfully evoked familiarity of touch, of taste, of the feel of a place, and also the place 'where absence began'. Our sense of belonging in the world, of knowing the world as ours, is both necessary and inescapable. Rich won't deny us that world that we so painfully construct for ourselves, and in fact she wants to direct attention to how tenacious and particular the world is; if the family narrative fails, home still retains its meaning:

> Even where love has run thin
> the child's soul musters strength
> calling on dust motes   song on the radio
> stray cat   piles of autumn leaves
> whatever comes along
> – the rush of purpose to make a life
> worth living past abandonment (section 7)

But this world-making is always a patching over of absence, building a 'tree-house' without a tree' she says in the final section. The image of the hole which 'will gape unseen again' garbles both the visual and the temporal – the obviousness of gaping remains unseen; the unseen, a negative fact that never happened, happens again. This visual and temporal disruption undermines narrative coherence, just as the home is always disrupted by death, difference, singularity, and change. Those excessive particulars of our material connection to home are embedded in history and yet excessive to the historical narratives; they are the contingent material of history and also a wild materiality complicating any discursive community.

The various meditations in sections 1 through 9 establish different and often contradictory perspectives on home, leaving the home as indistinct as the vague 'you' who is the subject of the poem. The attempt to speak to and for the 'you' never quite succeeds in dispelling the sense that 'you' is the speaker's self-address, an undecidability that fractures the coherence of the subject and also questions the possibility of community once again. But in section 10 Rich dramatically shifts tone. Here, she assumes the speaking 'I' for the first time and narrates a sharp-edged political and historical account of 'home' savagely opposed to the peaceful vision of the first section or the complacent dream of 'a porch with rubber-plant and glider' in section 9. This narrative also dispels the dreamy indeterminacy of previous sections:

> What if I told you your home
> is this continent of the homeless
> of children sold   taken by force
> driven from their mothers' land
> killed by their mothers to save from capture
> – this continent of changed names and mixed-up blood
> of languages tabooed
> diasporas unrecorded
> undocumented refugees
> underground railroads   trails of tears
> What if I tell you your home
> is this planet of warworn children
> women and children standing in line or milling
> endlessly calling each others' names
> What if I tell you, you are not different
> it's the family albums that lie
> – will any of this comfort you
> and how should this comfort you? (section 10)

Here where the poem is most blunt, most political, most melodramatic in some ways, Rich deploys a curious rhetorical strategy, repeating

'What if I told you', 'What if I tell you.' Her agency is gathered into the act of telling, fully acknowledged as telling. The self-reflexive acknowledgement points to her own agency in choosing to tell this story; both the voice and the story are her creations. This does not tend to undermine the information; it is a grand visionary meta-narrative of the histories of political violence undergirding the middle-class home, and it convinces by the sheer force of a catalogue of deprivation. But her seizing of political agency in the act of telling has uncertain consequences; indeed, the strength of this discursive voice is belied by the many questions which end this poem. Can the generalising and abstract narrative of the continent of the homeless intersect with our local narratives? The point of her telling is to move us from a personal sense of loss to a social and politicised view, to replace our small existential crises with historical ones. If this teaches us that the inadequacy of home is a political issue, that the personal is political, this may offer some comfort. But if it only replaces the abstraction of the ideal home with the abstraction of general homelessness, Rich wonders where comfort, that property of home, will come from. Will the abstract narrative itself offer a cold comfort? How will we recover those comforting excessive particulars, the body's world, those dust motes and kitchen faucets? Rich does not want the abstraction of political discourse to make us forget that this is what we talk about when we talk about the homeless: the most concrete stuff of our lives, the underpulse throbbing: *home, home!*

So after insisting that we hear this story, she ends the poem, not with the abstract political story, but with a more particularised vision attributed now neither to an 'I' or a 'you' but to the child who inhabits her own memories of home, who may or may not be the same as the child who makes a home 'where love runs thin' or even the homeless child of the preceding section. The turn to the child retains the political force of section 10, while also emphasising the human capacity for home-making:

> The child's soul carries on
> in the wake of home
> . . .
> finding places for everything
> the song   the stray cat   the skeleton
> the child's soul musters strength
> where the holes were torn
> but there are no miracles[.] (section 11)

The poem ends with another question about comfort: 'Who will number the grains of loss / and what would comfort be?' The unresolved question indicates the depth of her ambivalence about home and the difficulty of finding comfort, that most basic product of an ideal home, in a world of the homeless. If comfort seems too domesticated and conservative a goal either for revolutionary change or for a radical deconstructive vision, Rich reminds us that only a domestic vision can number the grains of loss, can see the particular texture of home and know the magnitude of loss.

Rich would change the idea of home from a nostalgic vision hiding political reality to a real, material goal of security and comfort. In the end her poem is unforgivingly blunt. If the materiality of our lives results in a confusing particularity, an undecidable shifting, the same materiality opens us to a quite determinate path. The body's world is what Rich wishes to protect; too often home is the least safe of places, too often the idea of home prevents us from finding the comfort we need. And yet home is also the site of speaking, the place of a shared language and of meaning, the place to find a voice to speak for those who have no home or voice. Rich will not leave home behind, but will keep it as a site of contradiction in a politics of location.

NOTES

1. Adrienne Rich, *Your Native Land, Your Life* (Norton, New York, 1986). Earlier poems by Rich referred to below can be found in *The Fact of a Doorframe: Poems Selected and New: 1950–1984* (Norton, New York, 1984).
2. Aimé Césaire, *Return to My Native Land* (Penguin, Harmondsworth, 1969).
3. Chantal Mouffe, 'Radical Democracy: Modern or Postmodern?', in Andrew Ross (ed.), *Universal Abandon? The Politics of Postmodernism* (University of Minnesota Press, Minneapolis, 1988), p. 44.
4. Judith Butler, *Gender Trouble: Feminism and the Subversion of Identity* (Routledge, New York, 1990); Paul Smith (ed.), *Discerning the Subject* (University of Minnesota Press, Minneapolis, 1988); Linda Nicholson (ed.), *Feminism/Postmodernism* (Routledge, New York, 1990); Biddy Martin and Chandra Mohanty, 'Feminist Politics: What's Home Got to Do With It?', in Teresa de Lauretis (ed.), *Feminist Studies/Critical Studies* (Indiana University Press, Bloomington, 1986).
5. Adrienne Rich, *Blood, Bread and Poetry: Selected Prose 1979–1985* (Norton, New York, 1986).

Chapter 15

Adrienne Rich

Consciousness raising as poetic method

Helen M. Dennis

for Sarah Barclay, Diana Basham, and Hanne Bramness

> I think that every feminist poet must long – I do – for real criticism of
> her work – not just descriptive, but analytic criticism which takes her
> language and images seriously enough to question them . . . I also need
> to know when in my work I am merely doing well what I know well
> how to do and when I am avoiding certain expressive risks. And while
> I can count on friends for some of this, it would be better for all feminist
> writers if such principled criticism were to come also from strangers – it
> would broaden the field in which we are working. (Adrienne Rich,
> 'Toward a More Feminist Criticism', *Blood, Bread and Poetry: Selected Prose
> 1978–1985* (London: Virago, 1987), p. 91)

Working, as I do, within the Academy, there is an institutional
imperative to be categorised and labelled. Therefore, I am an Anglo-
American gynocritic: I prefer to pronounce it with a hard 'g'. Despite
the hardness, I would define the gynocritic as she who is motivated
by love rather than hatred.[1] But love of female-author texts is
sometimes fuelled by hatred of patriarchal institutions and by female
anger. The gynocritic seeks to define an alternative, woman-centred
tradition of women's writing. She seeks out the literary foremothers;
she traces the continuities and relationships between women authors;
she establishes a descriptive account of recurrent themes in women's
writing which narrate women's experience, and she attempts to
validate and prioritise those aspects of, or perceptions of, women's
experience which appear to her and other women to have been
marginalised or neglected by the conventional, masculinist literary
traditions.

Within the Academy the Anglo-American gynocritic is characterised
as being intellectually naïve and unsophisticated, exhibiting all the
deficiencies of American pragmatism. She believes, erroneously, that
literary texts are transparent, and that there is some direct relation
between literature and life.[2] Beyond the Academy she is accused of
talking an irrelevant, oversophisticated and overspecialised language

that is more concerned to impress her colleagues and peers than to contribute actively to the ongoing struggles of the women's movement.[3] Put crudely, where do her allegiances lie: with literary theory or with women's lives?

In her own work, Adrienne Rich has confronted and resolved this dichotomy into a radical feminist cultural continuum. She is both a poet and a feminist critic. There is an interesting cross-fertilisation between these two literary modes in her work. Her poetry is informed by strategic feminist analysis and conceptualisation; her prose uses the strategies of confessional poetry to make connections between the autobiographical or 'personal' and the public, cultural arena, i.e. the 'political'.[4] This cultural practice has been arrived at by living through an era that has been as traumatic for the United States of America as any in its history. The resurgence of the women's movement in the 1960s and 1970s after the concerted effort in the 1950s to keep American women in the home; the disastrous practice of cold war politics; the military interventions in Korea and Vietnam; the growing awareness of encroaching complex ecological catastrophe; the acceleration of the nuclear arms race; the struggle for real political, social and economic equality by Afro-Americans and other ethnic minority groups: all these 'historical' scenarios have impacted variously upon individual Americans' lives. It can be argued that it is particularly the case with American women that political, 'public' events and conditions are registered on the private, personal self. The traumatic division of human functions and aspects into gender-specific roles, originating from the industrial revolution, has not yet been fully healed. Women are still more likely to experience cultural events in 'trivial', domestic situations. Woman still belongs chiefly, although not exclusively, to the domestic sphere.

By keeping an accurate register of her personal autobiographical and intellectual development, Rich has laid down a record of the changes in consciousness which have occurred for WASP women in the past forty years. (I am aware that WASP no longer refers to that which it denotes, i.e. White Anglo-Saxon Protestant, but rather, to the North-Eastern élitist culture that claims Rich despite her Jewish background).

The key, operative term here is 'consciousness raising': the process whereby individual women met together to scrutinise and reappraise their so-called 'personal' experience and to develop a discourse of political criticism to account for the underlying social, political and economic forces which led to its specific formation. Hence the individual and personal history became situated in a larger political 'herstory', and a thoroughgoing critique of patriarchal hegemony ensued. Two definitions will, hopefully, indicate why I believe consciousness raising to be so important for an understanding of Adrienne Rich's poetry.

> Once grasped at a general level ideas become like a kind of shorthand in our consciousness. But it is one thing to encounter a concept, quite another to understand it. In order to understand a general idea like hegemony it is necessary first to perceive in a whole series of separate moments how this has affected you. Then those moments have to be communicated. This is part of the total process of female self-recognition. It is the way through which we start to make our own language, and discover our own reflections. (Sheila Rowbotham, *Woman's Consciousness, Man's World*, 1973, p. 39)

> Feminism is the first theory to emerge from those whose interest it affirms. Its method recapitulates as theory the reality it seeks to capture. As Marxist method is dialectical materialism, feminist method is consciousness raising: the collective critical reconstitution of the meaning of women's social experience, as women live through it. (MacKinnon, 'Feminism, Marxism, Method and the State', O. Keohane, Rosaldo and Gelpi, *Feminist Theory: A Critique of Ideology*, 1982, p. 29)

Consciousness raising is both the romantic poet's conventional activity: self-reflection, recollection in relative tranquillity, the urge to order the random chaos of the transient; and at the same time it is the political method of an activist in a Women's Movement which is engaged in the struggle for socio-economic change and socio-political liberation.

Within Adrienne Rich's own poetic career there have been several phases in this consciousness-raising process:

1. Before her consciousness was raised Rich worked in a formalist, masculinist tradition. Female experience was marginalised, unnamed, suppressed and submerged – but one can still identify various tensions and unconsciously subversive strategies at work in the texts.
2. The tensions emerge – she is aware that she has learnt to speak a strange, alien, oppressive language which also controls her experience of her self in the world and of the world – not least the world of sexual politics.
3. She raises consciousness by naming this condition of inhabiting the oppressor's language. Definition of the problem is in itself an important stage in the process of revision. (This phase corresponds roughly to the theoretical work on women and language undertaken in the late 1970s, for example by Dale Spender in *Man-Made Language*.) The naming is accompanied by a shift towards

gynocentric texts – formal aspects, imaginative content, emotional and ideological expression are increasing overtly from female experience.

4. The next stage is a conscious experiment in reinventing a woman's/ feminist aesthetic – in *The Dream of a Common Language*. There she has moved right away from handling the problem with the asbestos gloves of masculinist formalism to a new immediacy and an emotive tenderness which is accompanied by the intellectual lucidity of the feminist voice, which seems to me to be quite *different* in kind from the early mode of 'intellectuality'.

5. The stage beyond is exemplified by *A Wild Patience has Taken me this Far* – where she consolidates the achievements of a woman-centred, woman identified work and world, to include, for example, foremothers in history and overtly lesbian love poems, as well as a radical feminist concern for ecology.

6. A further move is evidenced by her work of the past half-dozen years, to transcend the merely gynocentric, and to confront other, sometimes distinctly uncomfortable, issues. One of the most moving and honest poems of her recent work is to me the sequence, *Sources* (1983), which addresses those aspects of her past which ill-fitted the public persona of radical lesbian feminist: the Jewishness, which had remained muted for so long, and the formative relationships with her father and with her suicided husband.

Adrienne Rich has been writing and publishing poetry for forty years. In that time she has made the transition from a representative woman of twentieth-century American patriarchal culture whose 'female destiny' was decided for her, to a consciously radical feminist poet; from a dutiful daughter imitating the father's forms, to a women-centred woman renaming the world from the female perspective on the world and from the specificities of a white, American middle-class woman's experience of herself in the world.[5]

In 'When We Dead Awaken: Writing as Re-Vision' (1971), she reviews her career and the early stages when she experienced the split between woman as wife and mother, isolated in domesticity and with material responsibilities that put constant demands on time, energy, creative space – and required a type of traditional conservatism – and woman as writer, publishing 'successfully' and being received with approval by male reviewers for the 'gracefulness' of her work. And yet she felt a failure in both roles – experiencing an inauthenticity that she did not yet have the language and conceptual apparatus to define.

At the time (late 1950s early 1960s) – contemporary with *A Change of World* (1951) and *The Diamond Cutters* (1955) but before *Snapshot of a Daughter-in-Law* (1963), she wrote in her journal:

> Paralyzed by the sense that there exists a mesh of relationships – e.g., between my anger at the children, my sensual life, pacifism, sex (I mean sex in its broadest significance, not merely sexual desire) – an interconnectedness, which, *if I could see it, make it valid* would give me back myself, make it possible to function lucidly and passionately. Yet I grope in and out among these dark webs. (*On Lies, Secrets and Silence*, p. 44 (my emphasis))

Part of the problem had to do with her conception of what poetry should be: 'I had been taught that poetry should be universal, which meant, of course, nonfemale.' (Ibid.) And in the first two volumes one can see how well as an 'exceptional woman' she had learnt her lessons. Robert Frost is a dominant influence in monologues such as 'Autumn Equinox' and 'The Perennial Answer'. Dylan Thomas, Donne, Auden, MacNiece, Stevens, Yeats, are other acknowledged masters. What she learnt from them was elegance, formality, objectivity and distance, a certain allusive complexity coupled with a neat and graceful style. And yet the poems contain an alternative, woman's consciousness – *contain* being the operative word. Here I will consider an example of this where woman is confined to the domestic sphere, and where the 'foremother' provides a negative role-model for the present generation of women, namely, 'Aunt Jennifer's Tigers'.

Aunt Jennifer's Tigers

Aunt Jennifer's tigers prance across a screen,
Bright topaz denizens of a world of green.
They do not fear the men beneath the tree;
They pace in sleek chivalric certainty.

Aunt Jennifer's fingers fluttering through her wool
Find even the ivory needle hard to pull.
The massive weight of Uncle's wedding band
Sits heavily upon Aunt Jennifer's hand.

When Aunt is dead, her terrified hands will lie
Still ringed with ordeals she was mastered by.
The tigers in the panel that she made
Will go on prancing, proud and unafraid.

In three quatrains rhyming a,a,b,b; the poem is arguably influenced by Auden, although one can also perceive some Emily Dickinson influence in the poised sense of wit and paradox, but without the sinuous eccentricity of Dickinson's prosody. Rich's verse *form* holds no surprises and is perfectly balanced. The grammatical construction is contained by, or subsumed into, the formal requirements of the verse. The images and metaphors are slightly more startling and arresting. But the mode – or paradox – is both aware of the contradictions and apparently detached, disengaged from the female predicament that is stated. There is no exploration of the poet's own psychic geography in her treatment of the split.

The paradox in stanza one is understated. The image is of wild, free, savage creatures – unafraid of men – and 'in sleek chivalric certainty'. A male world order is invoked in relation to the tigers, although they actually stand for 'the world of green', i.e. nature (associated with women), or the world of tapestry – a woman's craft traditionally. Which is to say that Aunt Jennifer's tapestry 'screen' projects an image of her psyche as wild, free, unafraid – a creature that terrorises men – expressed in terms of a masculinist 'chivalric' code, and the language, e.g. 'Bright topaz denizens', reflects that notion of masculinist artefact. Yet this is a female craft – which is contained within the domestic sphere, and which contains the woman within the domestic realm. This aspect is expanded in stanza two, where the domestic is the material experience of marriage as patriarchal institution. The *image* of her tigers is merely that, an illusion – or even a delusion. It is produced at a cost – the cost is a woman's life-energies:

> Aunt Jennifer's fingers fluttering through her wool
> Find even the ivory needle hard to pull.

The alliteration on 'f' sets a light tone, which is then undermined – from 'even' to the end of the couplet. The 'ivory needle' still connotes the jungle and its produce – but the exotic freedom is subverted by the notion of the transformation of an elephant tusk into a commodity which has a part to play in women's servitude to domestic duties. The 'tigers prance' – but the fingers which produce them don't. They appear to 'flutter'. Yet this is not an image of lively freedom but of encroaching old age and loss of vitality; 'hard to pull' is the key, telling phrase. The next two lines make this explicit:

> The massive weight of Uncle's wedding band
> Sits heavily upon Aunt Jennifer's hand.

The rhymes, too, are masculine and heavy. The adjective – 'massive' and adverb – 'heavily', seem disproportionate if considered merely physically – but evidently there is a metaphysic present and expressed through this emblem, which is after all the most important symbol in most women's lives.

In stanza three – the 'fingers fluttering' are given a further and shocking explanation. They were 'terrified hands' – and the wedding ring weighed so heavy because it symbolised 'the ordeals she was mastered by'. The language here is both figurative, allusive and immediately explicit, hanging on the use of the verb 'ringed'. Aunt Jennifer was *terrified* and *mastered* by Uncle, through the institution of marriage – or by the institution of marriage through the particular agency of Uncle. The content is a strong prefiguration of Rich's radical feminist analysis. But the paradox, the tension is not allowed to explode the form. The poem ends with the paradox it began with, which is a substitute for an actual resolution:

> The tigers in the panel that she made
> Will go on prancing, proud and unafraid.

In a condition of oppression the psyche seeks imaginative compensation without changing the actual conditions of oppression. Aunt Jennifer's free spirit is expressed in her tapestry tigers, but that doesn't break the institutional bonds of wedlock. She is contained in the patriarchal institution and ideology, just as the tigers are contained in the screen or panel. And of course my implication is that Rich's awareness of the predicament and exposition of it is equally contained in a patriarchal verse form which is successful according to a masculinist preoccupation with style and formal considerations; but from a feminist point of view is a failure – it doesn't rock the boat or challenge assumptions – it doesn't channel the anger. The poet does not talk about herself – does not locate the political problem in her own experience; rather, she distances it. In her own words, she handles this hot material with 'asbestos gloves'. She makes it refer to an aunt – from a previous generation – hence the implication that this is no longer our problem.

One further example, 'For the Conjunction of Two Planets' is from the same collection, and is another poem which operates within the masculinist, formal tradition, and which seems to accept and use uncritically patriarchal conceptions and values. It also contains, still submerged and unrealised, a range of specifically female emotions, perceptions and stances, which unconsciously subvert the formal and thematic structure.

> For the Conjunction of Two Planets
>
> We smile at astrological hopes
> And leave the sky to expert men
> Who do not reckon horoscopes
> But painfully extend their ken
> In mathematical debate
> With slide and photographic plate.

> And yet, protest it if we will,
> Some corner of the mind retains
> The medieval man, who still
> Keeps watch upon those starry skeins
> And drives us out of doors at night
> To gaze at anagrams of light.
>
> Whatever register or law
> Is drawn in digits for these two,
> Venus and Jupiter keep their awe,
> Wardens of brilliance, as they do
> Their dual circuit of the west –
> The brightest planet and her guest.
>
> Is any light so proudly thrust
> From darkness on our lifted faces
> A sign of something we can trust,
> Or is it that in starry places
> We see the things we long to see
> In fiery iconography?

The poem reads to me like a lesson well learnt, but repeated somewhat hollowly. And yet it enacts a basic binary conceptual system – which goes something like:

light	dark
Expert men	Medieval man
Science	Superstition
Modern astronomy	Medieval astrology
Scientific, rational fact	Hope, emotion
Proved certainties	the seeking of symbols for human relations

Again the language is poised – and distanced by the impersonal 'we'. The searching for symbols in the stars is also a way of distancing the discussion about human love and sexual attraction. And, furthermore, the poem is trapped in a very traditional view of gender-roles and heterosexual love. This is supposedly about the personal and intimate experience of man and woman, but it is quite impersonal and 'out there'. The poet as woman/lover is functioning in myths of heterosexual roles that don't fit – there is nothing *from woman's experience* here – and the assertion of the importance of hope, aspiration, emotion, desire is framed as a question. The verse form reflects Rich's questioning perplexities and unease, while she is apparently completely at home in this phallocentric mode:

> Is any light so proudly thrust
> From darkness on our lifted faces
> A sign of something we can trust,

> Or is it that in starry places
> We see the things we long to see
> In fiery iconography?

To me the uneasiness is apparent in the extremely stylised images or 'emblems' of male and female roles, namely Jupiter and Venus. These emblems for human experience seem remote, somewhat static, not moved and informed by human emotion. This reflects a discontinuity between the sexual role culturally ascribed to men and women and how they are inhabited – or not. One could say that the poem is about 'sex in its broadest significance – not merely sexual desire' – for it is about 'expert men' and whatever it is that women stand for in relation to them – here the pressure is to go along with the experts – and about the traditional cultural image of woman as Venus – but even this is experienced somewhat cerebrally. This woman poet can only set against the modern, scientific masculinist ideology an older masculinist ideology, but one which is still phallocentric – the medieval man in our mind.

The awkwardness extends to her deployment of grammatical gender, which is a reflection of these cultural gender-specific roles. The 'we' is neutral and inclusive – presumably the 'expert men' and 'the medieval men' are similarly 'universal'. 'The medieval man . . . drives us out of doors at night / To gaze at anagrams of light' – not woman experiencing her own specifically female desire, but a cultural psychodrama she has inherited and internalised, though obviously not adequately enough, is pushing her to stare at this puzzle and work it out. Venus and Jupiter still have more power and force as cultural signifiers than as scientific 'facts', and a women's experience is forced to conform to these value-laden emblems. Yet the last line of stanza three is somehow shocking and subtly subversive. We get the feminine pronoun for the first time:

> The brightest planet and her guest.

Why is it that way round? There may be astronomical reasons. There probably are. Yet the effect in language is to make Venus the recipient, the receiver, the one who waits for her lover to call. Is this starry union actually equal after all? Not only is there a disjunction between the astral model and the human emotion which *questions* whether it should be looking to Venus and Jupiter for the paradigm for a heterosexual relationship, there is a further subversive message: that Venus may have the distinction of being the 'brightest planet' but she still has to wait for Jupiter to call.

The poised language both expresses and veils the impact of this submerged message. Hidden in the silences of the text is the recognition that 'woman' is a culturally defined social construct, that she ought to reflect the light of Venus. Moreover, the textual formality also hides the inarticulate acknowledgement that there is no adequate way of naming woman starting from the premises of a patriarchal, intellectual inheritance.

I want to jump from this early preconsciousness-raising stage to the time of transition, when the tensions and submerged, subversive elements actually surface and explode form and language. I will consider a poem which was uncollected until *Poems Selected and New: 1950–1974*, but which Rich does include in *The Fact of a Doorframe: Poems Selected and New 1950–1984*. I do not know why it was uncollected originally, but I conjecture that it did not appear to fit within the normal bounds of poetic (or feminine) decorum. The poem messily breaks down the divide between the public, political arena and her intimate, personal life. It doesn't distance either aspect sufficiently. The poem doesn't take much literary decoding, so obviously it is not art but, rather, an outpouring of an overemotional woman. From a radical feminist perspective, however, it validates woman's responses. It expresses woman's experience of the public and the private with stark and honest immediacy. It is located where we are located: in the domestic situation experiencing our powerlessness in the face of male hegemony, and searching for our power by naming the conditions of powerlessness and honestly naming our (sometimes degrading and undignified) responses to them. It is not graceful, it is not elegant, it is not balanced and poised. It is knocked off balance. It is angry, it is emotional, it is tearful, and to me it is overwhelmingly compelling.

Tear Gas

(*October 12, 1969: reports of the tear-gassing of demonstrators protesting the treatment of G.I. prisoners in the stockade at Fort Dix, New Jersey*)

This is how it feels to do something you are afraid of.
That they are afraid of.

(Would it have been different at Fort Dix, beginning to feel the full volume of tears in you, the measure of all you have in you to shed, all you have held back from false pride, false indifference, false courage

beginning to weep as you weep peeling onions, but endlessly, for the rest of time, tears of chemistry, tears of catalyst, tears of rage, tears for yourself, tears for the tortured men in the stockade and for their torturers

tears of fear, of the child stepping into the adult field of force, the
woman stepping into the male field of violence, tears of relief, that
your body was here, you had done it, every last refusal was over)

Here in this house my tears are running wild
in this Vermont of india-madras-colored leaves, of cesspool-stricken
    brooks, of violence licking at old people and children
and I am afraid
of the language in my head
I am alone, alone with language
and without meaning
coming back to something written years ago:
our words misunderstand us

wanting a word that will shed itself like a tear
onto the page
leaving its stain

Trying every key in the bunch to get the door even ajar
not knowing whether it's locked or simply jammed from long disuse
trying the keys over and over then throwing the bunch away
staring around for an axe
wondering if the world can be changed like this
if a life can be changed like this

It wasn't completeness I wanted
(the old ideas of a revolution that could be foretold, and once arrived
    at would give us ourselves and each other)
I stopped listening long ago to their descriptions
of the good society

The will to change begins in the body not in the mind
My politics is in my body, accruing and expanding with every act of
    resistance and each of my failures
Locked in the closet at 4 years old I beat the wall with my body
that act is in me still

No, not completeness:
but I needed a way of saying
(this is what they are afraid of)
that could deal with these fragments
I needed to touch you
with a hand, a body
but also with words
I need a language to hear myself with
to see myself in
a language like pigment released on the board
blood-black, sexual green, reds
veined with contradictions
bursting under pressure from the tube

staining the old grain of the wood
like sperm or tears
but this is not what I mean

these images are not what I mean
(I am afraid.)
I mean that I want you to answer me
when I speak badly
that I love you, that we are in danger
that she wants to have your child, that I want us to have mercy on
    each other
that I want to take her hand
that I see you changing
that it was change I loved in you
when I thought I loved completeness
that things I have said which in a few years will be forgotten
matter more to me than this or any poem
and I want you to listen
when I speak badly
not in poems but in tears
not my best but my worst
that these repetitions are beating their way
toward a place where we can no longer be together
where my body no longer will demonstrate outside your stockade
and wheeling through its blind tears will make for the open air
of another kind of action

(I am afraid.)
It's not the worst way to live.

The first thing I would note about 'Tear Gas' is that the whole paraphernalia of distanced, impersonal objectivity has been dropped. In Rukeyser's phrase, there are 'No more masks' here, not even a gas-mask. It starts from a personal reaction to a political event and works through to the politicisation of a personal situation. It does so without ambiguity, although it has the allusive quality of a private journal entry, where the situation need not be explained since the writer and her immediate family are her primary audience as well as protagonists in the drama.

On a first reading one might feel that there is something uncontrolled, invalid and 'Plath-like' in its subjectivity; that it is merely some journal jotting which reflects a moment of marital crisis – an eternal triangle in which Rich is being ousted and unhinged, hence is unable to watch or read news reports of some quite disconnected event without bursting into feminine tears.

Yet it strikes me that she is in control of language, even in a poem which articulates the problem as being, as much as anything, a problem of language. There are nuances which suggest that having analysed the conditions of oppression, the poet can also transform them into the basis for survival and for the active assumption of woman's power. (The theme is worked out more fully in the opening poem of *The Dream of a Common Language*: 'Power'.) For example, the modulation and qualification of the second line, transforms the basis of power:

> This is how it feels to do something you are afraid of.
> That they are afraid of.

In 'Aunt Jennifer's Tigers' the fear leads to suppression/repression and projection of the suppressed self in purely fantasy figures that reinforce and stabilise the *status quo*. But here the fear experienced by the anti-Vietnam protesters, and by the woman, is balanced by the recognition that the dominant majority, the 'oppressor' *is afraid too* when you protest. The balance of power is immediately altered.

The pronouns here recognise explicitly that poetry cannot be 'universal' – that there is a 'you' and a 'they'. 'They' are the other, at first the political, opponent. 'You' appears to be the self, still viewed at a slight remove. The self is imagining events that it hasn't as yet had the courage to participate in actively. It is the content that first directs our sense that this is woman writing from woman's experience: the experience of falsification and withholding expression. So the first phase of authentic engagement and recuperation of political power occurs as the tears are transformed into a symbol of power when shed freely as a political gesture. In the second prose paragraph the opening image centres on woman's experience and occupations:

> beginning to weep as you weep peeling onions . . .

Unlike the earlier poem 'Peeling Onions', this working of the motif makes the point that women's tears are not occasioned by our inherent weakness but by outside agencies (the onions we prepare or the political militaristic system we are ruled by). The poet is beginning to make imaginative connections so that the domestic and relatively harmless expands outwards to the enormity of the political. Her role is the traditional female role of mourning – the chorus commenting on the action. The woman's role is to be emotional, but this can become a power base. Tears of pathos can and do become 'tears of catalyst' through the process of consciousness raising. The fact that this is a woman speaking/weeping becomes increasingly overt:

> tears for the tortured men in the stockade and for their torturers
>
> tears of fear, of the child stepping into the adult field of force, the woman stepping into the male field of violence . . .

After these three prose/poem paragraphs which seem to work through sympathetic emotional response to a kind of imagined action and breakthrough: 'you had done it, every last refusal was over', the actual breakthrough in the poem is the shift from the pronoun 'you' which is still out there in the media-land to 'I', the 'I' that is 'Here in this house'. Like Aunt Jennifer's tigers, 'my tears are running *wild*' – but now this is perceived as the paradigm for the female aesthetic, and deployment of language.

> and I am afraid
> of the language in my head
> I am alone, alone with language
> and without meaning
> coming back to something written years ago:
> *our words misunderstand us*
> wanting a word that will shed itself like a tear
> onto the page
> leaving its stain
>
> . . .
>
> The will to change begins in the body not in the mind
> My politics is in my body, accruing and expanding with every act
> of resistance and each of my failures
> Locked in the closet at 4 years old I beat the wall with my body
> that act is in me still
>
> . . .
>
> I needed to touch you
> with a hand, a body
> but also with words
> I need a language to hear myself with
> to see myself in

Rich conceptualises language and woman's relation to language. The language available to her is *other* – it does not express her meanings, or understand her experience or emotions. Here she recognises the experience of that split, which is the first stage of consciousness raising in relation to language. As she wrote the same year, 1969, in 'Our Whole Life':

> All those dead letters
> rendered into the oppressor's language
> (*Poems Selected and New 1950–75*, p. 166)

The condition is described through a range of images; which again come from the domestic and household sphere, although there are echoes of Oedipus cutting through the sphinx's knot. Yet the description is precisely not 'rendered into the oppressor's language' this time:

> Trying every key in the bunch to get the door even ajar
> not knowing whether it's locked, or simply jammed from long disuse
> trying the keys over and over then throwing the bunch away
> staring around for an axe

Further down the page it becomes clear, too, that metaphorically she is locked in language and trying to get out – rather than trying to break an entry into the house of language. The image owes something to Emily Dickinson's sense of the female psyche as house – but for her analogy Rich draws on explicit personal psychological experience here. What the poem does with painful honesty is recover the suppressed personal and female experiences that should have been the basis of language and poetic expression from the start. The emotional responses which are judged trivial by the dominant masculinist culture are discovered to be a source of strength, not weakness:

> wanting a word that will shed itself like a tear
> onto the page
> leaving its stain

This is the paradigm. Not an empty shell the accomplished poet inherits and inhabits, but emotion, expressed through the bodily chemistry, and the body politic's chemistry too.

The final section goes even deeper into the hitherto suppressed or veiled area of personal and intimate detail. Talking of 'Aunt Jennifer's Tigers' she says: 'In those years formalism was part of the strategy – like asbestos gloves, it allowed me to handle materials I couldn't pick up bare-handed' (*On Lies, Secrets and Silence*, pp. 40–1). But now she does precisely that. She does more than that. The language also subtly questions and subverts the value-judgements that go with that formalism:

> I mean that I want you to answer me
> *when I speak badly*
>
> . . .
>
> that things I have said which in a few years will be forgotten
> matter more to me than this or any poem
> and I want you to listen
> *when I speak badly*
> not in poems but in tears
> *not my best but my worst*

I have already alluded to Rich's sense that when she succeeded in the patriarchal institutions of marriage and motherhood and in patriarchal poetry she experienced a sense of failure. Now this poem, over a decade later, inverts patriarchal values – the poem identified as Rich speaking at her best is not what she herself actually values. Her 'worst' is what really needs to be said and heard. And saying it does act as a catalyst. She returns to the opening images of women demonstrating outside the male stockade applies it to the personal and then moves on out beyond that 'you'/them or me/you situation.

The final couplet in a colloquial idiom recapitulates this transformation:

> (I am afraid.)
> It's not the worst way to live.

Fear is recognised. Hence it no longer paralyses. And she has moved beyond the patriarchal values of what is best and worst.

What makes this poem a remarkable achievement is the degree of honesty and recognition from a poet who was originally praised for her intellectuality, her dutiful iteration of a masculinist tradition. She is prepared to and has to let it all in. Consciousness raising achieves what formalism failed.

Male reactions to an earlier version of this paper interest me. Firstly, my interpretation of Venus, as 'waiting' for Jupiter to call, was questioned. Perhaps only other women know that experience of waiting, and the stranglehold of the cultural assumptions surrounding that experience.

I have also been accused of insufficient emphasis on Adrienne Rich's involvement in the protest movements of the 1960s. But I think the point about 'Tear Gas' is that she wasn't actually there. Rather, she experienced the American War in Vietnam, and the protest movement back home as so many of us did, through the television screen images. The television placed in the centre of the house, in the living room, or perhaps the newspaper at the breakfast table, connotes a new complexity to the simplistic dualism of private/public, personal/political. The militaristic and political is insistently present at the heart of the family drama. It presents itself as an immediate metaphor or metonym for the struggle to redefine gender-roles and the pain of sexual politics, and also for the female poet's power relations to patriarchal discourse. Feminist politics are emotional, whether we are discussing textual politics, the politics of the family, or the politics of expansionist military intervention. Both a male colleague and a male poet have tended to find the ghost of Walt Whitman in the poem.[6] While I do not deny his presence along with that of Dickinson, I think Rich's use of the first person singular pronoun differs from Whitman's. Hers is not the transcendent inflation of the individual ego, so much as the dredging up of an individual's specific experiences in the firm belief that they will provide a hitherto missing part of the emergent pattern of women's history.

I have chosen in this paper to look at two early poems by Rich which were first published in the year of my birth, and then to look at 'Tear Gas', because I believe it registered a breakthrough in consciousness raising, even if Rich did not realise this fully at the time. It is the poem in which all the suppressed connections surface and explode onto the paper. It is a poem of specific historical era. Rich's feminist analysis has progressed through several phases of increasing lucidity and integrity since then. But for me this poem will always remain one of the great poems that speaks from Rich's generation of women to my own.

NOTES

1. See Sydney Janet Kaplan, 'Varieties of Feminist Criticism', in Greene and Kahn (eds.), *Making a Difference* (Methuen, London, 1985).
2. Toril Moi, *Textual/Sexual Politics: Feminist Literary Theory* (Methuen, London, 1985).
3. Adrienne Rich, 'Blood, Bread and Poetry: The Location of the Poet (1984)', in *Blood, Bread and Poetry: Selected Prose 1979–1985* (Virago, London, 1986).
4. Maggie Humm, *Feminist Criticism: Women as Contemporary Critics* (Harvester, Brighton, 1986).
5. For her own discussion of this process, see 'When We Dead Awaken: Writing as Re-Vision', in *On Lies, Secrets & Silence: Selected Prose 1966–1978* (Virago, London, 1980).
6. John Goode, in an English Department Staff Seminar, University of Warwick, and Roy Fisher, in a Poetry Workshop, University of Warwick.

OTHER WORKS CITED, AND FURTHER BIBLIOGRAPHY

Anderson, Linda. 'Mapping the Self: The Poetry of Adrienne Rich'. *Writing Women*, 1,3 (June 1982), pp. 49–59.
Brogan, Hugh. *The Pelican History of the United States of America*. Harmondsworth, Penguin, 1986.
Daly, Mary. *Gyn/Ecology* (London, The Women's Press, 1979).
Gilbert, Sandra, and Susan Gubar (eds.). *Shakespeare's Sisters: Feminist Essays on Women Poets* (Bloomington, Indiana University Press, 1979).
Juhasz, Suzanne. *Naked and Fiery Forms: Modern American Poetry by Women: A New Tradition* (New York and London, Harper and Row, 1976).
Keohane, Nannerl O., Michelle Z. Rosaldo, and Barbara C. Gelpi. *Feminist Theory: A Critique of Ideology* (Brighton, Harvester, 1982).
Martin, Wendy. *An American Triptych: Anne Bradstreet, Emily Dickinson, Adrienne Rich* (Chapel Hill and London, University of North Carolina Press, 1984).
McDaniel, Judith. *Reconstituting the World: The Poetry and Vision of Adrienne Rich* (Spinsters, Ink, 1978).
Miller, Casey, and Kate Swift. *Words and Women: New Language in New Times* (New York, Anchor/Doubleday, 1976).

Neumann, Erich. *The Great Mother: An Analysis of the Archetype*. Trans. Ralph Manheim (Princeton NJ, Princeton University Press, 1972 (first published 1955)).

Olson, Tillie. *Silences* (London, Virago, 1980).

Ostriker, Alicia. *Writing Like a Woman* (Ann Arbor, University of Michigan Press, 1983).

Rich, Adrienne. *Poems Selected and New, 1950–74* (New York, Norton, 1975).

Rich, Adrienne. *Of Woman Born: Motherhood as Experience and Institution* (London, Virago, 1977).

Rich, Adrienne. *The Dream of a Common Language: Poems 1974–77* (New York and London, Norton, 1978),

Rich, Adrienne. *A Wild Patience Has Taken Me This Far: Poems 1978–81* (New York and London, Norton, 1981).

Rich, Adrienne. *The Fact of a Doorframe: Poems Selected and New, 1950–1984* (New York and London, Norton, 1984).

Rich, Adrienne. *Your Native Land, Your Life: Poems* (New York and London, Norton, 1986).

Rowbotham, Sheila. *Woman's Consciousness, Man's World* (Harmondsworth, Penguin, 1983).

Spender, Dale. *Man Made Language* (London, Routledge and Kegan Paul, 1980).

Chapter 16

'. . . if it's a statistic, it's not a woman':[1] a look at 'serious lessons learned' by Ntozake Shange

Helen Kidd

> Black feminism is not white feminism in blackface. Black women have particular and legitimate issues which affect our lives as Black women, and addressing those issues does not make us any less Black. . . .
>
> Despite our recent economic gains, Black women are still the lowest paid group in the nation by sex and race. This gives some idea of the inequity from which we started. . . .
>
> Black women speak as women because we are women and do not need others to speak for us. It is for Black men to speak up and tell us why and how their manhood is so threatened that Black women should be the prime targets. . . .[2]

In this essay I do not presume to speak for Black women as a white woman, but to speak to and about the poem, the writer, the reader, as a woman and writer who loves, and therefore cannot ignore, the diversity and the accomplishment of Black women writers. Moreover, it is this diversity, the richness of differences, both cultural and experiential, to which I shall repeatedly turn in the essay. As women I believe we should be able to speak from, and to celebrate, our own particularities. We are not a homogeneous group. We reject homogeneity, categorisation and statistics, just as Ntozake Shange rejects the abstract notion of woman in the poem. Woman, the arche/ stereotype, either suffering or nurturing, is a violation of our persons, and in just such a way being Black also defies categorisation into simplified areas of experience, either as totally down-trodden, totally 'primitive' (colourful, naïve, or barbaric), or happy-go-lucky and 'with a wonderful sense of rhythm'.

The poem, 'serious lessons learned', addresses this issue of being simultaneously labelled and then both taken for granted and belittled. But the poem is also many things. It is a gesture, a piece of music, a dance. It is essentially a performance poem which is rooted in the 'real' world, towards which it gestures continually, from which it springs. It is a piece of theatre, a *tete à tete* and an explicit exhortation. For all these reasons it is a Black poem, and for all these reasons it is a poem written by a woman. It is a woman's poem not simply because of its content, but also in the way in which it incorporates all these performance elements. I do not aim to speak about it in white European or North American critical terminology, that would be to do it unforgivable metacritical violence, but, rather, to address it in terms of the writer's own expectations of what a poem should aim to do, and also to set it in a cultural context. But firstly I stress that we must not make the mistake of imagining that the poem can be categorised as 'popular culture', any more than can the context from which it arises. In fact, I would like to dispense with these divisions altogether. 'Popular culture' is a term coined by those who recognise and promulgate literary and artistic canons. These are fundamentally imperialist distinctions which maintain European and white American male literature, art, and so on, at the top of a spurious league whose distinctions and criteria are formed by the cultural self-expressions of this particular and powerful group. These self-regarding criteria are considered, for no other reason than blind egoism, to be objective and universally relevant. Hence the terms 'high' and 'popular' culture stem from ignorance of cultural and racial differences and experiences.

So we will step aside from these criteria. This is a Black woman's poem, written by a particular Black woman, Ntozake Shange, about a particular experience, particularly common to North American Black women, and hence a warning to her sisters. I do not want to lose the poet and her relationship to the creation of the poem. Women writers have vanished into obscurity often enough throughout literary history. Black women writers have suffered this fate the worst. As Alice Walker says:

> How was the creativity of the black woman kept alive, year after year, century after century, when for most of the years black people have been in America, it was a punishable crime for a black person to read or write?[3]

I do not intend to contribute to the burial of the Black poet, or the woman poet, and, without succumbing to intentionalism, I want to use the poet's ideas about poetry.

In her introduction to *Nappy Edges*, 'things i wd say' Ntozake Shange says:

> . . . if we don't know the voice of a writer / the way we know 'oh . . .

that's trane' / something is very wrong. we are unfortunately / sellin ourselves down the river again. & we awready know abt that. if we go down the river again / just cuz we don't know or care to recognize our particularities / wont nobody come / cuz dont nobody care / if you dont know yr poets as well as yr tenor horns.[4]

She goes on to point out that this particularity is allowed to musicians but not to poets:

. . . i can tell you who is a poet from chicago / i cd say that's some west coast stuff / or some new york number / & there will be a great noddin of heads & uh-huhs / cuz we dont ask a poet to speak personally / we want a poet to speak like an arena / or like a fire station / to be everywhere / all at once / even if we never been there / . . . we expect a poet to clear a space / not her space / not a secret / not a closed room / but the town. we assume the poet to be the voice of everywhere we are not / as opposed to bein 'everything we are'. though what authentic musical criticism of our artists that exists / always allows them the space to be themselves.[5]

This then is a poem written by a particular woman, with a particular and recognisable style, and in order to do it justice we need to know about her. We cannot allow her as a woman, and as a Black writer, to remain an unknown. The poem asserts the right to selfhood, particularity, sexuality, gendered identity, not as part of a faceless category, or an echo of someone else's world. If we acknowledge the writer, we acknowledge the particularities, the variety of Black writing. We are saying, 'Yes, this must be Zaki. Not any other Black writer. This is Zaki's way of putting words onto the page. It is not Alice Walker, or Maya Angelou, because they write differently.' We begin to recognise the need to know the cultural lineage that contemporary Black writers are heir to. This is not a canon, nor even a challenge to 'the' canon. It simply is. Moreover, placed beside the Black writing, most of the white canon fades into insignificance.

This lineage is part of the experiences and artistic expression of the entire Diaspora, but Black American culture has its particular history. It is rooted in the experience of slavery. The Blues is one of the most renowned musical expressions that draws directly on this, rooted in the slave hollers and the lamentations of the South, and further back, behind Blues and Jazz, lie the various musics and ceremonials of Africa. All this may seem a long way back to Black Americans from New York or California, but to Black people in the South the fight for Civil Rights has never been completely won, and slavery and its kindred ills, are living memories.

So Shange can be seen both as a descendant of Phillis Wheatley and Zora Neale Hurston, but also of her Blues sisters, Bessie Smith, Billie Holiday and Memphis Minnie, to name but a few. These women performers also claimed a space for themselves. That space which they commanded made them powerful, if only for a while for some, because it is a space from which to be seen and heard. Like these singers Shange speaks to her own people. And this poem speaks primarily to women. If men take note, so much the better, but it is first and foremost for women. Similarly, it is also a Black poem. If white people listen, all well and good, but it is a Black poem for Black audiences, just as Blues is Black music for Black audiences, and some white fans.

The Bluesy complaints of these art forms are offset in this poem by the quirky spelling and the close representation of speech rhythms on the page. This couples the poem's lineage with jazz. Black music breathes through jazz; without Black music and Black musicians, jazz would not exist.

Finally, her approach to language and rejection of standard English as the correct medium for the page links Shange with the Creole and Patois poets of the Caribbean and, more recently, with the language of the Rastas. It is important to acknowledge these musical influences as Ntozake Shange also does:

> . . . my basic premise is that poets address themselves to the same issues as musicians / but that we give the musicians more space to run with / more personal legitimacy than we give our writers.[6]

or as she puts it in her best known short poem 'i live in music',

> i live in music
>   live in it
>   wash in it
> i cd even smell it
> wear sound on my fingers
> sound falls   so fulla music
> ya cd make a river where yr arm is &
> hold yrself
>   hold yrself in a music[7]

At this stage we need a short biographical interlude. We have been looking at the issue of individuality which the poem raises, and its relevance for Black writers. A community is made up of individuals, and a writing community is no different. So Ntozake Shange's biographical details, in brief, will help to place her and her work. She was born in 1948 in Trenton, New Jersey, and was originally called Paulette Williams. She changed her name in protest against Western influences. Ntozake is a Zulu word meaning 'she who comes with her own things', and Shange means 'she who walks like a lion'. Both names evoke strength, independence and originality, characteristics of her own work, and something she presents as inherent in many of her Black women speakers in her poetry and drama. Her involvement with the Black and women's movements have been major influences on her writing, and, while living in California, she became involved with poets, musicians, dancers and in creative workshops, all of which encouraged her to grow and to explore the interrelationships of dance, music and poetic performance on stage. Her well-known choreopoem *for colored girls who have considered suicide when the rainbow is enuf* was begun at this time, and evolved between the years 1974 and 1976. It was performed under and in various conditions, first in San Francisco and then in New York where it became a Broadway hit, was much exploited, and caused Ntozake Shange to distance herself from it.

The play is concerned with the same material that we find in *Nappy Edges*, and in her other work, the dramatic portrayal of the emotional lives of young Black women and the havoc created by social expectations and roles which interfere with personal relationships. 'serious lessons' is ironic, independent and wised up, whereas *'for colored girls'* moves through harrowingly honest dramatic moments to the realisation of independence achieved by the four women. Whereas 'serious lessons' suggests sexuality, autonomy, maturity and full awareness, other poems, such as 'chicago in sanfrancisco & you / me / waait / love is musik / touch me like sounds / chicago on my shoulder / yr hand / is now a kiss',[8] are overtly sensual and erotic, both as textual/textural surface play and in rhythm. This is not to deny the play of language, the ironies, the speech rhythms in 'serious lessons', but it has a violence, an abruptness of staccato sounds and phrases which emphasise the message, dramatise the particular moments of conflict and confrontation in a negative heterosexual relationship. For example:

> . . . & start talkin bout the fights when
> ya wanna be loved / or start not understandin english /
> quick / 'love / whatya mean love' /[9]

The music of the words used, the textures of sounds as well as the syncopation, abruption, or languorousness of phrasing constitutes the poetry's performance orientation, and equally its sensual/sensory nature. The inspiration, input and influences for this reached their apogee in the two-year gestation of *for colored girls*, and I want to include Ntozake Shange's account of that period, in order to emphasise the cross-fertilisation of arts and influences which were brought to bear on her writing.

> We started at the Bacchanal & worked through the winter at Ed Mock's Dance Studio with the assistance of West Coast Dance Works, setting pieces and cleaning up poems. I found two bands, the Sound Clinic (a

horn trio) & Jean Desarmes & His Raggae Blues Band, who agreed to
work with us if I found space. & I did The space we used waz the space
I knew: Women's Studies Departments, bars, cafes, & poetry centres.
With the selection of poems changing, dependent upon our audience &
our mood, & the dance growing to take space of its own, so that Paula
inspired my words to fall from me with her body, & the Sound Clinic
working with new arrangements of Ornette Coleman compositions &
their own, the Raggae Blue Band giving Caribbean renditions of Jimi
Hendrix & Redding, we set dates for Minnie's Can-Do Club in Haight
Ashbury. The poets showed up for us, the dancers showed up for us,
the women's community showed up, & we were listed as a 'must see'
. . . .[10]

I include this description of part of the genesis of *for colored girls* to
give you a picture of the poet's writing as one of process rather than
an end product, finished, static, fixed to the page. The intersection
of different creative forms becomes the poem itself. But this then
exists in a further dimension, as a performance, which constitutes
further opening and exploration.

'serious lessons' declares itself as performance poetry at its very
outset. It begins with the non-verbal utterance 'ah haaaa', a stagey
sound, an appeal to the audience's attention, and almost melodramatic.
The poem, furthermore, contains the insistence of the repeated
refrain-like 'beware'. The musicality of the poem, its score, so to
speak, lies in its presentation. It progresses as dance does, each sense
unit choreographed by the slashes, just as individual dance turns, or
the end of a movement sequence alters the direction of the dancer. It
is dramatic in that it adopts the monologist's persona, as well as
dramatising the illustrations of male *idées fixes* and emotional illiteracy
with snatches of direct and indirect reported speech.

The poem also has more conventional musical textures in its use of
alliteration, assonance and consonance. Take, for example, the first
line, those echoing vowels in 'beware' and 'dear' and 'ah haaaa', all
close to one another in sound quality; and the second line's alliterative
and consonantal pattern, 'rabid dogs' with the echo of the 'g' in
'gusanos with grenades'. This kind of musical patterning carries on
throughout the poem, as does the jazz phrasing. Long sense units are
alternated with bursts of short units, as, for example, in the opening
of the poem, the first four units ending on line four with a following
long improvisation on a theme, like a horn solo, ending on line nine
with a reiteration of the refrain 'beware beware'. The pattern is not
regular, in that the repetitions are not predictably placed, neither are
they complete repetitions, but are more exactly parallelisms. The long
improvisation at the beginning does not recur, but shorter, staccato,
drum-like sense units, bursts of short phrases interrupt the longer
units at frequent intervals, as in lines twenty three to twenty five:

> . . . / this man's got ya tied up in his fantasies
> yr fleshly & independent reality is insignificant
> unpredictable /

This section is succeeded by a series of shorter slashed passages which become shorter and shorter, more and more breathless, emphatic, urgent, as they move towards the next 'beware beware':

> . . . / touch for him is illusion
> is all he wants / a still photo of ya is his love
> forever / in control / watch to see
> if he likes ya to sit still
> be quiet / so he can / capture yr energy / beware beware.

The techniques of Ntozake's artistic collaborators with whom she has worked, and with whom she continues to work, can thus be seen to influence her poetry, even down to the presentation of the poetry on the page. Explaining the highly individual appearance of her poetry in print, she expresses it in terms of other influences,

> It bothers me on occasion, to look at poems where all the first letters are capitalized. It's very boring to me. That's why I use the lower-case alphabet. Also, I like the idea that letters dance, not just that the words dance; of course, the words also dance. I need some visual stimulation, so that reading becomes not just a passive act and more than an intellectual activity, but demands rigorous participation. Furthermore, I think there are ways to accentuate very subtle ideas and emotions so that the reader is not in control of the process. This means that I have to have more tricks than everybody else because I can't let you get away with thinking you know what I mean. After all, I didn't mean whatever you can just ignore. I mean what you have to struggle with, and in this transition the piece becomes special.
>
> The spellings result from the way I talk or the way the character talks, or the way I heard something said. Basically, the spellings reflect the language as I hear it.[11]

In this way the poem is again resisting the formal impositions of so-called standard English, an essentially authoritarian way of relating to syntax, grammar and spelling. Therefore it resists the 'ideal', the 'cerebratin', the notion of what it should be, and pays attention to its own particularity, its need for a specific, rather than universal, mode of being, something that formal notions would destroy, distort or deny, just as a 'cerebratin love affair' can destroy, distort or deny the 'truth of you'. The actual physicality, emotional needs, desires and 'fleshly & independent reality' of a particular woman are buried by the superimposition of an absolute, or ideal, and hence impossible notion of woman, the arche/stereotype. By emphasising the heterogeneity of women's emotional and physical needs and experiences, the poet is making a profoundly political statement. However, this does not come about because the aim of the poem is primarily

political. Indeed, she points out that this kind of pointedness can
stifle creativity. Talking about this in an interview, she has explained:

> The commercial people tell me that one of the reasons the rest of my
> work hasn't been as commercially successful as *For Colored Girls* is that
> it has *no point* that they could sell. That's because there's going to be *no
> more point*. I am not writing about a point. *For Colored Girls* doesn't have a
> point either, but they made a point out of it. Those girls were people
> whom I cared about, people whom I offered to you for you to see and to
> know. Black and Latin writers have to start demanding that the fact that
> we're alive is point enough![12]

Nevertheless, 'lessons learned' takes an oppositional stance. It is
the dramatic stance of a speaker who addresses her audience in a
warning voice, arguing for women's need to know that they can and
should expect more from relationships; that they have rights, that
these rights are to be allowed in order to be a completely fulfilled
person, not to fit an impossible image of some nebulous fictional
ideal. The speaker in the poem warns of the male-construct, 'women
in his head', and in this respect it is very much a poem for an
audience of women, a poem dramatising a problem. Ntozake Shange
has said that, for men, the idea can take over the needs of the poem,
just as, for men, the idea of 'Woman' can take over and deny specific
needs of particular women:

> In works by men there's usually an *idea* as opposed to a *reality* . . . Men
> also generally approach the conflicts involved in the sexual or political
> identity of a male character in a way that allows them to skim over
> whatever the real crisis is.[13]

She goes on to say:

> . . . women are more in touch with their feelings; therefore, they're able
> to identify what it is they're doing and feeling. I also think that women
> use their feelings to a greater degree and in more varied ways than men
> do.[14]

She qualifies this, however, when she points out that there are male
exceptions to this rule, and she has worked with them. More
importantly, she acknowledges that her growth, personally, and as
a writer, has been largely due to women's groups and collaboration
with women:

> i believe my work waz nourished & shaped to a large degree by the time
> i spent with women. in san francisco i waz isolated in this very close
> community of creative women. . . . we need ourselves to take care of
> ourselves. it's as simple as that.[15]

and she recognises that working with male artists can be an impedi-
ment:

> the collective recognition of certain realities that are female can still be

hampered, diverted, diluted by a masculine presence. yes. i segregated my work & took it to women. much like i wd take fresh water to people stranded in the mojave desert. i wdnt take a camera crew to observe me. i wdn't ask the people who had never known thirst to come watch the thirsty people drink.[16]

If this is, then, a Black poem because it acknowledges its Black American cultural roots in its jazz rhythms and dance, it is also a women's poem because it refuses the primacy of ideas over its poetic demands. Just as the rhythms of speech resist the dictatorship of formal syntax, and thus far it is both a Black poem resisting white 'standard English' and a women's poem resisting the male authoritarianism of ideals, so it is also a Black poem and a women's poem in that it acknowledges the external 'reality' from which it springs. It gestures defiantly towards that 'reality', proposing its own method of creation and approach as part of the alternative it would like to see take place. It celebrates feeling above intellect, touch above abstractions, but it is also a warning not to allow the old patterns of male dominance to continue:

> . . . mothers know that it's a dreadful proposition to give up one's life for one's family and one's mate and, therefore, lose oneself in the process of caring and tending for others. To send one's daughter off to that kind of self-sacrifice in silence with no preparation is a mortal sin to me. To do this without telling her that this is a sacrifice is so unnecessary. To break this silence is my responsibility, and I'm absolutely committed to it.[17]

Paradoxically this could be construed as a point, although in the process of a single poem it is simply enough to dramatise particular situations and celebrate others. To present problems, show and not tell, has to be the role of poetry, with which polemic has always been an uneasy bedfellow. She presents the problem of working with male poets in the witty and ironic prose piece 'wow . . . yr just like a man':

> he said hangin out with her waz just like hangin out witta man / she cd drink & talk pungently / even tell a risqué joke or two / more n that / she cd talk abt art / & that musta made her a man / cuz she sure cdnt scratch her balls / or pee further n him. . . .
> she waz very nice to the guys & sometimes fed them like their own mamas wd have / . . . sometimes when one of their women threw them out / they stayed at her house / cuz there waz never a man at her house / that waz one of the unspoken rules of her bein considered one of the fellas / or a poet / cuz if there waz a man at her house / like there waz one time / when she forgot that in order to be considered a poet she hadta be one of the guys / the poets who were men / got very indignant & walked out cuz she waz romancin some fella who waznt even a poet & wdnt be able to feed them that night. . . .[18]

The list of restrictions required to be a woman and also a poet grows and grows, until we are given the contrast of the woman writer becoming women-centred, and the consequences of celebrating this gender-specific area:

> she said / as a woman & a poet / i've decided to wear my ovaries on my sleeve / raise my poems on my milk / count my days by the flow of my mensis / the men who were poets were aghast / they fled the scene in fear of becoming unclean / they all knew those verses / & she waz left with an arena of her own / where words and notions / imply 'she' / where havin lovers is quite common regardless of sex / or profession / where music & mensis / are considered very personal / & language a tool for exploring space.[19]

It is precisely this use of language as a tool which makes Ntozake Shange such a riveting writer. While she is sensitive to the musical properties of language and phrasing, she is also alert to the demands of performance, the ceremonial occupation of the space on stage, and the celebration of the right to this. She asserts Black women's claim to this right as being as equally valid as their male counterparts, but at the same time she is aware of how the parameters of that space are defined and confining.

As regards personal space, the site of performance is merely an extension of this, a site whence the community can be recognised, celebrated and lamented in all its diversity, differences and short-comings, a site which presents to women others akin, but not identical, to themselves and from which serious lessons can indeed be learned, not through didacticism, but through empathy. 'serious lessons' is yet another means of answering Black male assumptions about women, which carries out some of the conclusions of 'wow . . . yr just like a man'.

> #1: when words & manners leave you no space for yrself / make a poem / very personal / very clear / & yr obstructions will join you or disappear /

> #2: if yr obstructions dont disappear / repeat over & over again / the new definitions / til the ol ones have no more fight in them / then cover them with syllables you've gathered from other dyin species /

> #3: a few soft words have sent many a woman to her back with her thighs flung open & eager / a few more / will find us standin up & speakin in our own tongue to whomever we goddam please.[20]

Let us not for a moment imagine that Ntozake Shange is alone in this project either as a woman poet, or a Black American poet. There are many, many women standing up and speaking to whomever they goddam please. The list of poets in this collection of essays must not be taken as representative of the broad spectrum of contemporary poetry. If we were to imagine that it is, then Black writing would appear to be in a parlous condition, and this is very far from the case. In this book Ntozake Shange is not only in a minority as a woman poet, but in the token position of being one of only two Black poets. If the canon is considered as a false construct and yet the focus still remains on white writers, then the notion of white artistic criteria being the ultimate arbiters, and the notion of white literature being superior, is bound to be reinforced.

The second implication of this is that this writer can appear to be indicative of the writings of the entire Diaspora, and hence both the individuality of this particular poet is lost, and also there is an assumed homogeneity of Black writing, and, by extension, Black experience, which does not in actuality exist, any more than we can say that Irish writers are the same as English writers, or Scots writers are the same as Australian writers. Colonial attitudes run deep and white communities are often blind to their own assumptions about white writers as the exemplars of literary criteria.

So the Black writer becomes white-washed, diluted, the writing robbed of its social and historical contexts, cut off from its cultural life-blood. It is presented as a minority grouping, patronised and simultaneously disempowered. Meanwhile, white literature founders in its quest for meaning, form, expression, rootling in the literary litter bins for the fag-ends of a devitalised, fragmented and played-out civilisation, and frequently disillusioned with its own roots. But other poetries stand waiting in the wings, to take the stage and reenergise language and literary and cultural perspectives. Academia requires (at the very least) a radical refocus and some useful humility. There is much to be learned, but not from a position of superiority. By looking at Black and Asian literature, very many of our invisible criteria will be called to account, and that *is* rigorous academic enquiry. I believe the answers to many teasing literary and political questions lie with Black writing, and it is long past the time when we should have begun to listen. To include an essay like this at all in the collection is, at best, a toehold, a beginning; but it is not enough.

Black poets will continue to write whether whites read them or not. Women poets will continue to write whether read by men or not, and within both these spheres you will find that the particular, the diverse, the different are not so much cause for division but for celebration. As Audre Lorde puts it:

> Somewhere, on the edge of consciousness, there is what I call a *mythical norm*, which each one of us within our hearts knows 'that is not me' . . . It is with this mythical norm that the trappings of power reside in this society.[21]

In 'serious lessons' Ntozake Shange insists that women deserve so much more than society and their male partners usually allow. As with all her work, there is a beckoning to her sisters to love themselves. Audre Lorde puts it this way:

> In this country, Black women traditionally have had compassion for everybody else except ourselves. We have cared for whites because we had to for pay or survival; we have cared for our children and our fathers and our brothers and our lovers. History and popular culture . . . are full of tales of Black women who had 'compassion for misguided black men'. Our scarred, broken, battered and dead daughters and sisters are a mute testament to that reality. We need to learn to have care and compassion for ourselves, also.[22]

'serious lessons' addresses the moment before the violence, the idea that carries the act of violation, of diminution, of betrayal. 'this love is not for ya' Shange says, but this is ambiguous; not only is this love the love of an idea that the man has 'a cerebratin love affair' in fact, but this love should not have to be for anyone, this 'whip across the back', this implied slavery. This moment is a moment of understanding, a revelation, a wisdom shared. It is not part of world history, but one of those small moments which in all their multiplicity go to make world history. Let Ntozake Shange have the last word:

> as we demand to be heard / we want you to hear us. we come to you the way leroi jenkins comes or cecil taylor / or b.b. king. we come to you alone / in the theater / in the story / & the poem. like with billie holiday or betty carter / we shd give you a moment that cannot be re-created / a specificity that cannot be confused. our language shd let you know who's talkin, what we're talkin abt & how we cant stop sayin this to you. some urgency accompanies the text. something important is going on. we are speakin. reachin for yr person / we cannot hold it / we dont want to sell it / we give you ourselves / if you listen . . .
>
> you cd imagine us like music & make us yrs /
>
> *we can be quiet & think & love the silence*
> *we need to look at trees more closely*
> *we need to listen*[23]

NOTES

1. Claudia Tate (ed.), *Black Women Writers at Work* (Oldcastle, Harpenden, 1985), p. 159.
2. Audre Lorde, 'Sexism: An American Disease in Blackface', in *Sister Outsider: Essays and Speeches* (The Crossing Press, New York, 1984), p. 60.
3. Alice Walker, 'In Search of our Mother's Gardens', in *In Search of Our Mother's Gardens: Womanist Prose* (The Women's Press, London, 1984), p. 234.
4. Ntozake Shange, 'things i wd say: takin a solo / a poetic possibility a poetic imperative', *Nappy Edges* (Methuen, London, 1987), p. 4. Shange's other works

include *Three Pieces* (St Martin's Press, New York, 1981 and Penguin, London, 1982); *A Daughter's Geography* (St Martin's Press, New York, 1984 and Methuen, London, 1984); *Riding the Moon in Texas* (St Martin's Press, New York, 1987). She has also published two novels, *Sassafrass, Cypress and Indigo* (St Martin's Press, New York, 1982 and Methuen, London, 1983) and *Betsey Brown* (St Martin's Press, New York, 1985).
5. Ntozake Shange, *Nappy Edges*, pp. 4–5.
6. Ibid., p. 5.
7. Ibid., p. 126.
8. Ibid., p. 142.
9. Ibid., pp. 110–11.
10. Ntozake Shange, 'introduction', in *for colored girls who have considered suicide when the rainbow is enuf* (Methuen, London, 1978), pp. xii–xiii.
11. Claudia Tate, *Black Women Writers*, p. 163.
12. Ibid., p. 171.
13. Ibid., p. 160.
14. Ibid., p. 161.
15. Ntozake Shange, *Nappy Edges*, p. 22.
16. Ibid., p. 22.
17. Claudia Tate, *Black Women Writers*, p. 162.
18. Ntozake Shange, *Nappy Edges*, p. 13–15.
19. Ibid., p. 16.
20. Ibid., p. 16.
21. Audre Lorde, 'Age, Race, Class and Sex: Women Redefining Difference', in *Sister Outsider: Essays and Speeches*, p. 116.
22. Ibid., 'Sexism', p. 62.
23. Ntozake Shange, *Nappy Edges*, pp. 11–12.

Afterword

'What are you against?'
'What have you got?'
                    Sheriff's daughter and Brando character in *The Wild One*

A trick of thought that the Saussurean, 'structuralist' moment in modern literary theory has bequeathed to us is the habit of posing the question, to any phenomenon in any field: 'in opposition to what?'

So we may reasonably ask: poetry is now opposed – to what? To answer that is to see that, variously, at different times poetry has found itself in a position that can be plotted in terms of a number of opposed categories: between speech and writing, between natural, normal or ordinary language and the artificial, between the language of power and its others.

In the past the obvious other to poetry has often been natural speech and writing. Poetry has been placed in the position of being the un-ordinary against a normal or ordinary language which was plain, unadorned, unelaborated, unconsidered, spontaneous, 'low'. Accordingly, poetry defined itself as formal, decorated, considered and 'high'.

In our present moment, natural and ordinary language is not necessarily speech. Conversational speech, both face-to-face and in its simulacral media versions, of course proliferates, yet the truly forceful language of our time is easy enough to spot, for it is the ordinary language of power. It is what the Weberian bureaucrat writes, what the serious newspapers print, what at a more playful level seeks to charm us into market-economy participation via advertising, what at a more instructive level piles up as the language of research reports, scholarly articles and books, and legal judgments. Our normal (or norm/al) language is the totality of typical sentences generated within the global hegemony of corporate ownership, market consumption and Western technology. And there is one kind of poetry which, for a variety of reasons, has failed to recognise the date on the calendar and so in the very act of striving to separate itself from natural language has unwittingly reproduced it.

Yet while normal language goes about its business by striving to repeat itself endlessly – and, if possible, universally – poetry now more than ever is destined to be other. For it cannot escape the treadmill of being different, of being other to itself according to that necessity Pound spelt out as 'Make It New!' and exemplified when he wrote (parenthetically) in Canto LXXXI 'to break the pentameter, that was the first heave'. Particular poets may want to hold onto the sonnet in opposition to the deadness of the memo, or to incorporate the scientific report into verse in opposition to the deadness of the sonnet. But the relation between poetry past and poetry (not) now serves to define, negatively, the space within which the poetry of our moment emerges.

The best of this poetry seems to crystallise in this space in one of two modes.

Against a bureaucratese which displays a numbingly generalising style and yet emanates from regimes which cannot deliver the truly grand generalisation of rights encapsulated in the formula of 1789, 'Liberty, Equality, Fraternity', emerges a poetry of emotion, confession, plain speech, lived experience, recrimination – where the experience and anger is that of those whom the system marginalises. The roll-call of the underprivileged may by now be well-known – women, workers, blacks, gays, the poor in the West, the poorer in the developing world, the handicapped, the young, the old – but within each category (and no doubt blocked by the very categorisation) are voices which demand to be heard *as* poetic. So there is a poetry here that claims to be working against power, and to that degree against what is currently 'natural'.

Equally against bureaucratic language but *also* against everyday natural speech itself, with its rule-governed syntax, semantics and pragmatics, its tendency to efface itself as sounds, words and sentences in the service of friction-free communication lies a poetic practice of defamiliarisation which is calculated to frustrate the demand for communication, a practice which has been given attention throughout this volume. As coeditors we solicited essays linking theory to a particular poem or group of poems. Although in no sense sharing a party line, an unanticipated number of contributors volunteered to write from a general sympathy with a position perhaps most explicitly set out by advocates of 'Language' poetry. The name 'Language Poetry', saluting the seminal journal $L=A=N=G=U=A=G=E$ through which a community of practitioners of this poetry was established, is, as labels go, not a bad one, however cross it may make practitioners of speech-based poetry of reported experience and reflection, who can equally claim to be using language. What makes Language Poetry more 'language-y' than the typical respectable poetry-workshop-generated text is its preparedness to explore new ways of making language *resist* – in the sense in which Lacan, defining the Real as that which resists, comes strangely into alignment with Dr Johnson's famous, simple-minded, idealism-refuting kick. Toe against stone; tongue and eye 'against' a language which thereby becomes felt, no longer transparent and bodiless.

To the extent that modern literary theory is radical in its intention it should gravitate towards engagement with either or both of the radicalities just described: a poetry of the marginalised voice, a poetry which, by injecting the principles of the margin *into* the voice, torques or fractures the 'sayable' irremediably.

Both these poetries require considerable courage from their practitioners. In one case, it is daring to speak when you have been told by the powerful that you had better reconcile yourself to having been cast in a non-speaking role. In the other case, it is daring to speak so as not to be understood, and not to be understood *in principle* (these are not 'difficult' poems simply awaiting New Critical explication or even the sort of annotation that is undeniably of help to the reader of Pound or of Olson once scholars put in the work).

Nothing guarantees that literary theory's new paradigm might not be used against, rather than in support of, the most vital tendencies of poetry now. A mechanical application of Derridean distrust of the age-old privileging of speech over writing, or of 'anti-humanist' distrust of the speaking subject's autonomy, might work to the disadvantage of the poetry of speech from the margin, and of its poets. At the same time a Stanley Fish-like relativistic notion of 'interpretive' communities, liberal-minded and open though it seems, does assume poetry to be open to interpretation, and this 'Language' poetry typically refuses.

A rather different problem is posed by theory's own 'opposed to what?' status. The new paradigm has generally seemed at its most radically vigorous when applied to the apparently 'staid' texts sanctified by the canon: whether challenging their canonical status, laying bare the conditions under which they have been produced and received, or tapping their latent transgressiveness, criticism has liked to address works to which it could posit itself as other even as it revisioned them productively. This is not so easy to do when the text that theory is to handle threatens to be stranger, more baffling, more political, more personal than theory itself.

We hope nevertheless that the discussions collected here speak in the main from a position of serious (which is not to say uncritical) sympathy with the poems that are the objects of discussion. Writing about contemporary poetry is itself a courageous venture; the lifeless, automaton-like nagging and head-patting that characterises most current reviewing practice reflects a real difficulty in finding an honourable 'commentary mode' where poetry is concerned. The new critical paradigm, in its reflexiveness and openness, may make it possible at last for the poetries of today to be written of in a manner which properly testifies – classically enough! – to their particular beauty and their particular truth.

Notes on Contributors

Peter Brooker teaches critical theory and modern literature at Thames Polytechnic where he helped found and edit *Literature and History*. He has written on Ezra Pound, modern theory and literature, and English studies. Most recently he was the author of *Bertolt Brecht, Dialectics, Poetry, Politics* (1988) and coeditor of *Dialogue and Difference, English into the Nineties* (1980). He is presently completing a Critical Reader on modernism and postmodernism for Longman and writing a kind of fiction.

Dympna Callaghan is an Assistant Lecturer in the Department of English, University of Syracuse, New York. She has published extensively in the field of both Renaissance and twentieth-century women's literature.

Joseph Chadwick is an Associate Lecturer in the Department of English, University of Hawaii. He has published articles on Joyce, Yeats, Beckett and Kafka.

Steve Connor has taught since 1979 at Birkbeck College, London, where he is Senior Lecturer in English and Director of the Centre for Interdisciplinary Research in Culture and the Humanities. He has published three books: *Charles Dickens* (1985); *Samuel Beckett: Repetition, Theory and Text* (1988); *Postmodernist Culture: An Introduction to Theories of the Contemporary* (1989). At present he is completing a book entitled *Cultural Values* and a study of the discourses of Victorian mythography.

Harriet Davidson is Associate Professor of English and Comparative Literature at Rutgers University and author of *T.S. Eliot and Hermeneutics* (1985), as well as articles on contemporary poetry and contemporary theory. She is editing a forthcoming volume of theoretical essays on T.S. Eliot for the Longman Critical Reader series and is currently working on a book about contemporary poetry, theory and politics.

Helen M. Dennis is a lecturer in English and American Literature at the University of Warwick and also a member of the Graduate School of Women's Studies there. Her doctorate, taken at the University of York, is entitled *A New Approach to the Poetry of Ezra Pound: through the Medieval Provencal Aspect*. She runs the Contemporary Poetry Archive at the University of Warwick, and is currently working on *A Comparative Survey of American Women Authors, 1860–1990*. She is a single parent and has three children, two sons and a daughter.

Thomas Docherty teaches English, theory and film at University College, Dublin. Author of *Reading (Absent) Character* (1983), *John Donne, Undone* (1986), *On Modern Authority* (1987), *After Theory: Postmodernism/Postmarxism* (1990) and numerous articles on theory and on twentieth-century literature, he is presently editing *The Postmodernist Reader* for Harvester Press, *The Deleuze Reader* for Blackwell, and is preparing a study of *Criticism and Modernity*.

Antony Easthope is Professor of English and Cultural Studies at Manchester Polytechnic. His publications include *Poetry as Discourse* (1983), *British Post-Structuralism* (1988) and *Poetry and Phantasy* (1989).

Helen Kidd is a poet and coeditor of a small poetry magazine. Currently completing a thesis on women poets in Britain and Ireland, she is a contributor to *Diverse Voices: Twentieth Century Women's Writing from Around the World* and coeditor of the *Virago Book of Women's Love Poetry*. Helen Kidd is a part-time lecturer in English at Oxford Polytechnic and mother of three children.

Jerome McGann is Commonwealth Professor of English at the University of Virginia. He has just completed volumes VI and VII of his edition of Byron's *Complete Poetical Works*, and his most recent critical book – *The Textual Condition* – will appear shortly.

Peter Middleton teaches in the Department of English at Southampton University. He has published poetry in *Temblor* and other small press magazines in Britain and the United States, and articles on Blake, Eliot and various contemporary poets. He is completing a book on masculinity and modernity.

Peter Nicholls is lecturer in English and American Literature at the University of Sussex. He is the author of *Ezra Pound: Politics, Economics and Writing* (1984), and of recent articles on postmodernism, expressionist theatre, and the New Historicism. He is currently completing *Modernism: A Literary Guide* for Macmillan.

Marjorie Perloff's most recent book is *Poetic License: Essays in Modernist and Postmodernist Lyric* (1990). She is now completing a study of late twentieth-century poetics in relation to the media, to be called *Radical Artifice* and published by the University of Chicago Press. She teaches English and Comparative Literature at Stanford University.

Richard Rand teaches English at the University of Alabama and is at work on a book about Coleridge and Wordsworth.

Andrew Ross teaches English at Princeton University, and is the author of *The Failure of Modernism* (1986), *No Respect: Intellectuals and Popular Culture* (1989) and *Strange Weather: Culture Science and Technology in the Age of Limits* (forthcoming). He is also the editor of *Universal Abandon? The Politics of Postmodernism* (1988) and coeditor of *Technoculture* (1991).

Rick Rylance is Senior Lecturer and Field Leader in English at Anglia Polytechnic, Cambridge. His published work includes *Debating Texts: A Reader in Twentieth-Century Literary Theory* (1987). He is presently completing a book on Roland Barthes and a history of nineteenth-century psychological theory.

John O. Thompson is a Lecturer in the School of Politics and Communication Studies at the University of Liverpool. He is coauthor, with Ann Thompson, of *Shakespeare, Meaning and Metaphor* (1987); his collection of poetry, *Echo and Montana*, appeared in Canada in 1980.

Geoffrey Ward is a Lecturer in the Department of English Language and Literature, University of Liverpool. His book on the New York Poets will be published by Macmillan in 1991. He has published five collections of poetry, most recently *Not in the Hand Itself* (1984), and has written numerous articles on contemporary poetry.